OFFICE 2003
Simplified®

Visual

by Sherry Willard Kinkoph

WILEY

Wiley Publishing, Inc.

OFFICE 2003 SIMPLIFIED®

Published by
Wiley Publishing, Inc.
111 River Street
Hoboken, NJ 07030-5774

Published simultaneously in Canada

Library of Congress Control Number: 2005933524

ISBN-13: 978-0-7645-9959-0

ISBN-10: 0-7645-9959-3

Manufactured in the United States of America

10 9 8 7 6 5 4 3 2

Trademark Acknowledgments

Contact Us

For general information on our other products and services please contact our Customer Care Department within the U.S. at (800) 762-2974, outside the U.S. at (317) 572-3993, or fax (317) 572-4002.

For technical support please visit www.wiley.com/techsupport.

WILEY

Wiley Publishing, Inc.

Sales

Contact Wiley
at (800) 762-2974 or
fax (317) 572-4002.

Praise for Visual Books

"Like a lot of other people, I understand things best when I see them visually. Your books really make learning easy and life more fun."

John T. Frey (Cadillac, MI)

"I have quite a few of your Visual books and have been very pleased with all of them. I love the way the lessons are presented!"

Mary Jane Newman (Yorba Linda, CA)

"I just purchased my third Visual book (my first two are dog-eared now!), and, once again, your product has surpassed my expectations."

Tracey Moore (Memphis, TN)

"I am an avid fan of your Visual books. If I need to learn anything, I just buy one of your books and learn the topic in no time. Wonders! I have even trained my friends to give me Visual books as gifts."

Illona Bergstrom (Aventura, FL)

"Thank you for making it so clear. I appreciate it. I will buy many more Visual books."

J.P. Sangdong (North York, Ontario, Canada)

"I have several books from the Visual series and have always found them to be valuable resources."

Stephen P. Miller (Ballston Spa, NY)

"Thank you for the wonderful books you produce. It wasn't until I was an adult that I discovered how I learn — visually. Nothing compares to Visual books. I love the simple layout. I can just grab a book and use it at my computer, lesson by lesson. And I understand the material! You really know the way I think and learn. Thanks so much!"

Stacey Han (Avondale, AZ)

"I absolutely admire your company's work. Your books are terrific. The format is perfect, especially for visual learners like me. Keep them coming!"

Frederick A. Taylor, Jr. (New Port Richey, FL)

"I have several of your Visual books and they are the best I have ever used."

Stanley Clark (Crawfordville, FL)

"I bought my first Visual book last month. Wow. Now I want to learn everything in this easy format!"

Tom Vial (New York, NY)

"Thank you, thank you, thank you...for making it so easy for me to break into this high-tech world. I now own four of your books. I recommend them to anyone who is a beginner like myself."

Gay O'Donnell (Calgary, Alberta, Canada)

"I write to extend my thanks and appreciation for your books. They are clear, easy to follow, and straight to the point. Keep up the good work! I bought several of your books and they are just right! No regrets! I will always buy your books because they are the best."

Seward Kollie (Dakar, Senegal)

"Compliments to the chef!! Your books are extraordinary! Or, simply put, extra-ordinary, meaning way above the rest! THANK YOU THANK YOU THANK YOU! I buy them for friends, family, and colleagues."

Christine J. Manfrin (Castle Rock, CO)

"What fantastic teaching books you have produced! Congratulations to you and your staff. You deserve the Nobel Prize in Education in the Software category. Thanks for helping me understand computers."

Bruno Tonon (Melbourne, Australia)

"Over time, I have bought a number of your 'Read Less - Learn More' books. For me, they are THE way to learn anything easily. I learn easiest using your method of teaching."

José A. Mazón (Cuba, NY)

"I am an avid purchaser and reader of the Visual series, and they are the greatest computer books I've seen. The Visual books are perfect for people like myself who enjoy the computer, but want to know how to use it more efficiently. Your books have definitely given me a greater understanding of my computer, and have taught me to use it more effectively. Thank you very much for the hard work, effort, and dedication that you put into this series."

Alex Diaz (Las Vegas, NV)

 Credits

Project Editor
Sarah Hellert

Acquisitions Editor
Jody Lefevere

Product Development
Manager
Lindsay Sandman

Copy Editor
Kim Heusel

Technical Editor
Don Passenger

Editorial Manager
Robyn Siesky

Manufacturing
Allan Conley
Linda Cook
Paul Gilchrist
Jennifer Guynn

Illustrators
Steven Amory
Matthew Bell
Elizabeth Cardenas-Nelson
Kristin Corley
Ronda David-Burroughs
Cheryl Grubbs
Sean Johanessen
Jacob Mansfield
Rita Marley
Paul Schmitt III

Book Design
Kathie Rickard

Production Coordinator
Maridee V. Ennis

Layout
Carrie A. Foster
Jennifer Heleine
Amanda Spagnuolo

Screen Artist
Jill A. Proll

Proofreader
Tricia Liebig

Quality Control
Laura Albert

Indexer
Joan Griffitts

Vice President and
Executive Group Publisher
Richard Swadley

Vice President and
Publisher
Barry Pruett

Director of Composition
Services
Debbie Stailey

About the Author

Sherry Willard Kinkoph has written and edited over 70 books over the past 10 years covering a variety of computer topics ranging from hardware to software, from Microsoft Office programs to the Internet. Her recent titles include *Master VISUALLY eBay Business Kit, Teach Yourself VISUALLY Photoshop Elements 3.0,* and *Teach Yourself VISUALLY Office 2003.* Sherry's ongoing quest is to help users of all levels master the ever-changing computer technologies. No matter how many times they — the software manufacturers and hardware conglomerates — throw out a new version or upgrade, Sherry vows to be there to make sense of it all and help computer users get the most out of their machines.

Author's Acknowledgments

Special thanks go out to publisher Barry Pruett and to acquisitions editor Jody Lefevere for allowing me the opportunity to tackle this exciting project; to project editor Sarah Hellert for her dedication and patience in guiding this project from start to finish; to copy editor Kim Heusel, for ensuring that all the i's were dotted and t's were crossed; to technical editor Don Passenger for skillfully checking each step and offering valuable input along the way; and finally to the production team at Wiley for their able efforts in creating such a visual masterpiece. Special thanks also to my dearest sister, Melissa Cannon. Thank you for being the Sam to my Frodo during this journey.

Table of Contents

Part I: Office Features

1

Office Basics

2

Working with Files

Part II: Word

3

Adding Text

4

Formatting Text

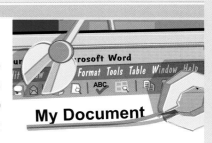

My Document

You can use Word's basic formatting commands – **bold**, *italic*, and <u>underline</u> – to quickly add formatting to your text. These three formatting styles are the most common ways to change the appearance of the text.

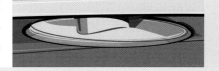

Table of Contents

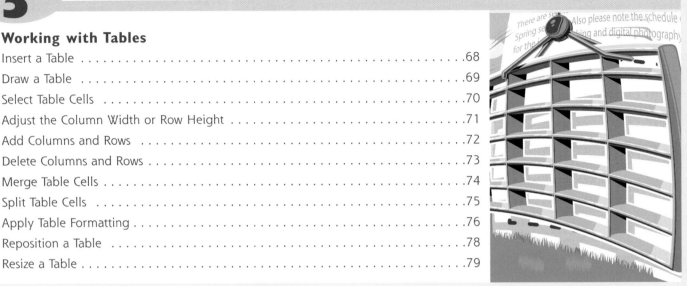

7

Previewing and Printing Documents

Part III: Excel

8

Building Spreadsheets

Table of Contents

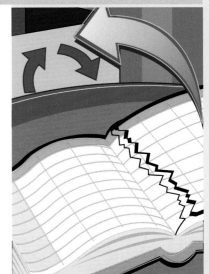

11

Formatting Worksheets

12

Working with Charts

Table of Contents

Part IV: PowerPoint

13

Presentation Basics

14

Creating Slides

15

Assembling a Slide Show

16

Presenting a Slide Show

Table of Contents

Part V: Access

17

Database Basics

18

Adding Data Using Tables

19

Adding Data Using Forms

20

Finding and Querying Data

Table of Contents

Part VI: Outlook

21

Organizing with Outlook

22

E-mailing with Outlook

Part VII: Publisher

23

Publisher Basics

24

Fine-Tuning a Publication

Table of Contents

Part VIII: Internet and Graphics

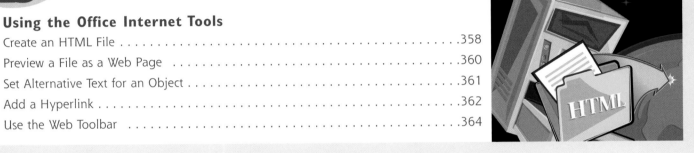

25

Using the Office Internet Tools

26

Using the Office Graphics Tools

Part 1

Office Features

Every Office application shares a common look and feel. You can find many of the same features in each program, including toolbars, menus, and task panes. Many of the tasks you perform, such as creating and working with files, share the same processes and features throughout the Office suite. When you learn how to perform a task in one program, you can use the same procedure to perform the task in another program. This makes learning the programs easier.

In this part, you learn how to navigate your way around the common Office features and basic tasks.

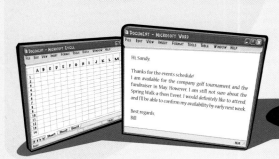

Start and Exit Office Applications

Before you begin working with any of the Microsoft Office programs, you must first open a program. When you finish your work, you can close the program. If applicable, you can save your work before exiting a program completely.

Start and Exit Office Applications

START AN OFFICE APPLICATION

① Click **Start**.

② Click **All Programs**.

③ Click **Microsoft Office**.

④ Click the name of the program you want to open.

Note: Depending on which programs you installed, not all of the Office programs may be listed in the menu.

The program you selected opens in a program window.

Note: See the next section to learn how to identify different areas of the program window.

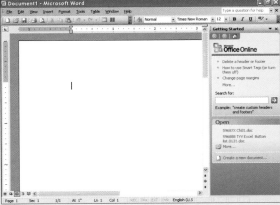

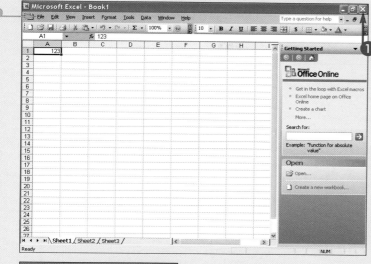

EXIT AN OFFICE APPLICATION

1 Click the **Close** button (⊠).

● You can also click **File** and then **Exit**.

If you have not yet saved your work, the program prompts you to do so before exiting.

Note: *Outlook does not prompt you to save anything before closing, unless you have unsaved e-mail messages you were composing.*

2 Click **Yes** to save.

The program window closes.

● If you click **No**, the program closes without saving your data.

● If you click **Cancel**, the program window remains open.

Can I create a shortcut icon for an Office application?

Yes. You can create a shortcut icon that appears on the Windows desktop. Any time you want to open the program, simply double-click the shortcut icon. Follow these steps:

1 Right-click over a blank area of the desktop and click **New**.

2 Click **Shortcut**.

The Create Shortcut dialog box appears.

3 Click **Browse**, navigate to the Office program, and double-click the filename.

4 Click **Next**.

5 Type a name for the shortcut.

6 Click **Finish**.

The new shortcut icon is added to the desktop.

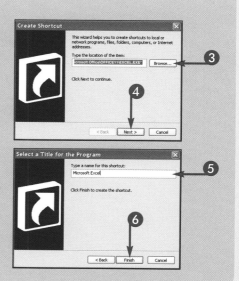

Navigate the
Program Windows

All of the Microsoft Office programs share a common appearance and many of the same features, such as menu bars, toolbars, and scroll bars. When you learn your way around one program, you can easily use the same skills to navigate the other Office programs. If you are new to Office 2003, take a moment and familiarize yourself with the types of on-screen elements you can expect to encounter.

Title Bar
Displays the name of the open file and the Office Program.

Menu Bar
Displays menus which, when clicked, reveal commands.

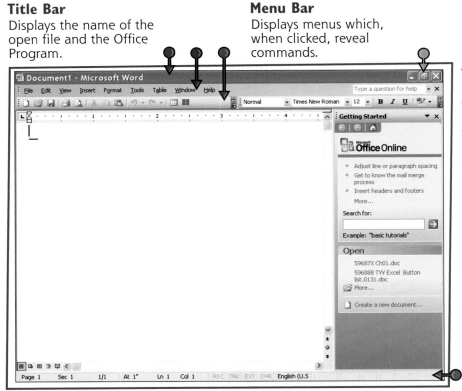

Toolbars
Display shortcut buttons to common tasks. The Standard and Formatting toolbars share on-screen space in Word and Excel.

Program Window Controls
Use these three buttons to minimize, maximize, or close the program window.

Status Bar
Displays information about the current worksheet or file.

Formula Bar

Use this bar, found in Excel, to type and edit formulas and perform calculations on your worksheet data.

Window Controls

Use these buttons to minimize, maximize, or close the current document.

Task Pane

This pane offers links to common program tasks. The task pane can display several different panes of information or controls.

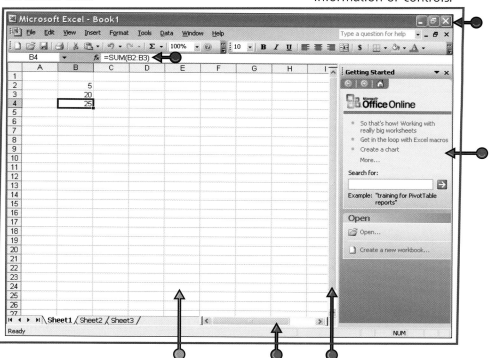

Work Area

The main work area is where you add and work with data in a program. Depending on the Office program, the work area may be a document, a worksheet, or a slide.

Scroll Bars

Use the vertical and horizontal scroll bars to scroll through the item displayed in the work area, such as a document or worksheet.

Work with
Task Panes

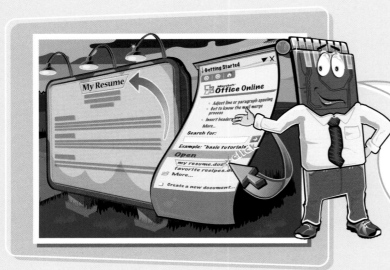

You can use the task pane to access common commands and controls. You can display more than one pane in the task pane area, and you can use the navigation buttons to view open panes. New to Office 2003, the task pane is displayed on the right side of every program window by default, with the exception of Publisher, which displays the pane on the left side of the window. You can close the task pane at any time to free up workspace on-screen.

Work with Task Panes

DISPLAY PANES

1. Click here to display a list of available panes.

2. Click a pane.

Note: If the task pane is not displayed, click **View** and then **Task Pane**.

The pane appears.

Note: The task pane is not available in Outlook.

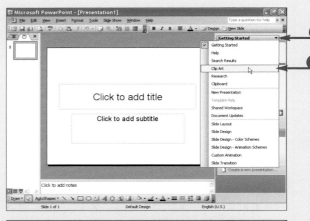

- If two or more panes are displayed, you can click the navigation buttons (◙ and ◙) to move between panes.

- You can click a link to activate a feature.

- You can click the **Home** button (🏠) to return to the default task pane, the Getting Started pane.

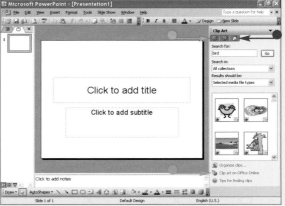

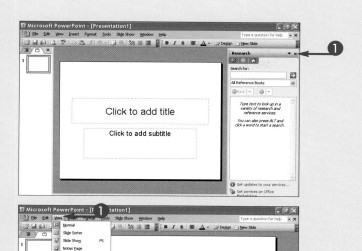

CLOSE THE TASK PANE

① Click ☒.

The task pane closes.

REOPEN THE TASK PANE

① Click **View**.

② Click **Task Pane**.

The task pane opens.

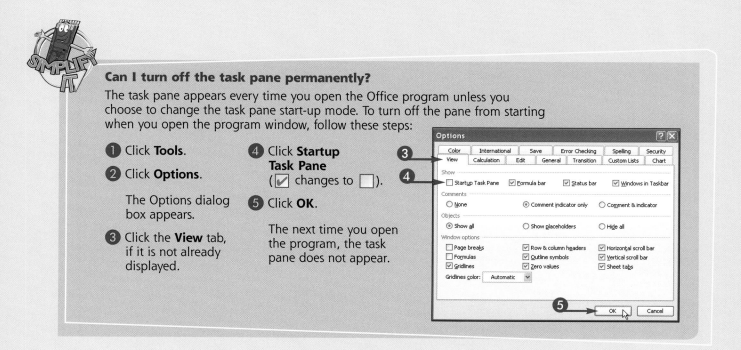

Can I turn off the task pane permanently?

The task pane appears every time you open the Office program unless you choose to change the task pane start-up mode. To turn off the pane from starting when you open the program window, follow these steps:

① Click **Tools**.

② Click **Options**.

The Options dialog box appears.

③ Click the **View** tab, if it is not already displayed.

④ Click **Startup Task Pane**
(☑ changes to ☐).

⑤ Click **OK**.

The next time you open the program, the task pane does not appear.

Work with Menus and Toolbars

In Word, Excel, and PowerPoint, the Standard and Formatting toolbars share the same row on-screen. You can use the Toolbar Options button to display all the buttons for a particular toolbar.

You can use menus and toolbars to activate commands and carry out tasks in the Office programs. A menu displays commands in a drop-down list, while toolbars display commands as buttons you can click. By default, the personalized menus and toolbars display the commands and buttons you use the most, making it easier to select the same commands again and again. You can display the full menu or all the available toolbar buttons when you need to activate another command or feature.

Work with Menus and Toolbars

DISPLAY A FULL MENU

1 Click a menu name.

At first, the menu displays the most recently used commands.

2 Click 🖫.

Note: *If the full menu already appears, the personalized menu option is turned off.*

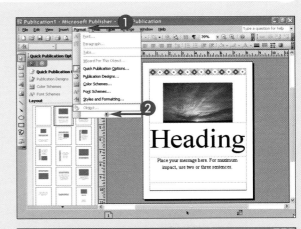

● The full menu appears.

Note: *You can also wait a few seconds after clicking a menu name and the full menu appears.*

You can now click the command you want to activate.

Note: *See the tip in this section to learn how to turn personalized menus on or off.*

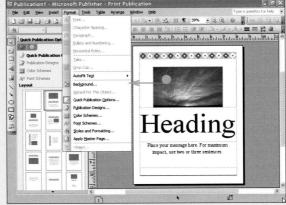

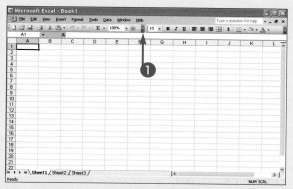

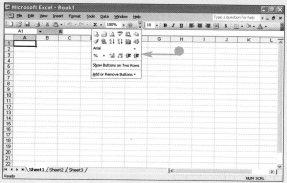

DISPLAY A FULL TOOLBAR

1 Click 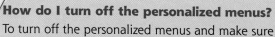.

The full list of available toolbar buttons appears.

● You can click the button you want to activate.

Note: *To learn how to hide and display toolbars, see the next section.*

How do I turn off the personalized menus?

To turn off the personalized menus and make sure every menu command is displayed in full every time you open a menu, follow these steps:

1 Click **Tools**.

2 Click **Customize**.

The Customize dialog box appears.

3 Click the **Options** tab, if it is not already displayed.

4 Click **Always show full menus** (☐ changes to ☑).

5 Click **Close**.

The next time you open a menu, it displays in full.

If the personalized menus option is already turned off, you can follow these steps to turn the option on again.

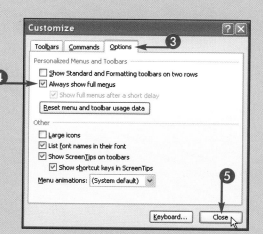

Display and Hide Toolbars

You can use toolbars to quickly activate common tasks and commands with a click of a button. By default, some of the Office programs, such as Word and Excel, display the Standard and Formatting toolbars side by side at the top of the program window. Because of the shared space, lesser-used buttons may not appear on the toolbars but remain hidden from view in the Toolbar Options drop-down list.

You can control which buttons appear on any of the toolbars, adding and subtracting buttons to suit the way in which you work. To learn more about customizing toolbars, see the next section.

Display and Hide Toolbars

DISPLAY FULL TOOLBARS

① Click **Tools**.

② Click **Customize**.

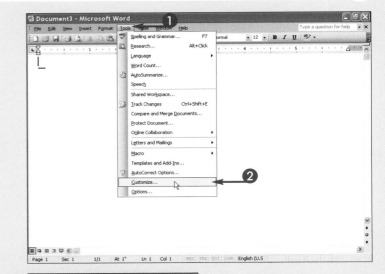

The Customize dialog box appears.

③ Click the **Options** tab if it does not already appear in front.

④ Click **Show Standard and Formatting toolbars on two rows** (☐ changes to ✔).

⑤ Click **Close**.

CHAPTER

Office Basics

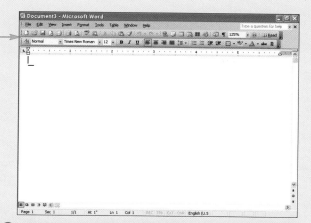

● The toolbars appear on separate rows, displaying all the available buttons.

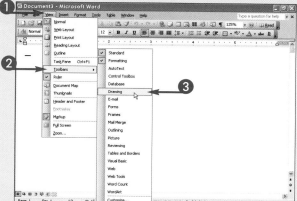

HIDE OR DISPLAY A TOOLBAR

1. Click **View**.

2. Click **Toolbars**.

3. Click the toolbar you want to display or hide.

   A check mark (☑) next to the toolbar name indicates the toolbar is displayed.

If my toolbars appear side by side, how do I view the hidden buttons?
You can click the **Toolbar Options** button (▮) to display a menu of buttons that are not currently visible on the toolbar. Then click the button you want to activate. By default, the Standard and Formatting toolbars show only the most recently used buttons. You can also click the **Show Buttons on Two Rows** command on the drop-down menu to turn on the full toolbar display.

How do I find out what a particular button does?
If you move your mouse pointer over a button on any toolbar, a ScreenTips box appears identifying the button's name. By default, the ScreenTips feature is turned on in all of the Office programs. To learn more about customizing toolbars or turning the feature off, see the next section.

13

Customize Toolbars

You can customize any Office toolbar, or even create your own toolbar containing only the buttons you use the most. Every Office toolbar includes a set of default buttons. You can add commands to the button set, or subtract commands from the set to tailor the toolbar to work the way you want.

Customize Toolbars

1 Click **Tools**.

2 Click **Customize**.

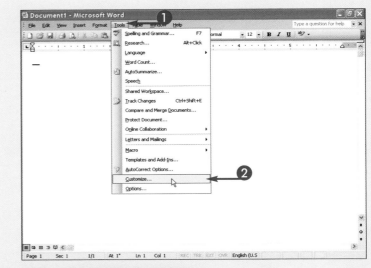

The Customize dialog box appears.

3 Click the **Toolbars** tab.

4 Click the toolbar you want to customize (☐ changes to ☑).

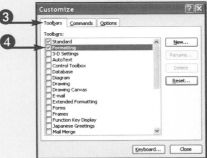

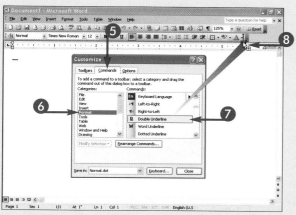

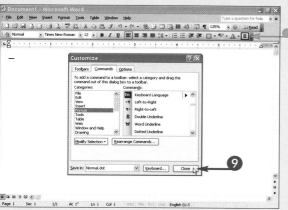

5 Click the **Commands** tab.

6 Click a command category.

7 Scroll to the command you want to add.

8 Click and drag the command from the list box and drop it on the toolbar where you want it to appear.

● The button is added to the toolbar.

You can continue adding more buttons to the toolbar as needed.

To remove a button from the toolbar, click and drag it off the toolbar.

9 When finished, click **Close**.

Note: You can also use the Customize dialog box to add and subtract commands from your menus.

How do I create a brand-new toolbar from scratch?
You can build a new toolbar and assign it a unique name. You can then add buttons to the toolbar to create a customized toolbar. To do this, repeat Steps **1** to **3** shown in this section to open the Customize dialog box. Click **New**, and in the New Toolbar dialog box that appears, type a name for the toolbar. Click **OK**, and the new toolbar appears on-screen. Repeat Steps **5** to **9** to add buttons to the toolbar. After you create a new toolbar, it is added to the list of available toolbars you can use with the program.

Find Help with Office

You can use the Office Help tools to assist you when you run into a problem or need more explanation about a particular task. With an Internet connection, you can use Microsoft's online help files to quickly access information about an Office feature. The Help pane offers tools for searching for topics you want to learn more about.

You must log on to your Internet connection in order to use the online help files.

Find Help with Office

① Display the task pane.

Note: See the section "Work with Task Panes," earlier in this chapter, to learn more about viewing task panes.

② Click the **Other Task Panes** button (⬇).

③ Click **Help**.

The Help pane opens.

④ Type a word or phrase you want to learn more about.

⑤ Click the **Start Searching** button (➡).

You can also press **Enter** to start the search.

● You can also click this link to look for topics in the table of contents.

Note: You may need to log on to the Internet to access Microsoft's online help files.

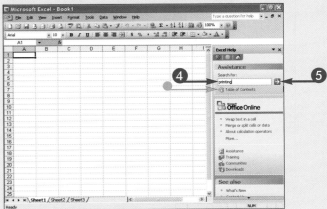

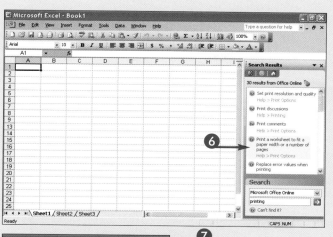

The Search Results pane opens, displaying a list of possible matches.

6 Click a link to learn more about a topic.

The Microsoft Help window opens, and you can read more about the topic.

● You can click a link to learn more about a subject.

● You can use the **Back** (⇦) and **Forward** (⇨) buttons to move back and forth between help topics.

● You can click **Print** (🖨) to print the information.

7 Click ✕ to close the window.

SIMPLIFY IT

Can I use the Type a question for help box on the menu bar to find help?
Yes. To use the box, follow these steps. Click inside the box and type the question, phrase, or word about which you want to know more. Press **Enter**. The Search Results pane appears, listing possible matches. You can click a topic to learn more about the subject.

What does the Office Assistant do?
You can use the animated Office Assistant to help you with various tasks you perform in the Office programs. To turn the Assistant on, click the **Help** menu and then click **Show the Office Assistant**. The assistant animates when you perform a common task or when it offers you assistance. It stays out of the way until needed. To ask a question, click the animated assistant, type a question or keyword, and then press **Enter**. To turn the assistant off again, click the **Help** menu and then **Hide the Office Assistant**.

Start a
New File

With the exception of Outlook, you can create new files any time you want to add data to an Office program. Depending on the program you are working with, you can create different types of new files. When you create a new file in Word, it is called a *document*. In Excel, a new file is called a *workbook*. In Access, new files are called *databases*. If you start a new file in PowerPoint, it is called a *presentation*. In Publisher a new file is called a *publication*.

Start a New File

USE THE NEW BUTTON

① Click the **New** button (🗅) on the Standard toolbar.

Note: *To learn more about viewing toolbars, see Chapter 1.*

The Office program opens a new blank file.

In this example, a new file opens in Word.

If you click 🗅 in Access, the New File task pane appears, and you can start a blank database.

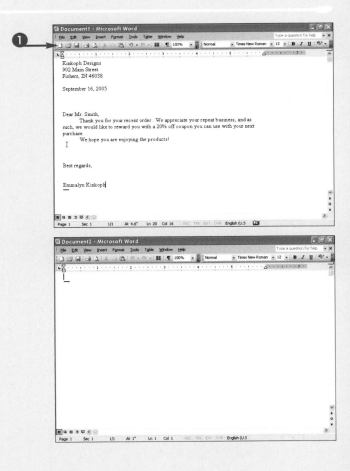

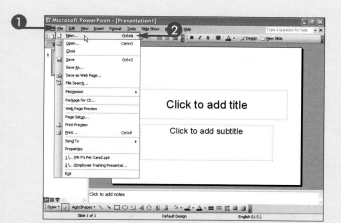

START A FILE WITH THE TASK PANE

1. Click **File**.

2. Click **New**.

   If the task pane is already open, you can click ▼ and then **New**.

   The task pane opens a pane for creating a new document, workbook, presentation, database, or publication.

   In this example, the New Presentation pane opens in PowerPoint.

3. Click the type of file you want to create.

   A new file opens on-screen.

   Note: See Chapter 1 to learn more about working with the Office task panes.

How do I create a new file based on a template?

Many of the Office programs allow you to build a new file based on a template. For example, in Word, you can choose from letters, faxes, memos, reports, and more. Templates are simply preformatted layouts you can use to create files, substituting your own text for the placeholder text found in the template. In PowerPoint and Publisher, you use a template every time you choose a presentation or publication design. In Word, Excel, and Access, you can choose from a library of templates that install with the program. Simply click the appropriate templates link in the New Document, New Workbook, or New File task pane.

Where else can I find templates to use with my Microsoft Office programs?

Using your Internet connection, you can find more Office templates on the Microsoft Web site. Click the **Templates on Office Online** link to access the site and download any templates you like. You can also find additional templates created by other users. Conduct a Web search for the templates related to the Office program you want to use.

Save a File

Each Office program saves to a default file type. For example, when you save an Excel workbook, the XLS file format is assigned.

You can save your data to reuse it or share it with others. It is also good practice to frequently save any file you are working on in case of a power failure or computer crash. When you save a file, you can give it a unique filename, and choose to store it in a particular folder or drive.

Save a File

1 Click the **Save** button (🔲) on the Standard toolbar.

Note: To learn more about viewing toolbars, see Chapter 1.

● You can also click **File** and then **Save** or **Save As**.

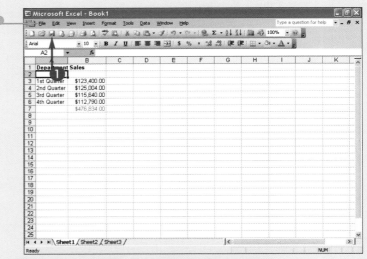

The Save As dialog box appears.

2 Click here to navigate and select the folder or drive to which you want to save the file.

3 Click here and type a name for the file.

4 Click **Save**.

The Office program saves the file and the new filename appears on the program window's title bar.

Open an Existing File

You can open a file you previously worked on to continue adding or editing data. Regardless of whether you store a file in a folder on your computer's hard drive, on a floppy disk, or a CD, you can easily access files using the Open dialog box.

With the exception of Outlook, each Office program automatically lists your most recent files for quick access at the bottom of the File menu or in the Getting Started task pane.

Open an Existing File

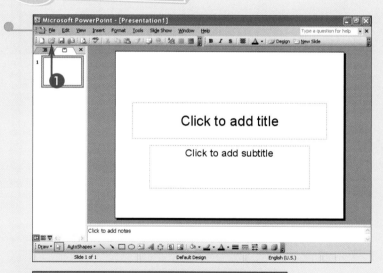

① Click the **Open** button ([image]) on the Standard toolbar.

Note: To learn more about viewing toolbars, see Chapter 1.

● You can also click **File** and then **Open**.

You can also use the Getting Started or New Workbook panes to open existing files.

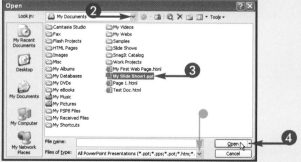

The Open dialog box appears.

② Click here to navigate to and select the folder or drive where you stored the file.

● You can look for a specific file type using the format drop-down list.

③ Click the name of the file you want to open.

④ Click **Open**.

The file opens in the program window.

21

Close
a File

The document window controls are not available in Publisher, Access, or Outlook.

You can close a file you are no longer using without closing the entire program window. Closing unnecessary files frees up processing power on your computer.

Close a File

1 Click the **Close Window** button (☒) on the Menu bar.

● You can also click **File** and then **Close**.

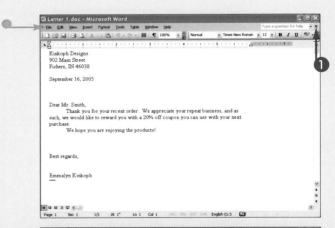

The file closes.

In this example, the Word program window remains open.

Note: To learn how to close the program entirely, see Chapter 1.

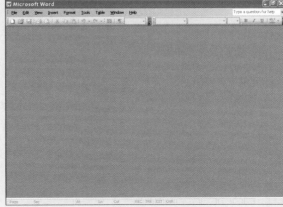

Find
a File

If you are looking for a file you recently worked on, the Getting Started task pane and the File menu lists recently used files.

You can use the Basic File Search task pane to search for an Office file. This pane is only available through the File Search command. You can use the pane to look for a particular filename as well as search through specific folders or drives. This technique is not applicable in Outlook.

Find a File

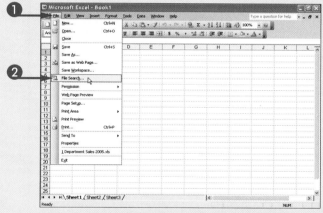

1 Click **File**.

2 Click **File Search**.

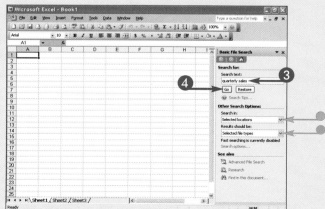

The Basic File Search pane appears.

3 Type a search keyword or filename.

● To search a particular folder or drive, click the **Search in** ⏷ and choose a folder or drive.

● To search for a specific file type, click the **Results should be** ⏷ and choose a file format.

4 Click **Go**.

The Office program conducts a search for the file and displays any matching results in the task pane.

Preview
a File

In Word, Excel, PowerPoint, Publisher, and Access, you can preview a file to see how it appears before it is printed. The Print Preview window includes options for viewing multiple pages, changing the view magnification, and printing the file.

Preview a File

① Click **File**.

② Click **Print Preview**.

The Print Preview window appears.

● You can change your magnification level using this drop-down list.

● If your file contains more than one page, you can view multiple pages on-screen by clicking the **Multiple Pages** button (🖹).

● You can click the **Print** button (🖨) to print the file.

③ Click **Close**.

Print Preview closes.

Print a File

If you have a printer connected to your computer, you can print your Microsoft Office files. You can send a file directly to the printer using the default printer settings, or you can open the Print dialog box and make changes to the printer settings. The printer settings may vary slightly among Office programs.

Print a File

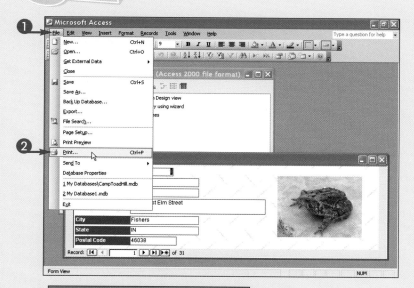

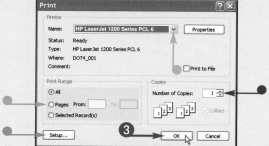

① Click **File**.

② Click **Print**.

To print a file without adjusting any printer settings, click the **Print** button (🖨) on the Standard toolbar.

The Print dialog box appears.

● You can choose a printer from this drop-down list.

● You can print a selection from the file, or specific pages using the available settings.

● You can specify a number of copies to print.

● For more printer options, click here.

③ Click **OK**.

The Office program sends the file to the printer for printing.

25

Cut, Copy, and Paste Data

The Copy command makes a duplicate of the selected data, while the Cut command removes the data from the original file entirely. When you copy or paste data, it is placed in the Windows Clipboard until you are ready to paste it into place.

You can use the Cut, Copy, and Paste commands to copy data within a program, or move and share data among Office programs. For example, you might copy a graphic from Word and place it in a PowerPoint slide, or copy data from Excel to display in a Publisher publication. You can also drag and drop data to move and copy it within a file.

Cut, Copy, and Paste Data

CUT AND COPY DATA

1 Select the data you want to cut or copy.

2 Click the **Cut** button (⬚) to move data, or the **Copy** button (⬚) to copy data.

Note: *You can also use keyboard shortcuts to cut and copy. Press* `Ctrl` + `X` *to cut or* `Ctrl` + `C` *to copy.*

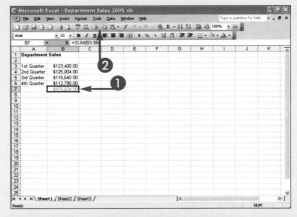

The data is placed in the Windows Clipboard.

3 Click the point where you want to insert the cut or copied data.

You can also open another file to copy to.

4 Click the **Paste** button (⬚).

Note: *You can also press* `Ctrl` + `V` *to paste data.*

The data appears in the new location.

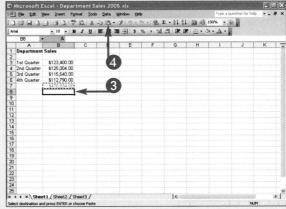

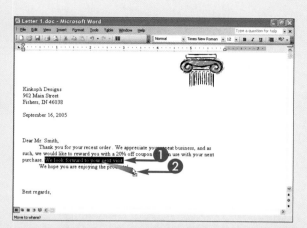

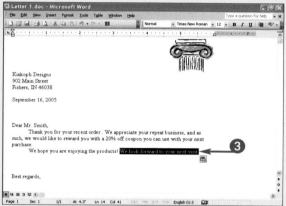

DRAG AND DROP DATA

1 Select the data you want to cut or copy.

2 Click and drag the data to a new location.

To copy the data as you drag it, press and hold `Ctrl`.

3 Release the mouse button to drop the data in place.

The data appears in the new location.

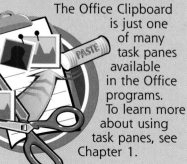

When I cut or copy data, an icon appears. What is it?

The Paste Options smart tag (📋▾) may appear when you perform any cut or copy task. You can click the smart tag to view a drop-down list of related options for the task you are performing. You can click an option from the list to activate the option. If you prefer not to use the smart tag, you can ignore it. The tag disappears if you continue to work on the file. If the Paste Options smart tags are turned off, you can click **Tools**, click **Options**, and then select the **Show Paste Options** check box (☐ changes to ☑) on the **Edit** tab to turn the feature on again.

Can I cut or copy multiple pieces of data?

Yes. You can cut or copy multiple pieces of data, and the Office Clipboard task pane opens. The Office Clipboard holds up to 24 items. You can paste them in whatever order you choose, or you can opt to paste them all at the same time. The Office Clipboard is just one of many task panes available in the Office programs. To learn more about using task panes, see Chapter 1.

Link and Embed Data

With linked data, any changes you make to the data in the client program are automatically updated in the source file. With embedded data, no update occurs if you make changes to the client data; however, the data still retains a connection to the source data and you can use this connection to quickly return to the source data and make changes.

You can use object linking and embedding (OLE) to share data across Microsoft Office programs. With OLE, data maintains a connection with the original program, called the *source* file. The recipient of the linked or embedded data is called the *client* file.

Link and Embed Data

1 Select the data you want to link or embed.

2 Click 📋.

● You can also click **Edit** and then click **Copy**.

The data is placed in the Windows Clipboard.

3 Open the file in which you want to link or embed the data.

4 Click where you want the data to appear in the file.

5 Click **Edit**.

6 Click **Paste Special**.

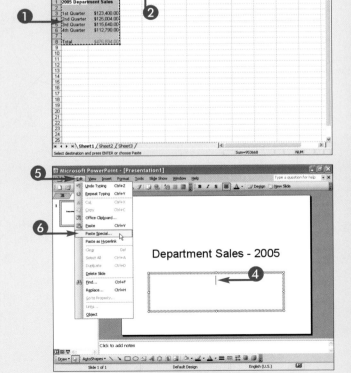

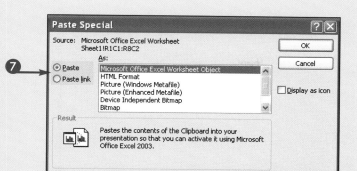

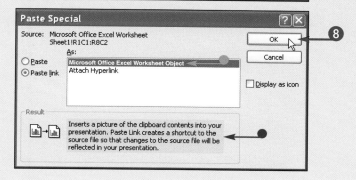

The Paste Special dialog box appears.

⑦ Click the option you want to apply (◯ changes to ◉).

You can select the **Paste link** option to link the data, or you can select the **Paste** option to embed the data.

● You can select a format for the linked or embedded data here.

● The Result box displays notes about the action.

⑧ Click **OK**.

The data is linked or embedded.

How do I return to the source data if my data is embedded?

You can double-click the embedded data to reopen the source file. This technique allows you to open the source file directly without first opening the program used to create the file and then opening the file itself. After you open the source file, you can make changes to the original data, and then copy and paste it into the client file.

What happens if I move the source file?

If you rename, delete, or move the source file, the link is broken and an error message appears in the client file. You can edit your links using the Links dialog box, including changing the source or breaking a link. To access the dialog box, click **Edit** and then **Links**.

Assign a Password to a File

You can add security to your Word, Excel, and PowerPoint data by assigning passwords to your files. You can assign a password that makes the file inoperable unless the user knows the password, or you can assign a password that allows other users to open the file but not make any changes to it.

The very best passwords contain a mix of upper- and lowercase letters, numbers, and symbols.

Assign a Password to a File

① Click **Tools**.

② Click **Options**.

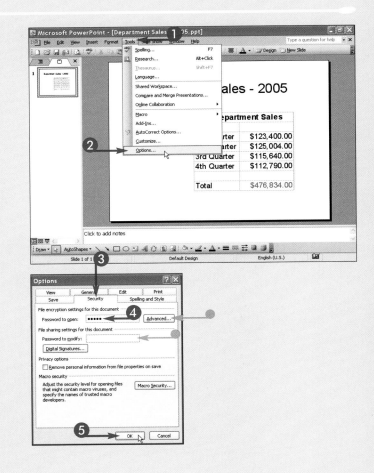

The Options dialog box appears.

③ Click the **Security** tab.

④ Click in the **Password to open** box and type a password.

● To allow users to view the file but not make changes, type a password here.

⑤ Click **OK**.

● If you want to set an encryption type, click **Advanced** and choose an encryption.

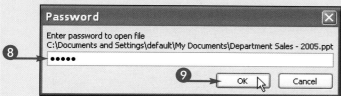

The Confirm Password dialog box appears.

6 Retype the password exactly as you typed it in Step **4**.

7 Click **OK**.

The password is assigned to the file.

The next time you open the file, the Office program prompts you for the password.

8 Type the password.

9 Click **OK** to open the file.

What happens if I forget a password?

It is crucial that you remember your Office passwords. If you lose a password, you can no longer open the file. Lost passwords cannot be recovered. Consider writing the password down and keeping it in a safe place. Be sure to keep a record of which password goes with which file.

How do I remove a password?

To remove a password you no longer want, reopen the Options dialog box following the steps in this section and click the **Security** tab. Delete the current password and click **OK**. You can also reset the password by typing and confirming a new password.

Part II

Word

Word is the number one selling word processing program on the market today. You can use Word to tackle any project involving text, such as correspondence, reports, mass mailings, and more. Word's versatile formatting features allow you to enhance your text documents with ease, and add additional elements such as tables, headers and footers, lists, and more. Word offers a variety of editing tools to help you make your document look its best.

In this part, you learn how to build and format Word documents and tap into Word's many tools to preview, proofread, and print your documents.

Change Word's Views

As you begin working with Word, you can choose several ways to view the documents you create. For example, you can use the Zoom tool to control the magnification of your document. You can also choose from five different layout views: Normal, Print Layout, Outline, Web Layout, and Reading Layout.

Normal view displays only the text area of the document. Print Layout view shows margins, headers, and footers. Use Outline view to work with outline levels in a document. Web Layout view displays a Web page preview of your document. Reading Layout view optimizes your document for easy reading and less strain on the eyes.

Change Word's Views

USE THE ZOOM TOOL

1. Click the **Zoom** ☐ on the Standard toolbar.

2. Click a zoom level.

   You can also type a zoom percentage in the text field and press `Enter` to change the view.

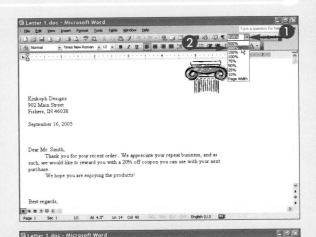

Word applies the magnification to the document.

In this example, Word magnifies the view to 200 percent.

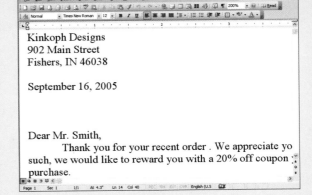

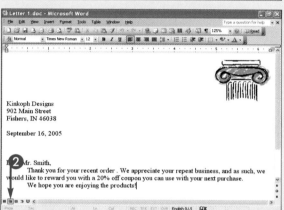

SWITCH LAYOUT VIEWS

① Click a layout view button.

Word immediately displays the new view.

● You can also switch views using the View menu.

In this example, Print Layout view displays all the positioning of text, graphics, and other elements on the page.

② Click another layout view icon.

In this example, Web Layout view displays all the positioning of text, graphics, and other elements as they appear in a Web browser.

How can I make more room in the workspace area to view my document?

You can turn off different Word elements to free on-screen viewing space for your documents. For example, closing the task pane can free up quite a bit of room on the right side of the document. See Chapter 1 to learn more about hiding the task pane. You can also hide the ruler and toolbars to gain more workspace area. You can click the **View** menu and turn off the ruler or individual toolbars.

What can I do in the Outline layout view?

If you create documents built on a structure such as headings, subheadings, and body text, you can use the Outline view to see and make changes to the document structure. When you activate the Outline view, the Outlining toolbar appears. You can use the buttons on the toolbar to change heading styles and levels to modify your document's structure.

Type and Edit Text

When you open Microsoft Word, a blank document appears, ready for you to start typing text. Whether you want to write a letter, a memo, or a report, you can use Word to quickly type and edit text.

Type and Edit Text

TYPE TEXT

1. Start typing your text.

   Word automatically wraps the text to the next line for you.

   - The insertion point, or cursor, marks the current location where text appears when you start typing.

   - This symbol marks the end of the document.

2. Press **Enter** to start a new paragraph.

   - You can press **Enter** twice to add an extra space between paragraphs.

   - You can press **Tab** to quickly create an indent for a line of text.

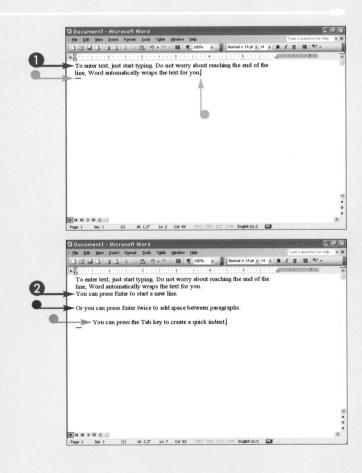

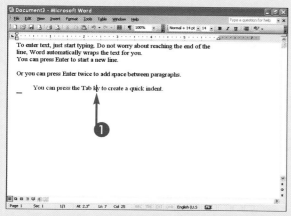

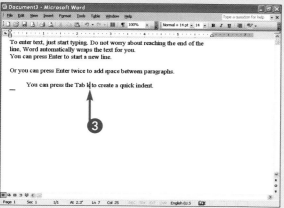

EDIT TEXT

1 Click in the document where you want to fix a mistake.

2 Press **Backspace** to delete characters to the left of the cursor.

3 Press **Delete** to delete characters to the right of the cursor.

You can also delete selected text.

Note: See the next section to learn how to select characters, words, and paragraphs in Word.

Note: If you make a spelling mistake, Word's AutoCorrect feature comes into play, either correcting the mistake or underlining it in red.

Note: Learn more about AutoCorrect in Chapter 7.

How do I add lines to my Word documents?

With some special characters, if you type three or more and press **Enter**, Word replaces the characters with a line style. For example, if you type three asterisks and press **Enter**, Word displays a dotted line. Use this table for more line styles you can add:

Character	Line Style
•	Dotted line
=	Double line
~	Wavy line
#	Thick decorative line
_	Thick single line

What is the difference between Insert and Overtype mode?

By default, Word is set to Insert mode, which means anywhere you insert the cursor and start typing, the existing text moves over for any new text you type. If you switch to Overtype mode, any existing text is overwritten with the new text. You can toggle between Insert and Overtype modes by double-clicking the **OVR** setting on the status bar or by pressing **Insert** on the keyboard.

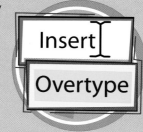

Select Text

You can select text in your document to perform different tasks, such as editing and formatting. For example, you can select a word and make it italicized, or select a paragraph to remove it from the document. When you select text, it appears highlighted in a black box on-screen. Word offers several different selection techniques you can apply to select a single character, a word, a sentence, a paragraph, or the entire document.

Select Text

CLICK AND DRAG TO SELECT TEXT

1 Click in front of the word or character you want to select.

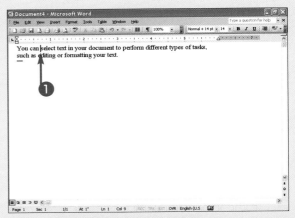

2 Drag across the text you want to select.

Word selects any characters you drag across.

You can use this technique to select characters, words, sentences, paragraphs, and more.

To deselect selected text, simply click anywhere outside the text or press any keyboard arrow key.

Note: To select all the text in a document, click the **Edit** menu and then click **Select All**.

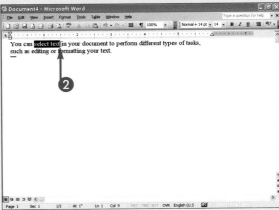

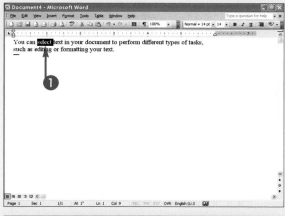

SELECT TEXT WITH A MOUSE CLICK

❶ Double-click anywhere inside a word you want to select.

Word selects the text.

You can also triple-click anywhere inside a paragraph to select a paragraph.

SELECT TEXT USING THE MARGIN

❶ Click inside the left margin.

Word selects the entire line of text.

You can double-click inside the left margin to select a paragraph.

You can triple-click inside the left margin to select all the text in the document.

Can I also use my keyboard to select text?

Yes. You can use keyboard shortcuts to select text in your document. You can use the ↓ , ← , → , and ↑ keys to move around the document. To select text, use one of these shortcuts:

To select a single word, press Ctrl + Shift + ← or Ctrl + Shift + → .

To select a paragraph, press Ctrl + Shift + ↓ or Ctrl + Shift + ↑ .

To select all the text from the cursor onward, press Ctrl + Shift + End .

To select all the text above the current cursor location, press Ctrl + Shift + home.

To select the entire document, press Ctrl + A.

Move and
Copy Text

You can move text from one location to another in your document. You can also duplicate text and paste a copy in another spot on the page. You can use the Cut, Copy, and Paste commands to move or copy a single character, a word, or an entire paragraph.

Move and Copy Text

DRAG AND DROP TEXT

1 Select the text you want to move or copy.

Note: *See the previous section to learn how to select text.*

2 Drag the text to a new location in the document.

To copy the text, press **Ctrl** while dragging.

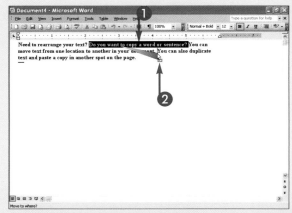

3 Drop the text in place.

Word moves or copies the text.

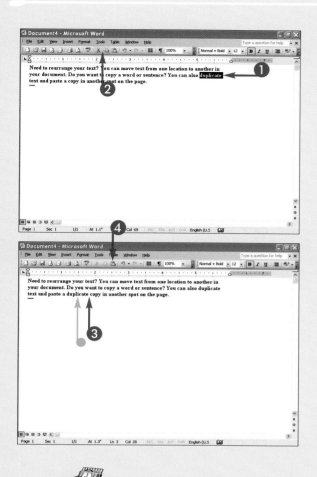

MOVE OR COPY TEXT WITH TOOLBAR BUTTONS

1 Select the text you want to move or copy.

2 Click 🔏 to move the text, or click 🖹 to copy the text.

3 Click where you want to insert the cut or copied text.

4 Click 🖺.

● Word pastes the text in place.

How do I use the smart tag to paste text?

As soon as you finish pasting text into place, Word displays a smart tag icon. You can click the icon to display a menu of related moving or copying options for the text, such as copying formatting along with the word. You can click the smart tag to reveal the list of options. You can ignore the smart tag and it goes away when you continue working in the document.

How do I turn off the smart tags in Word?

By default, the smart tags are turned on in Word to help you with common tasks. To turn the feature off, click **Tools** and then **Options** to open the Options dialog box. In the **Edit** tab, deselect the **Smart cut and paste** option (☑ changes to ☐). Click **OK** to apply your changes. The next time you move or copy an item, the smart tag no longer appears.

Save Time with AutoText

You can speed up your text entry tasks by using Word's AutoText tool. For example, if you repeatedly type the same company name over and over again with your documents, you can add the name to the list of AutoText entries. The next time you begin to type the name, AutoText immediately enters the name for you.

The AutoText feature is one of several correction features you can find in Word. You can find additional correction features in the AutoCorrect dialog box. See Chapter 7 to learn more about the AutoCorrect feature.

Save Time with AutoText

ADD AN AUTOTEXT ENTRY

1 Select the text you want to add to the AutoText feature.

Note: See the section "Select Text," earlier in this chapter, to learn how to select text.

2 Click **Insert**.

3 Click **AutoText**.

4 Click **New**.

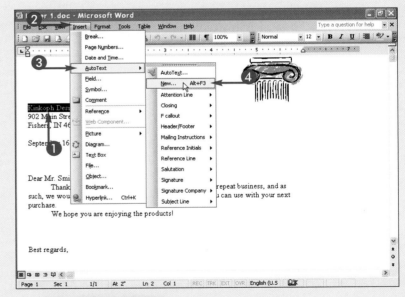

The Create AutoText dialog box appears.

5 Type a name for the entry, or use the default name suggestion.

6 Click **OK**.

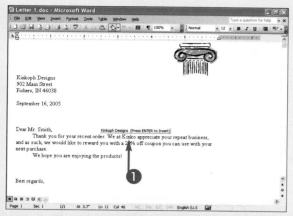

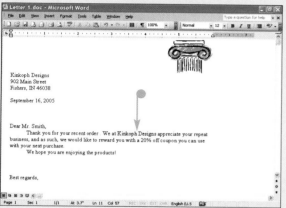

INSERT AUTOTEXT

1 To insert an AutoText entry, start typing the first few letters of the text.

AutoText displays an AutoComplete tip containing the full entry.

2 Press **Enter**.

● Word inserts the AutoText entry into the document.

What does the AutoText toolbar do?

The AutoText toolbar offers you another way to create AutoText entries. To open the toolbar, click **View**, **Toolbars**, and then **AutoText**. To turn text into an entry, select the text and click **New** from the AutoText toolbar. To open the AutoText library of entries, you can click the **AutoText** button (▦).

How do I remove an AutoText entry?

You can remove an AutoText entry you no longer need. Click **Insert**, **AutoText**, and then **AutoText** to open the AutoText tab of the AutoCorrect dialog box. You can also click the **AutoText** button (▦) on the AutoText toolbar to open the dialog box. Next, select the entry that you want to remove. Click **Delete** to remove the entry, and then click **OK** to close the dialog box. If you want to add more entries to the library, leave the dialog box open and click **Insert** to add more entries.

Insert Symbols

From time to time, you might need to insert a special symbol or character into your Word document, such as a trademark symbol or an em dash character. You can use the Symbol dialog box to access a wide range of special characters and symbols, including mathematical and Greek symbols, architectural symbols, and more.

Insert Symbols

INSERT A SYMBOL

① Click where you want to insert a symbol.

② Click **Insert**.

③ Click **Symbol**.

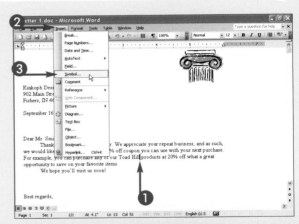

The Symbol dialog box appears.

④ To add a symbol, click the **Symbols** tab.

⑤ Click a symbol.

⑥ Click **Insert**.

● Word inserts the symbol.

The dialog box remains open so you can add more symbols to your text.

● This area displays recently used symbols you can quickly click to insert again.

⑦ When finished, click **Close**.

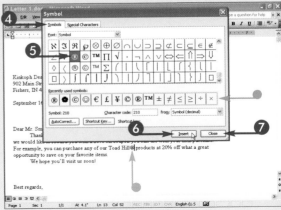

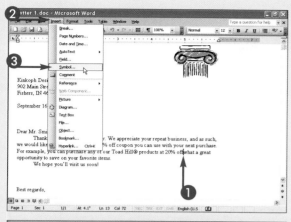

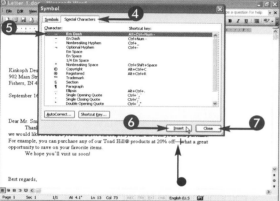

INSERT A SPECIAL CHARACTER

1 Click where you want to insert a character.

2 Click **Insert**.

3 Click **Symbol**.

The Symbol dialog box appears.

4 To add a special character, click the **Special Characters** tab.

5 Click the character you want to insert.

6 Click **Insert**.

● Word adds the character to the current cursor location in the document.

The dialog box remains open so you can add more characters to your text.

7 When finished, click **Close**.

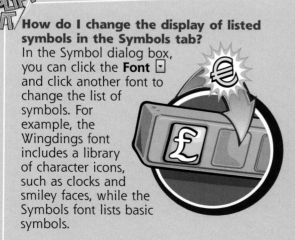

How do I change the display of listed symbols in the Symbols tab?
In the Symbol dialog box, you can click the **Font** ⊡ and click another font to change the list of symbols. For example, the Wingdings font includes a library of character icons, such as clocks and smiley faces, while the Symbols font lists basic symbols.

When I type some special characters on the keyboard, Word inserts a symbol for me. Why?
Word's AutoCorrect feature automatically inserts common symbols for certain keyboard combinations. For example, if you type (c), AutoCorrect immediately changes it to the copyright symbol, ©. To undo the occurrence, simply click the **Undo** button (⟲) immediately to return to (c). To learn more about AutoCorrect, see Chapter 7.

Add Basic Formatting

Word features a variety of formatting options you can apply to control the appearance of your document. Text formatting, such as bold and italics, changes the appearance of characters. You can apply text formatting to a single character, a word, a sentence, a paragraph, or an entire document.

You can use Word's basic formatting commands — bold, italic, and underline — to quickly add formatting to your text. These three formatting styles are the most common ways to change the appearance of text in a document.

Add Basic Formatting

① Select the text you want to format.

Note: See Chapter 3 to learn how to select text.

② Click a formatting button.

Click **Bold** (B) to make text bold.

Click **Italic** (I) to italicize text.

Click **Underline** (U) to add an underline to the text.

Note: See Chapter 1 to learn how to use toolbars.

Word applies the formatting to the text.

● In this example, bold formatting is applied to the text.

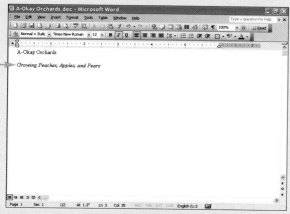

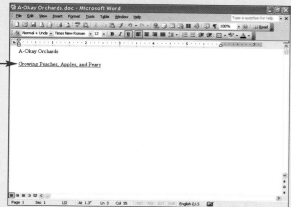

- In this example, the text is italicized.

  You can apply one format, a combination of formats, or all three formats to your text.

- In this example, underline formatting is applied to the text.

How do I remove the basic formatting from my text?

You can apply the same steps for assigning bold, italics, or underlining to turn the formatting off again. Simply select the data or cell and de-activate the appropriate button by clicking it again. The formatting buttons toggle the command on or off. If you make a mistake with any of the formatting you just applied, you can click the **Undo** button (⟲).

Are there keyboard shortcuts for applying basic formatting?

Yes. You can use keyboard shortcuts to quickly apply any of the three basic formatting styles. To apply bold formatting, press `Ctrl` + `B`. To apply italics to your text, press `Ctrl` + `I`. To add underlining to your text, press `Ctrl` + `U`.

Change the Font

You can change the font to change the appearance of text in a document. For example, you might change the font of the title of your document. By default, Word applies Times New Roman to every new document you create. You can change the font using the Formatting toolbar or the Font dialog box.

A *font* is simply a design you can apply to text in a document. Fonts come in all kinds of designs, ranging from plain and simple to scripts and artistic styles. Every font has a unique name. Times New Roman and Arial are two very popular fonts for text. Your own selection of fonts will vary based on what is stored on your computer.

Change the Font

QUICKLY CHANGE THE FONT

1 Select the text you want to format.

Note: See Chapter 3 to learn how to select text.

2 Click the **Font** ⊡ on the Formatting toolbar.

3 Click a font.

● Word applies the font to the text.

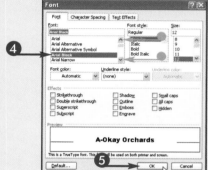

USE THE FONT DIALOG BOX

1 Select the text you want to format.

Note: See Chapter 3 to learn how to select text.

2 Click **Format**.

3 Click **Font**.

The Font dialog box appears.

● You can use the scroll arrows to view the available fonts.

4 Click the font you want to apply.

You can also use this dialog box to change the font style and size, and to set other text effects.

5 Click **OK**.

Word applies the font.

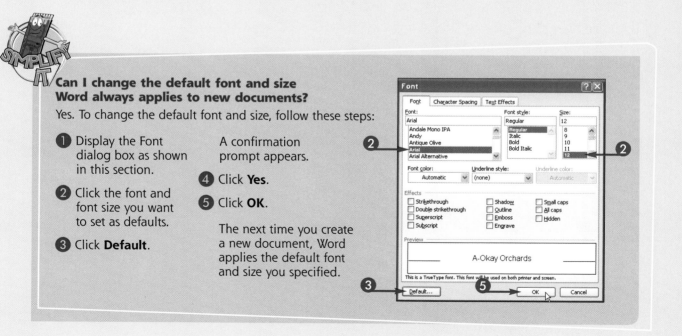

Can I change the default font and size Word always applies to new documents?

Yes. To change the default font and size, follow these steps:

1 Display the Font dialog box as shown in this section.

2 Click the font and font size you want to set as defaults.

3 Click **Default**.

A confirmation prompt appears.

4 Click **Yes**.

5 Click **OK**.

The next time you create a new document, Word applies the default font and size you specified.

Change the Font Size

You can change the font size to change the appearance of text in a document. For example, you can increase title text to appear larger than the other text in your document. Font sizes are measured in points. By default, Word applies 10-point size to every new document you create. You can change the font size using the Formatting toolbar or the Font dialog box.

When setting different sizes for your text, always consider the legibility of the document. If you set the font size too small, the text becomes difficult to read.

Change the Font Size

QUICKLY CHANGE THE FONT SIZE

1. Select the text you want to format.

   Note: See Chapter 3 to learn how to select text.

2. Click the **Font Size** ⊡ on the Formatting toolbar.

3. Click a size.

- Word applies the font size to the text.

   In this example, 20-point size is applied to the text.

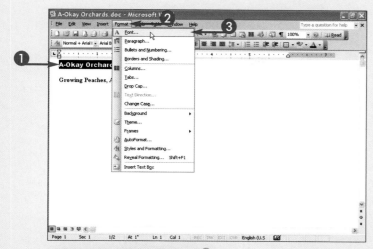

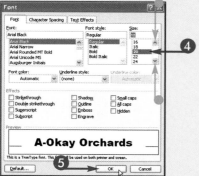

USE THE FONT DIALOG BOX

1 Select the text you want to format.

   Note: *See Chapter 3 to learn how to select text.*

2 Click **Format**.

3 Click **Font**.

The Font dialog box appears.

4 Click the font size you want to apply.

● You can use the scroll arrows to view the various sizes.

   You can also type a size directly into the Size box.

   You can also use this dialog box to change the font style and size, and to set other text effects.

5 Click **OK**.

   Word applies the font size.

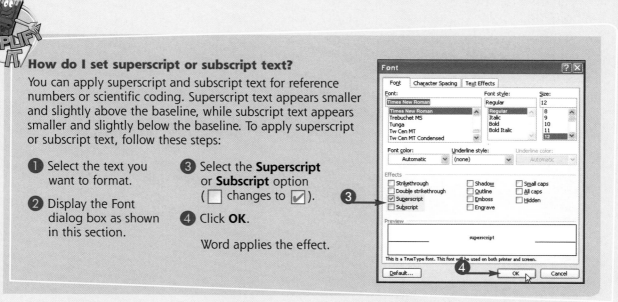

How do I set superscript or subscript text?

You can apply superscript and subscript text for reference numbers or scientific coding. Superscript text appears smaller and slightly above the baseline, while subscript text appears smaller and slightly below the baseline. To apply superscript or subscript text, follow these steps:

1 Select the text you want to format.

2 Display the Font dialog box as shown in this section.

3 Select the **Superscript** or **Subscript** option (☐ changes to ☑).

4 Click **OK**.

   Word applies the effect.

Add Color to Text

You can add color to your Word text to further enhance the appearance of a document or add emphasis to your text. When selecting text colors, be careful not to choose a color that makes your text difficult to read, whether the intended audience reads the text on-screen or on a printed page.

Add Color to Text

1. Select the text you want to format.

   Note: See Chapter 3 to learn how to select text.

2. Click the **Font Color** ⬛ on the Formatting toolbar.

3. Click a color.

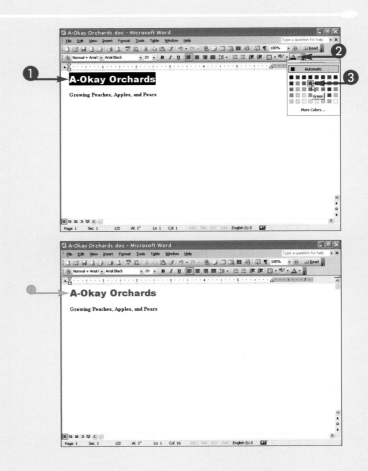

Word applies the color to the text.

● In this example, green is applied to the text.

Copy
Formatting

You can use the Format Painter feature to copy formatting to other text in your document. For example, perhaps you have applied a variety of formatting to a paragraph to create a certain look. When you want to re-create the same look elsewhere in the document, you do not have to repeat the same steps you applied to assign the original formatting. Instead, you can paint the formatting to the other text in one action.

Copy Formatting

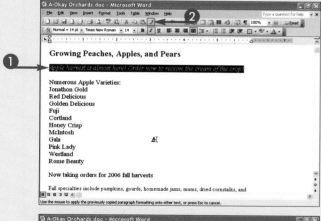

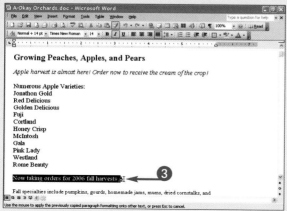

1. Select the text containing the formatting you want to copy.

   Note: See Chapter 3 to learn how to select text.

2. Click the **Format Painter** button (image) on the Standard toolbar.

   The ⌖ changes to 📋.

3. Click and drag over the text to which you want to copy the formatting.

   Word immediately copies the formatting to the new text.

   Note: To copy the same formatting multiple times, double-click (image).

   Note: You can press Esc to cancel the Format Painter at any time.

Align Text

You can use Word's alignment commands to change the way in which text is positioned horizontally on a page. By default, Word assigns the Left Align command. You can also choose to center your text on a page, align it to the right side of the page, or justify it so it lines up at both the left and right margins of the page.

Align Text

1. Select the text you want to format.

2. Click an alignment button on the Formatting toolbar.

   Click the **Align Left** button (■) to left-align text.

   Click the **Center** button (■) to center text.

   Click the **Align Right** button (■) to right-align text.

   Click the **Justify** button (■) to justify text between the left and right margins.

   Word applies the alignment to the text.

   ● In this example, the text is centered on the document page.

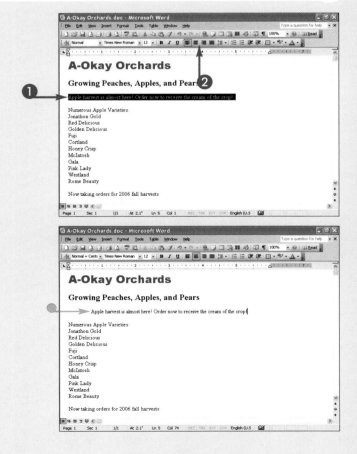

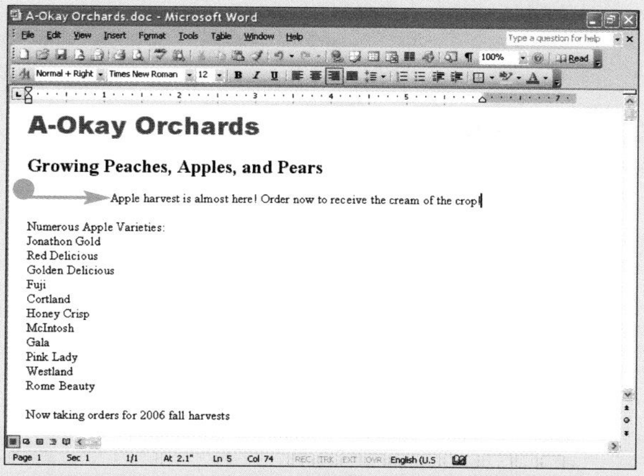

- In this example, the text is right-aligned on the document page.

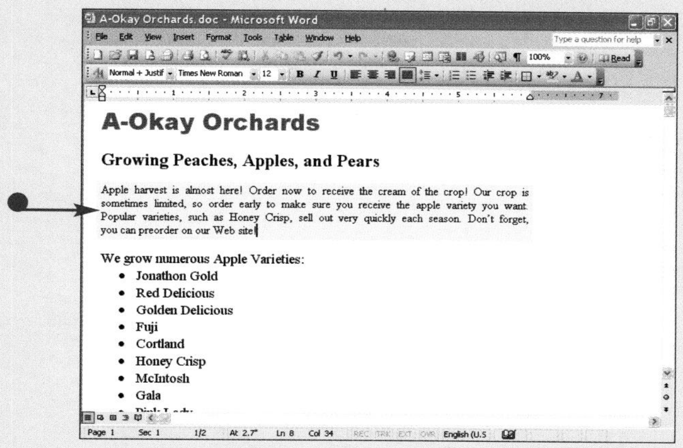

- In this example, the text is justified on the document page.

SIMPLIFY IT

Is there a way to control the vertical alignment of text on my page?

Yes. You can use the Page Setup dialog box to specify vertical alignments, such as centering title text on a title page. Follow these steps to apply vertical alignment in Word:

1. Click **File**.
2. Click **Page Setup**.

   The Page Setup dialog box appears.
3. Click the **Layout** tab.
4. Click the **Vertical alignment** ⌄ and click an alignment.
5. Click **OK** to exit the dialog box and apply the alignment.

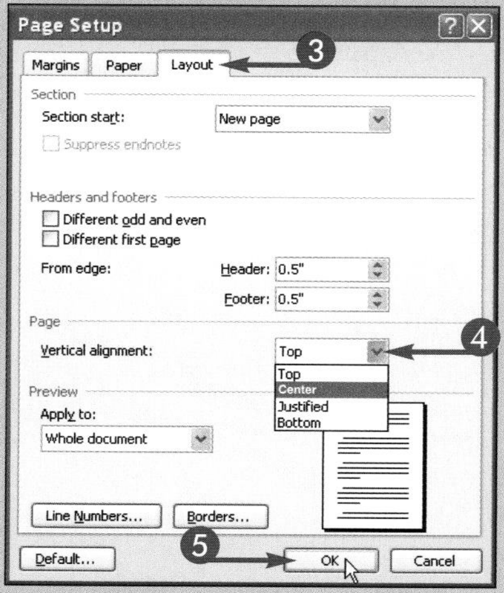

Indent Text

You can use indents as another way to control the horizontal positioning of text in a document. Indents are simply margins that affect individual lines of text or paragraphs. You can use indents to make paragraphs distinguishable on a page.

SET QUICK INDENTS

1. Click anywhere in the text line or paragraph you want to indent.

2. Click an **Indent** button on the Formatting toolbar.

   Click the **Decrease Indent** button (📑) to decrease the indentation.

   Click the **Increase Indent** button (📑) to increase the indentation.

● Word applies the indent.

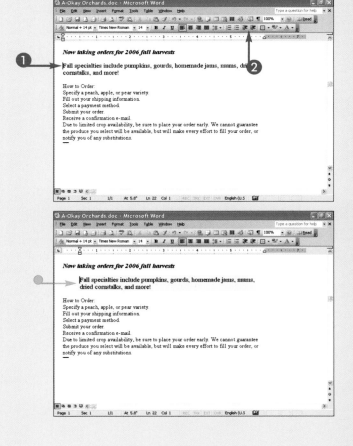

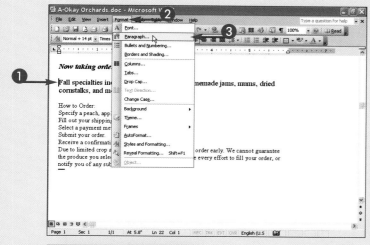

SET PRECISE INDENTS

1 Click anywhere in the text line or paragraph you want to indent.

2 Click **Format**.

3 Click **Paragraph**.

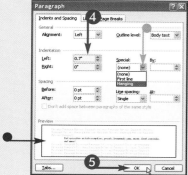

The Paragraph dialog box appears.

4 Type a specific indentation in the **Left** or **Right** indent boxes.

You can also click the ⬍ buttons to set an indent measurement.

● To set a specific kind of indent, click ⬇ and click an indent.

● The Preview area shows a sample of the indent.

5 Click **OK**.

Word applies the indent to the text.

What is the difference between an indent and a tab?

You can use tabs to create columnar text across a page, while indents control where a paragraph or line of text starts in relation to the margins. You can, however, press Tab to quickly create an indent for a line of text or the first line of a paragraph. Pressing Tab indents the text by 0.5 inches by default.

Can I set indents using the Word ruler?

Yes. You can drag the indent marker (☐) on the ruler bar to quickly set an indent. (If the ruler is not displayed, click **View** and then **Ruler**.) The ruler displays markers for changing the left indent, right indent, first-line indent, and hanging indent. You can move ⬚ over the marker to identify the correct marker if ScreenTips are turned on.

Set Tabs

You can use tab stop alignments to control how text is aligned. For example, you can align tab text to the right edge of the tab column, center the text in the column, use a decimal tab to line up decimal points, or a bar tab to set a vertical bar between columns.

You can use tabs to create vertically aligned columns of text in your Word document. By default, Word creates tab stops every 0.5 inches across the page, and aligns the text to the left of each tab column. You can set your own tab stops using the ruler or the Tabs dialog box. You can also change the tab alignment, and specify an exact measurement between tab stops.

Set Tabs

SET QUICK TABS

① Click the Tab marker area on the ruler to cycle through to the type of tab marker you want to set.

⌊ sets a left tab.

⌊ sets a center tab.

⌋ sets a right tab.

⌊ sets a decimal tab.

⌊ sets a bar tab.

② Click on the ruler where you want the tab inserted.

③ Click the beginning of the text you want to tab.

④ Press Tab.

Word applies the tab.

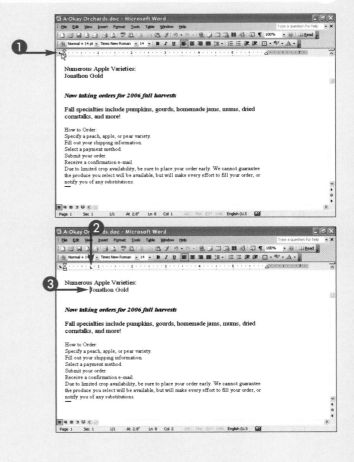

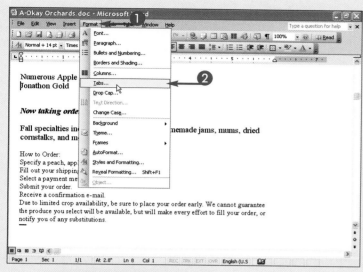

SET PRECISE TABS

① Click **Format**.

② Click **Tabs**.

The Tabs dialog box appears.

③ Click in the **Tab stop position** box and type a new tab stop measurement.

④ Click a tab alignment (○ changes to ⊙).

● If needed, you can also select a tab leader character here (○ changes to ⊙).

⑤ Click **Set**.

Word saves the new tab stop.

⑥ Click **OK**.

Word exits the dialog box, and you can use the new tab stops.

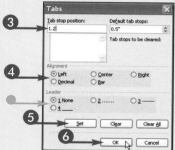

How do I remove tab stops I no longer need?

To remove a tab stop from the ruler, simply drag the tab stop off of the ruler. To remove a tab stop in the Tabs dialog box, you can select it and click **Clear**. To clear every tab stop you saved in the Tabs dialog box, click **Clear All**.

What are leader tabs?

You can use leader tabs to separate tab columns with dots, dashes, or lines. Leader tabs can help readers follow the information across tab columns. You can set leader tabs using the Tabs dialog box, as shown in this section.

Create Bulleted or Numbered Lists

You can set off lists of information in your documents using bullets or numbers. A bulleted list adds bullet dots in front of each list item, while a numbered list adds numbers in front of each list item. Bulleted and numbered lists can help you keep your information organized and orderly.

Create Bulleted or Numbered Lists

SET QUICK LISTS

① Select the text you want to format.

② Click a formatting button.

Click the **Bullets** button (☰) to create a bulleted list.

Click the **Numbering** button (☰) to create a numbered list.

● Word applies the formatting to the list.

This example shows a bulleted list.

● To add more text to the list, click at the end of the line and press Enter; Word immediately starts a new line in the list with a bullet or number.

Note: To turn off a bulleted or numbered list, press Enter twice after the last item in the list or click ☰ or ☰.

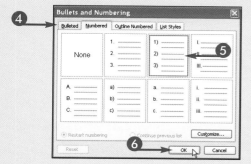

CHANGE BULLET OR NUMBER STYLES

1 Select the text you want to format.

2 Click **Format**.

3 Click **Bullets and Numbering**.

The Bullets and Numbering dialog box appears.

4 Click the **Bulleted** tab to change bullet styles or the **Numbered** tab to change number styles.

5 Click a style.

6 Click **OK**.

Word applies the new style.

Can I customize a style?

Yes. You can create a customized style or control the positioning of bullets and numbers. Follow these steps to learn how:

1 Display the Bullets and Numbering dialog box, as shown in this section.

2 Click the style you want to edit.

3 Click **Customize**.

The Customize dialog box appears.

4 Set any options for the format and position of the bullets or numbers.

5 Click **OK** to close the Customize dialog box.

6 Click **OK** to close the Bullets and Numbering dialog box.

The customized style is applied.

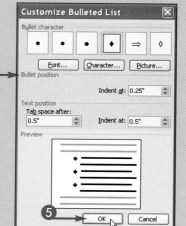

Set Margins

You can control the margins of your document pages. By default, Word assigns a 1-inch margin at the top and bottom of a page, and a 1.25-inch margin on the left and right side of a page with every new document you create. You can set wider margins to fit more text on a page, or set smaller margins to fit less text on a page.

Set Margins

SET MARGINS USING PAGE SETUP

1. Click **File**.

2. Click **Page Setup**.

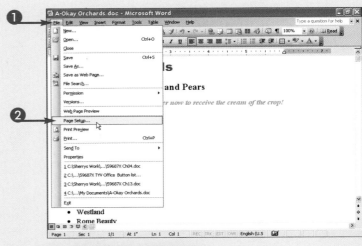

The Page Setup dialog box appears.

3. Click the **Margins** tab.

4. Type the margin settings you want to apply or click 🔼 to set new margins.

- The Preview area shows a sample of the new margin settings.

5. Click **OK**.

Word applies the new settings.

You can click 🔳 to switch to Print Layout view if you want to see the actual margins.

Note: See Chapter 3 to learn more about Word's views.

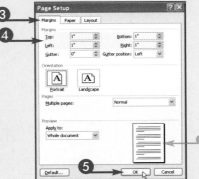

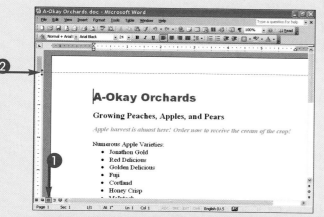

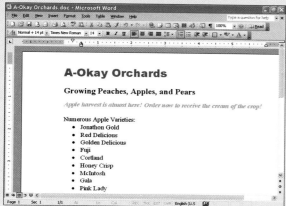

SET MARGINS USING THE RULER

1 Click 🔲 to switch to Print Layout or Print Preview mode.

Note: See Chapter 3 to learn more about Word's views.

2 Click and drag a margin area to move a margin.

Word immediately adjusts the margin in the document.

How do I set new default margins for all my Word documents?

If your company or organization consistently uses the same margins, you can choose those settings as the default for every new document you open in Word. Simply follow the steps for setting margins in the Page Setup dialog box, shown in this section, set the new margins, and click **Default**.

I set new margins, but my printer did not follow them. Why not?

Use caution when setting margins too narrow or wide. Some printers have a minimum margin in which nothing can be printed. For example, with many printers, anything less than 0.25 inches is outside the printable area. Be sure to test the margins, or check your printer documentation for more information.

Set the Line Spacing

You can adjust the amount of spacing that appears between lines of text for your paragraphs. For example, you may need to assign double-spacing to allow for handwritten edits, or set 1.5 spacing to make the paragraphs easier to read. By default, Word assigns single spacing for all new documents you create.

Set the Line Spacing

SET QUICK LINE SPACING

1. Select the text you want to format.
2. Click the **Line Spacing** button (⊟) on the Formatting toolbar.
3. Click a line spacing option.

Word immediately applies the new spacing.

- In this example, 2.0 line spacing is applied.

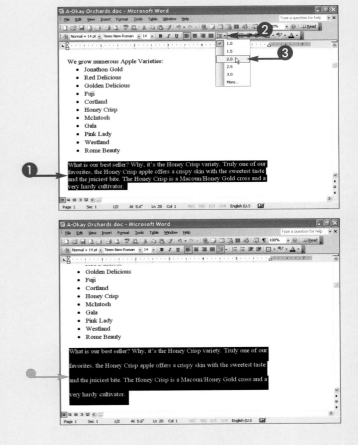

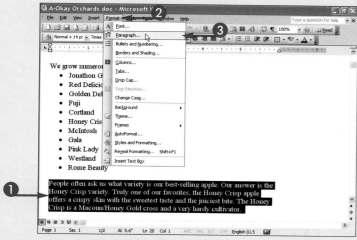

USE THE PARAGRAPH DIALOG BOX TO SET SPACING

1 Select the text you want to format.

2 Click **Format**.

3 Click **Paragraph**.

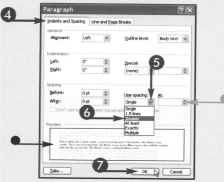

The Paragraph dialog box appears.

4 Click the **Indents and Spacing** tab.

5 Click the **Line spacing** ⌄.

6 Click a spacing option.

● To set an exact spacing, click here and type a measurement.

● An example of the spacing appears here.

7 Click **OK**.

Word applies the new spacing.

How do I add extra space before or after a paragraph?

To control the spacing surrounding a paragraph, you can use the **Before** and **After** options in the Paragraph dialog box. In the Spacing section in the **Indents and Spacing** tab, you can use the **Before** and **After** options to add a specified amount of space, measured in points, before and after a paragraph. This feature can help you add more breathing room for your text, or set a paragraph apart from surrounding text in a document.

I set new line spacing, but now my text appears cut off. Why?

If your line of text includes characters or a graphic that is larger than the surrounding text, Word may cause the larger text or object to appear cut off. To remedy the situation, set a larger measurement for the line spacing using the Paragraph dialog box.

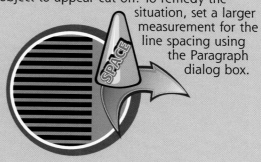

Format
with Styles

Word comes with a collection of preset styles you can use, or you can customize the styles as well as create your own new styles.

You can use Word's styles to apply a collection of formatting specifications all at the same time. For example, if a corporate report requires specific formatting for every heading, you can assign the formatting to a style and apply it whenever you need it. This can save you time otherwise spent assigning multiple formatting settings over and over again.

Format with Styles

① Format the text as desired.

② Select the text or click anywhere within the formatted text.

③ Click inside the **Style** list box and type a name for the style.

④ Press Enter.

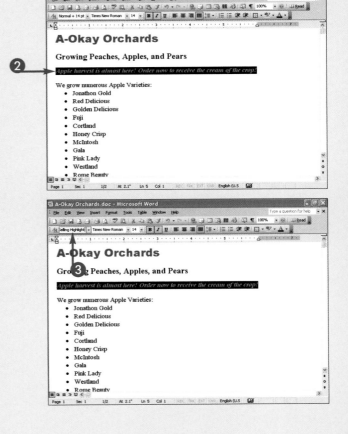

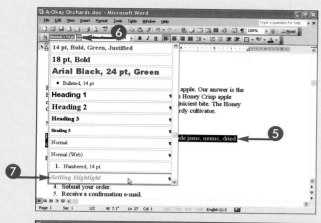

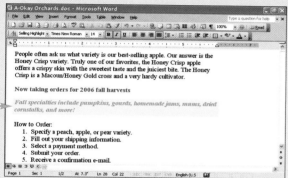

Word adds the style to the list.

⑤ To apply the new style, select the text you want to format.

⑥ Click the **Style** ▾.

⑦ Click the style name you want to apply.

● Word immediately applies the style.

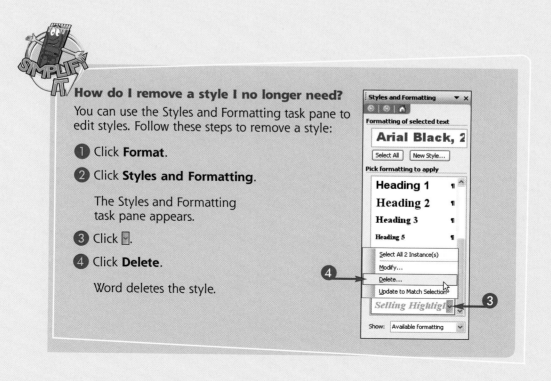

How do I remove a style I no longer need?

You can use the Styles and Formatting task pane to edit styles. Follow these steps to remove a style:

① Click **Format**.

② Click **Styles and Formatting**.

The Styles and Formatting task pane appears.

③ Click ▾.

④ Click **Delete**.

Word deletes the style.

Insert a Table

You can use tables to present data in an organized fashion. For example, you can add a table to your document to display a list of items or a roster of classes. Tables are built with columns and rows that intersect to form *cells*. You can insert all types of data in table cells, including text and graphics.

After you create a table, you can use Tab **to move from one cell to another, or you can click in the cell in which you want to add or edit data. As you type data, Word wraps the text to fit the current cell size.**

Insert a Table

① Click in the document where you want to insert a table.

② Click the **Insert Table** button (▥) on the Standard toolbar.

③ Drag across the number of columns and rows you want to set for your table.

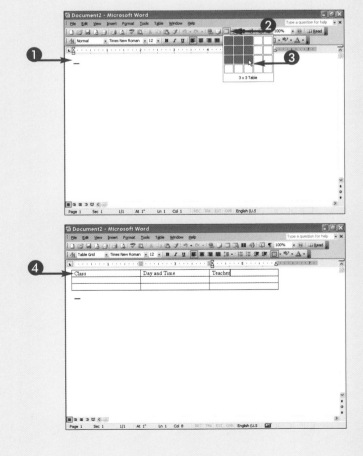

Word adds the table to the document.

④ Click inside a cell and type your data.

Draw a Table

You can create a customized table by drawing the table size and controlling how the rows and columns appear in your table. Using the Tables and Borders toolbar buttons, you can customize the line style, line thickness, and line color of the borders you draw for your table cells.

Draw a Table

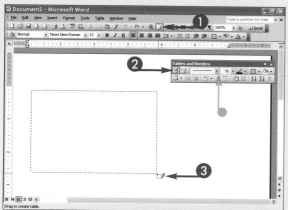

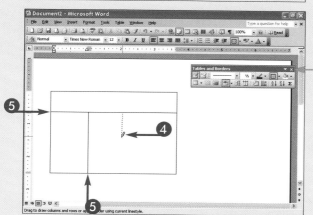

1 Click the **Tables and Borders** button ([]) on the Standard toolbar.

Word switches to Print Layout view and displays the Tables and Borders toolbar.

2 Click the **Draw Table** button ([]), if it is not already selected.

● You can set a line style, line weight, and border color for the table using these buttons.

3 Drag across the document to draw an outside border for your table.

4 Drag an internal line to delineate a row or column in your table.

5 Continue adding inner lines to build your table cells.

You can click inside a cell and type your table data.

● You can click ✕ to close the toolbar when you finish.

Note: *You can use the Tables and Borders toolbar to add and subtract rows and columns, format tables, and more.*

Select
Table Cells

You can select table cells, rows, and columns in a table to perform editing tasks and apply formatting to all the selected areas of the table. For example, you might select an entire column to apply bold formatting to all the text.

Select Table Cells

① Click and drag over the cells you want to select.

Any cell you drag over becomes a part of the selection.

● You can also use the **Table** menu to select parts of your table.

② Release the mouse button, and everything you dragged over is selected.

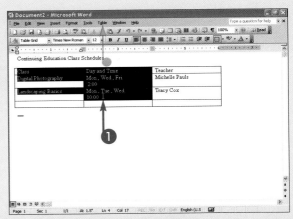

To select a single cell, you can triple-click the cell to select everything in the cell.

● To select an entire column or row, move the mouse pointer near the border and click.

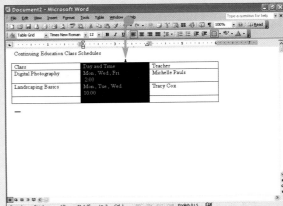

After you create a table, you can control the sizing of the inner cells by making adjustments to the column width or row height. For example, you may need to make a cell wider to accommodate a long line of text, or you may need to make a cell large enough in depth to hold a particular graphic or chart.

Adjust the Column Width or Row Height

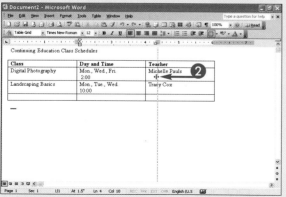

① Move the mouse pointer over the edge of the cell where you want to adjust the size.

The ⇧ changes to ◄╟►.

② Click and drag the border in the desired direction to adjust the column width or row height.

If you drag the top or bottom border of a cell, the row height adjusts as you drag.

If you drag the left or right border of a cell, the column width adjusts as you drag.

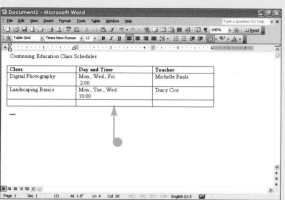

③ Release the mouse.

Word adjusts the column width or row height.

● In this example, the column is widened.

Add Columns and Rows

You can add columns and rows to your Word tables to add more data. For example, you can add a row to add another item to a list. Adding columns and rows increases the overall size of the table on the document page.

① Click in the row or column where you want to add another row or column, or select the column or row.

Note: *If you select more than one row or column, Word duplicates the number when you activate the Insert command.*

② Click **Table**.

③ Click **Insert**.

④ Click the type of insertion you want to create.

Click **Columns to the Left** or **Columns to the Right** to insert a column.

Click **Rows Above** or **Rows Below** to insert a row.

● Word adds a column or row to the table.

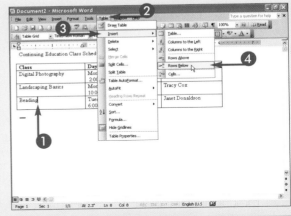

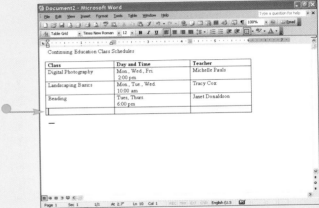

Delete Columns and Rows

> You can remove a column or row you no longer need in your table. When you remove a column or row, Word restructures the remaining cells to fill the void.

Delete Columns and Rows

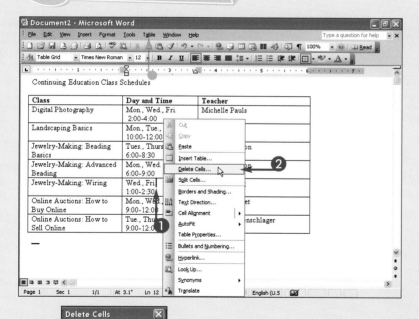

① Right-click the column or row you want to remove.

② Click **Delete Cells**.

● You can also use the **Table** menu to delete table elements.

The Delete Cells dialog box appears.

③ Select an option to delete a column or row (○ changes to ◉).

● You can delete interior cells rather than an entire row or column by selecting from these options (○ changes to ◉).

④ Click **OK**.

Word deletes the column or row.

73

Merge Table Cells

You can combine two or more table cells to create a larger cell. For example, you might merge cells to create a title across the top of your table, or you may merge two interior cells to create one large cell for a graphic or chart.

Merge Table Cells

1. Select the cells you want to merge.

   Note: See the section "Select Table Cells," earlier in this chapter, to learn how to select cells.

2. Click **Table**.

3. Click **Merge Cells**.

● Word creates one large cell.

Split
Table Cells

You can split table cells to create additional cells within your table. For example, you might split a cell and show two different choices in a column or row.

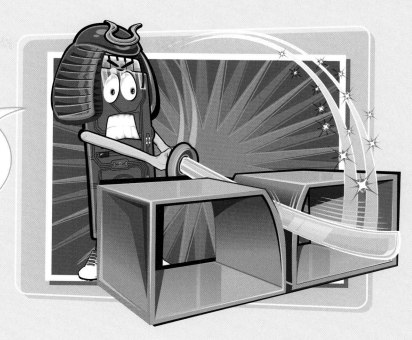

Split Table Cells

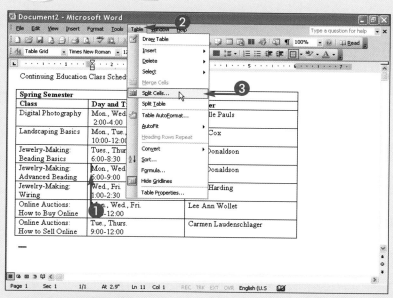

1 Click inside or select the cell you want to split.

Note: See the section "Select Table Cells," earlier in this chapter, to learn how to select cells.

2 Click **Table**.

3 Click **Split Cells**.

The Split Cells dialog box appears.

4 Designate how many columns or rows you want to create in the split cell.

You can type a number, or click the arrow buttons to designate a number.

5 Click **OK**.

Word divides the cell.

Apply Table Formatting

You can add instant formatting to your Word tables by assigning one of the many formatting styles designed specifically for tables. Table styles offer a variety of designs that include shading and color, borders, and fonts. Rather than apply individual formatting commands yourself, you can use the Table AutoFormat feature to quickly turn a plain table into an interesting visual element on a page.

Apply Table Formatting

① Click anywhere in the table you want to format.

② Click **Table**.

③ Click **Table AutoFormat**.

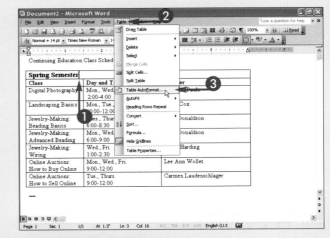

The Table AutoFormat dialog box appears.

④ Click a table style you want to apply.

● The Preview area displays a sample of the style.

● You can use the scroll bars to view all the available styles.

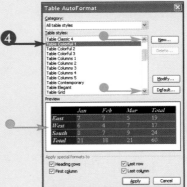

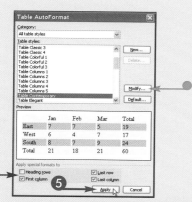

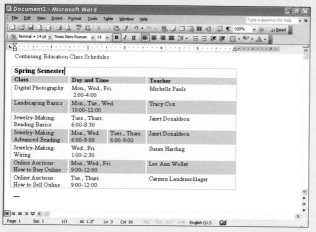

- You can select these options to apply any special formatting to your table (☐ changes to ☑).

- To modify an existing table style, click **Modify** to make changes to the formatting.

5 Click **Apply**.

Word applies the new formatting to the entire table.

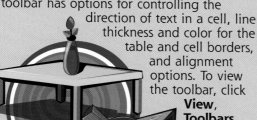

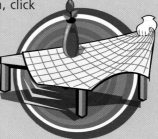

Can I apply my own formatting to a table?

Yes. If you prefer to assign your own formatting to table elements, you can do so using the Formatting toolbar. You can also use the tools available on the Tables and Borders toolbar. The Tables and Borders toolbar has options for controlling the direction of text in a cell, line thickness and color for the table and cell borders, and alignment options. To view the toolbar, click **View**, **Toolbars**, and then **Tables and Borders**.

How do I remove the gridlines in my table?

You can hide the table and cell borders to make your table data resemble a neatly organized list. Click **Table** and then **Hide Gridlines**. If you print the table with the borders hidden, no borders appear on your printed copy. To turn the borders on again, click **Table** and then **Show Gridlines**.

Reposition a Table

You can move a table around your document to better position it on a page. You must switch to Print Layout or Web Layout view to move a table.

See Chapter 3 to learn more about using Word's views.

① Move the mouse over the upper left corner of the table.

● A selection handle appears.

② Click and drag the table handle to move the table to a new area in the document.

A dotted line marks the table location as you move.

③ Release the mouse button.

Word moves the table.

Note: *You can control the text wrap around a table using the Table Properties dialog box. Right-click the table and click **Table Properties** to open the dialog box. Click the **Table** tab to view text wrapping options.*

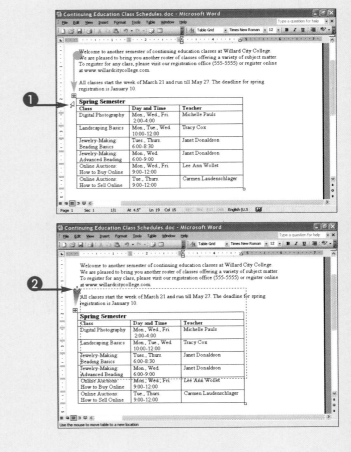

Resize a Table

You can resize a table to adjust its appearance in a Word document. For example, you may need to enlarge a table to make it more legible, or you may need to reduce the table size to fit it in with other text on the page.

You must switch to Print Layout or Web Layout view to resize a table. See Chapter 3 to learn more about using Word's views.

Resize a Table

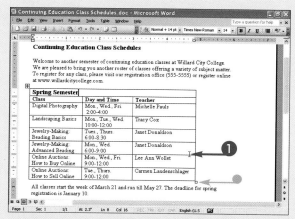

① Move the mouse over any area of the table.

● A sizing handle appears in the lower right corner of the table.

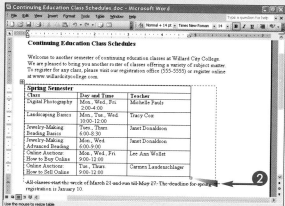

② Click and drag the resizing handle to enlarge or reduce the table size.

Note: *If you make the table too small, Word shortens the table width but tries to fit all the text in each cell, increasing the table depth.*

③ Release the mouse button.

Word resizes the table.

Note: *You can control the text wrap around a table using the Table Properties dialog box. Right-click the table and click* **Table Properties** *to open the dialog box. Click the* **Table** *tab to view text wrapping options.*

Add Borders and Shading to Text

Be careful not to add too many effects to your document or it becomes difficult to read. When adding shading behind text, choose a fill color that does not make the text illegible.

You can add borders and shading to your document text to add emphasis or make the document aesthetically appealing. For example, you can add a border to a paragraph to bring attention to the text, or you can add shading behind a title.

Add Borders and Shading to Text

ADD A BORDER

① Click anywhere in the text or select the text to which you want to add a border.

② Click **Format**.

③ Click **Borders and Shading**.

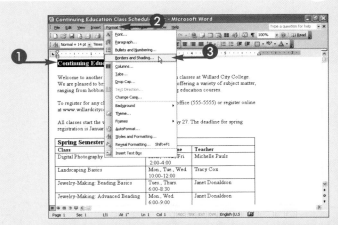

The Borders and Shading dialog box appears.

④ Click the **Borders** tab, if it is not already selected.

⑤ Click a border setting.

● The Preview area displays a sample of the border.

⑥ Click a border style.

● You can choose a color and line weight here.

⑦ Click **OK**.

Word applies the border.

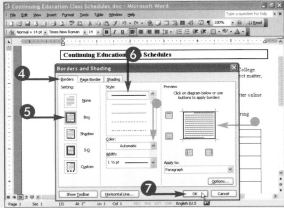

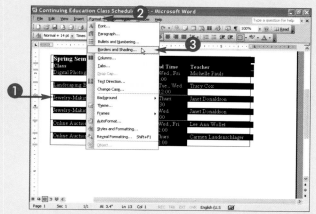

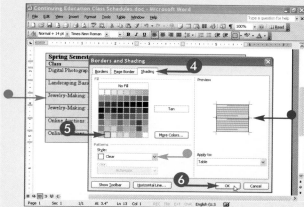

ADD SHADING

① Click anywhere in the text or select the text to which you want to add shading.

② Click **Format**.

③ Click **Borders and Shading**.

The Borders and Shading dialog box appears.

④ Click the **Shading** tab.

⑤ Click a Fill color.

● The Preview area displays a sample of the shading.

● You can click the **Style** and choose a pattern for your shading effect.

⑥ Click **OK**.

● Word applies the shading.

How do I add a border to the entire page?

You can click the **Page Border** tab in the Borders and Shading dialog box to find options for setting a border around the perimeter of a page. Like a text or paragraph border, you can control the page border's style, color, and line thickness. You can also choose to display only certain sides of the border, such as the top and bottom.

Can I use the Outside Border button to add a border to my text?

Yes. The **Outside Border** button (▣) on the Formatting toolbar includes a drop-down list of border styles you can apply immediately to selected text. Simply click ▣ to display the list and click a border style. For a greater variety of customizing effects, use the Borders and Shading dialog box.

Create Columns

You can create columns in Word to present your text much like a newspaper or magazine format. For example, if you are creating a brochure or newsletter, you can use columns to make text flow from one block to the next.

You must switch to Print Layout or Web Layout view to create and view columns. See Chapter 3 to learn more about using Word's views.

Create Columns

① Select the text you want to place into columns.

② Click **Format**.

③ Click **Columns**.

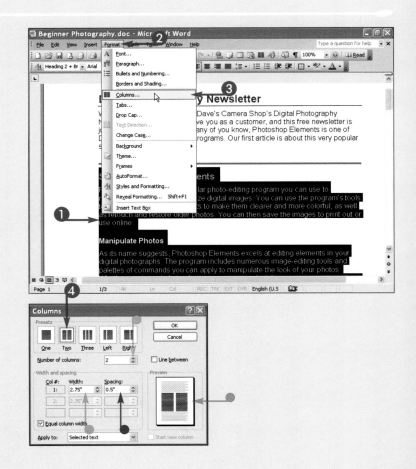

The Columns dialog box appears.

④ Click a preset for the type of column style you want to apply.

● You can also specify the number of columns here.

● You can set an exact column width here.

● You can control the spacing between columns using this setting.

● The Preview area displays a sample of the columns.

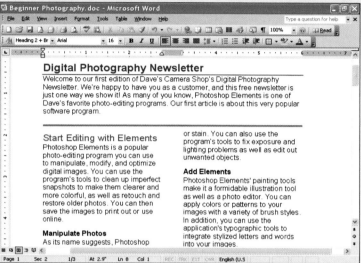

- To apply the column format to a portion of your document, click the **Apply to** ⏷ and specify whether you want the columns to apply to the selected text or the entire document.

- To include a vertical line separating the columns, select this option (☐ changes to ☑).

5 Click **OK**.

Word applies the column format to the selected text.

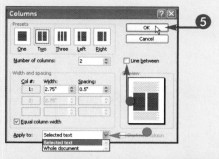

Is there a quicker way to assign columns?

You can click the **Columns** button (▦) on the Standard toolbar to quickly create columns in your document. First select the text you want to turn into columns, and then click ▦ and drag across the number of columns you want to create. Word immediately assigns the column format to your text.

How do I create a break within a column?

You can add a column break by first clicking where you want the break to occur and then pressing Ctrl + Shift + Enter . To remove a break, select it and press Delete . To stop the column format entirely, click ▦ and then select the single-column format.

Add Headers and Footers

You can use headers and footers to add text that appears at the top or bottom of every page. Headers and footers are useful for making sure every page prints with a page number, document title, author name, or date. Header text appears at the very top of the page outside the text margin. Footers appear at the very bottom of a page.

Headers and footers are built with *fields* that hold places for information that updates, such as page numbers or dates. To view header and footer text, switch to Print Layout view.

Add Headers and Footers

1 Click **View**.

2 Click **Header and Footer**.

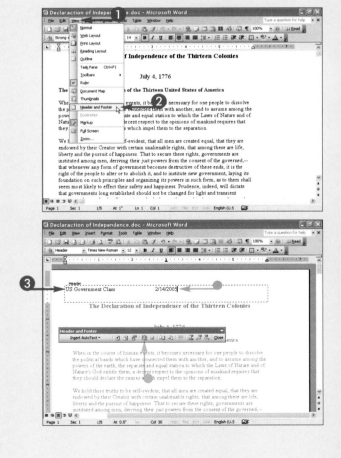

Word switches to Print Layout view and displays the Header and Footer toolbar.

3 To create header text, click in the header area and type your text.

● To insert a particular field — page number, date, or time — click that field button in the toolbar.

● This example adds a date field to the header.

You can press Tab to insert fields at intervals across the header or footer area.

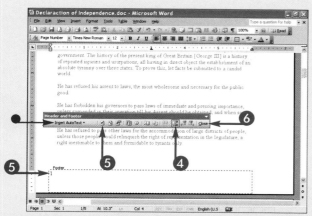

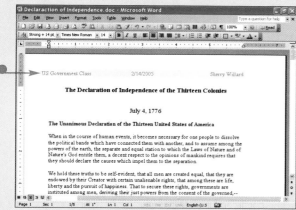

4 To create footer text, click the **Switch Between Header and Footer** button ().

5 Type your text in the footer area or use the toolbar buttons to insert a particular field.

● You can also insert one of several AutoText entries.

6 When finished, click **Close**.

● Word displays the header and footer text in Print Layout view.

Note: You can only view headers and footers in Print Layout. To learn more about view modes, see Chapter 3.

Can I remove a header or footer for the first page and keep it for the remaining pages?

Yes. Click **File** and then click **Page Setup**. This opens the Page Setup dialog box. Click the **Layout** tab. Under the Headers and Footers options, select the **Different first page** option. If you want to remove the header or footer for odd or even pages, select the **Different odd and even** option (☐ changes to ✔). You can also use this dialog box to control the positioning of the header or footer from the edge of the page. Click **OK** to exit the dialog box and apply any changes.

How do I remove a header or footer I no longer want?

Follow the steps in this task to view headers and footers again. Select the header or footer text and press Delete . If you need to remove several headers and footers, click the **Show Previous** () or **Show Next** () buttons on the Headers and Footers toolbar to move back and forth between headers and footers.

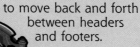

Insert Comments

You can add comments to your documents to make a note to yourself about a particular section or task or as a note for other users to see. For example, if you share your documents with other users, you can use comments to leave feedback about the text without typing directly in the document. Word displays comments in a balloon or in the Reviewing pane.

Comments are especially important if you and your colleagues utilize Word's tracking and revision features. To learn more about tracking and reviewing document changes, see Chapter 7.

Insert Comments

① Click where you want to insert a comment.

② Click **Insert**.

③ Click **Comment**.

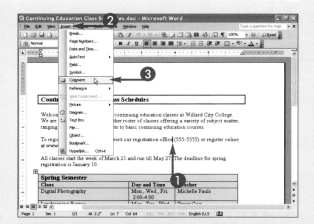

● A comment balloon appears, along with the Reviewing toolbar.

Note: If you activate the Comment command while the Tracking Changes feature is on, the Reviewing pane and Reviewing toolbar appear.

④ Type your comment.

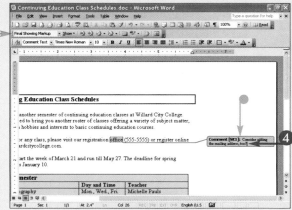

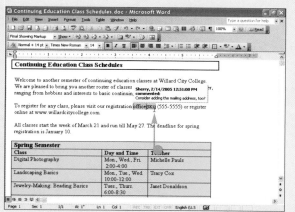

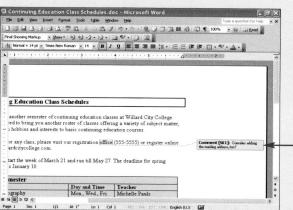

- In Normal view, you can move the mouse pointer over the comment to view the comment details as a ScreenTip.

  The ScreenTip displays information about the author, time, and date of the comment.

- In Print Layout view, the comment appears in the right margin.

How do I remove a comment?
Open the Reviewing pane by clicking **View, Toolbars,** and then **Reviewing**. Click the **Previous** (🔼) or **Next** (🔽) buttons on the toolbar to move to the comment you want to delete. Click the **Delete Comment** button (🔲). Word removes the comment. To remove all the comments in the entire document, click the 🔲 button ▾ and then click **Delete All Comments in Document**.

How do I respond to a comment?
You can add a comment to a comment by typing a new comment adjacent to the existing comment. Navigate to the comment using the 🔽 or 🔽 buttons on the Reviewing toolbar, and then click the **Insert Comment** button (🔲). Word inserts a new comment.

Insert Footnotes and Endnotes

You can add footnotes and endnotes to your document to include additional information. Footnotes and endnotes help identify sources or reference other material. Footnotes appear at the bottom of a page, while endnotes appear at the end of the document.

Insert Footnotes and Endnotes

1. If adding a footnote, click where you want to insert the footnote number.

2. Click **Insert**.

3. Click **Reference**.

4. Click **Footnote**.

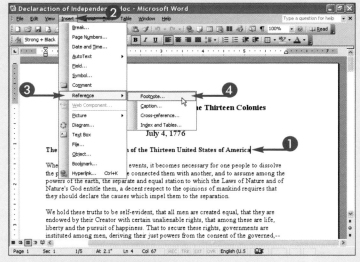

The Footnote and Endnote dialog box appears.

5. Select the **Footnotes** or **Endnotes** option (○ changes to ●).

- You can click ⌄ to specify where the footnote or endnote appears.

- You can use the Format options to control the numbering for your notes.

6. Click **Insert**.

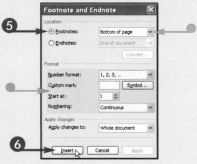

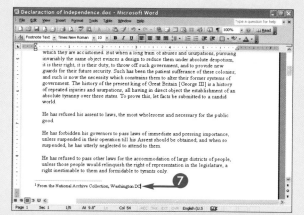

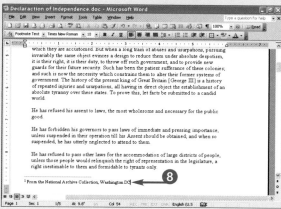

7 If adding a footnote, type your note text at the bottom of the current page.

The footnote number appears automatically.

Note: *You can also add footnote or endnote text using the Reviewing pane. See Chapter 7 to learn more about Word's document reviewing features.*

8 If adding an endnote, type your note text at the bottom of the last page of the document.

The endnote number appears automatically.

How can I reset the footnote number in my document?

If you need to reset the number, perhaps for a new chapter in the document, you can reopen the Footnote and Endnote dialog box and specify a start number. Click inside the **Start at** box and type a number or use the arrow button (⬍) to set a new number. Click **Apply** to apply the changes to the document.

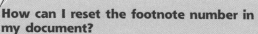

What other referencing tools can I use in Word?

The Reference menu, a submenu of the Insert menu, offers several other referencing tools you can apply, such as indexing features, captioning, and cross-reference features. For example, if you click **Insert**, **Reference**, and then **Caption**, the Caption dialog box appears, and you can set a caption for a figure or table in your document. See the Word help files to learn more about the other referencing tools available.

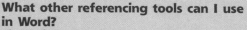

Insert Page Numbers and Page Breaks

You can add page numbers and page breaks to your documents to make the pages more manageable. For example, adding page numbers to longer documents can help you keep the pages in order after printing. Adding page breaks can help you control which text appears on which page of the document.

Insert Page Numbers and Page Breaks

INSERT PAGE NUMBERS

1 Click **Insert**.

2 Click **Page Numbers**.

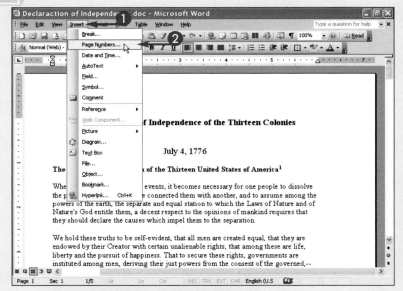

The Page Numbers dialog box appears.

3 Click the **Position** ⬇ to change where the page numbers appear.

4 Click the **Alignment** ⬇ to change how the page numbers are aligned.

● To omit a page number on the first page, deselect this option (☑ changes to ☐).

5 Click **OK**.

Word assigns page numbers to your document.

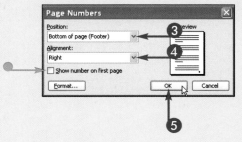

Note: You can see page numbers in Print Layout view.

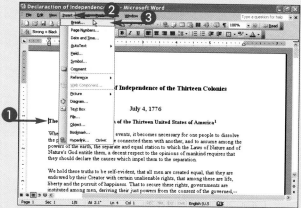

INSERT PAGE BREAKS

1 Click in the document where you want to insert a page break.

2 Click **Insert**.

3 Click **Break**.

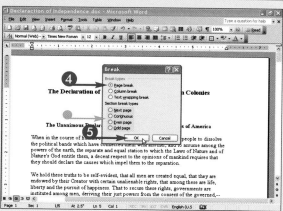

The Break dialog box opens.

4 Select the **Page break** option (○ changes to ◉).

● You can also insert section breaks and control the location for the breaks by selecting one of these options (○ changes to ◉).

5 Click **OK**.

Word assigns the page break.

Is there a faster way to insert a page break?

You can insert a manual page break by pressing `Ctrl` + `Enter` . Page breaks appear as dotted lines in Normal view. In Print Layout view, the break displays the page as a new document page. You can also insert a soft break. Press `Shift` + `Enter` to insert a soft break.

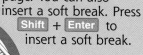

Can I change the style of numbers used in my document's page numbers?

Yes. Click **Format** in the Page Numbers dialog box. This opens the Page Number Format dialog box. You can change the number style to Roman numerals, alphabetical numbering, and more. You can also include chapter numbers with your page numbers.

Find and Replace Text

You can use Word's Find tool to search your document for a particular word or phrase. You can use the Replace tool to replace instances of a word or phrase with other text. For example, you may need to sort through a long document replacing a reference with another name.

Find and Replace Text

FIND TEXT

1 Click **Edit**.

2 Click **Find**.

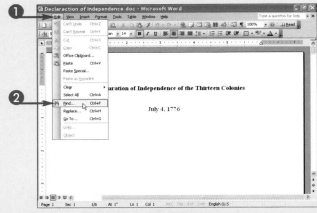

The Find and Replace dialog box appears with the Find tab displayed.

3 Type the text you want to find.

4 Click **Find Next** or press Enter.

● Word searches the document and finds the first occurrence of the text.

You can click **Find Next** again to search for the next occurrence.

5 When finished, click **Cancel** to close the dialog box.

Note: If Word displays a prompt box when the last occurrence is found, click **OK**.

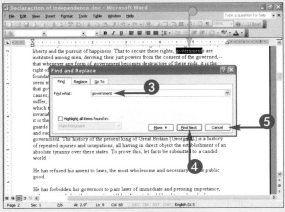

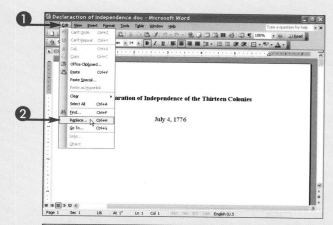

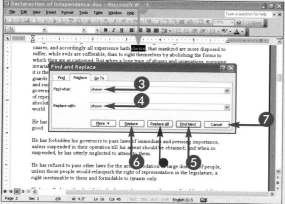

REPLACE TEXT

1 Click **Edit**.

2 Click **Replace**.

3 In the Find and Replace dialog box, type the text you want to find.

4 Type replacement text.

5 Click **Find Next**.

● Word locates the first occurrence.

6 Click **Replace** to replace the occurrence.

● To replace every occurrence in the document, click **Replace All**.

7 When finished, click **Cancel**.

Click **OK** if Word displays a prompt when the last occurrence is found.

Where can I find detailed search options?

You can click **More** in the Find and Replace dialog box to reveal additional search options you can apply. For example, you can search for matching text case, whole words, and more. You can also search for specific formatting or special characters by clicking **Format** and **Special**. To hide the additional search options, click **Less**.

How can I search for and delete text?

To search for a particular word or phrase using the Find and Replace dialog box and remove the text completely from the document, start by typing the text in the **Find what** text field. Leave the **Replace with** box empty. When you activate the search, Word looks for the text and deletes it without adding new text to the document.

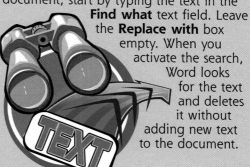

Check Spelling and Grammar

By default, Word checks for spelling and grammar problems automatically. Misspellings appear underlined with a red wavy line. Potential grammar errors are underlined with a green wavy line.

You can use Word's Spelling and Grammar check features to check your document for spelling and grammatical errors. Although both features are helpful, they are never a substitute for good proofreading with your own eyes. Both features can catch some errors, but not all, so take time to read over your documents for misspellings.

Check Spelling and Grammar

CORRECT A MISTAKE

1. When you encounter a spelling or grammar problem, right-click the underlined text.

   The menu that appears shows possible corrections.

2. Click a correction from the menu.

   • To ignore the error, click **Ignore All**.

   • To add the word to the built-in dictionary, click **Add to Dictionary**.

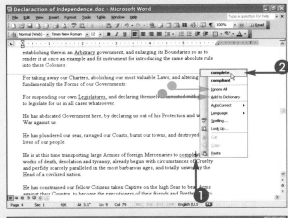

RUN THE SPELL CHECKER

1. Click the **Spelling and Grammar** button ( ) on the Standard toolbar.

   To check only a section of your document, select the section before activating the spell check.

   • You can also click **Tools** and then **Spelling and Grammar**.

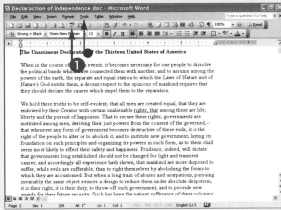

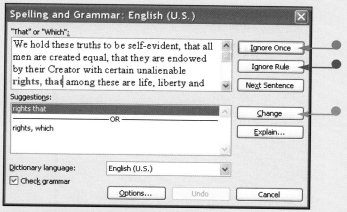

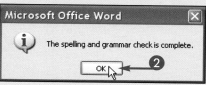

Word searches the document for any mistakes and displays the Spelling and Grammar dialog box if it finds an error.

● Click **Change** to make a correction.

To correct all the misspellings of the same word, click **Change All**.

● To ignore the error one time, click **Ignore Once**.

● To ignore every occurrence, click **Ignore All** or **Ignore Rule**.

When the spell check is complete, a prompt box appears.

② Click **OK**.

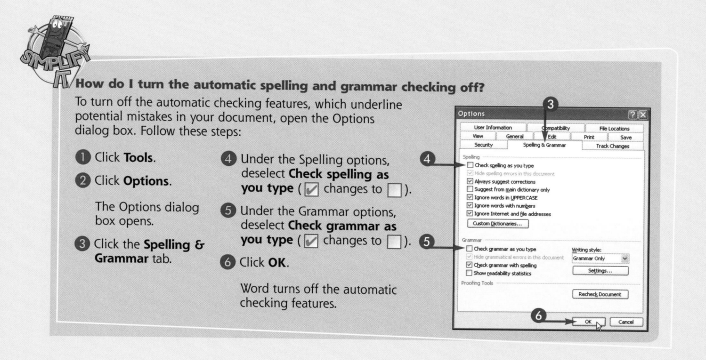

How do I turn the automatic spelling and grammar checking off?

To turn off the automatic checking features, which underline potential mistakes in your document, open the Options dialog box. Follow these steps:

① Click **Tools**.

② Click **Options**.

The Options dialog box opens.

③ Click the **Spelling & Grammar** tab.

④ Under the Spelling options, deselect **Check spelling as you type** (☑ changes to ☐).

⑤ Under the Grammar options, deselect **Check grammar as you type** (☑ changes to ☐).

⑥ Click **OK**.

Word turns off the automatic checking features.

Work with AutoCorrect

You may have already noticed the AutoCorrect feature kicking in as you typed in a document. The corrections this feature makes are performed automatically. AutoCorrect comes with a list of preset misspellings; however, the list is not comprehensive. To speed up your own text entry tasks, consider adding your own problem words to the list.

You can use the AutoCorrect feature to quickly correct words you commonly misspell. For example, if you find yourself continually misspelling the same term over and over again, you can add the word to the AutoCorrect dictionary. The next time you mistype the word, AutoCorrect fixes your mistake for you.

Work with AutoCorrect

ADD A MISSPELLING

① Click **Tools**.

② Click **AutoCorrect Options**.

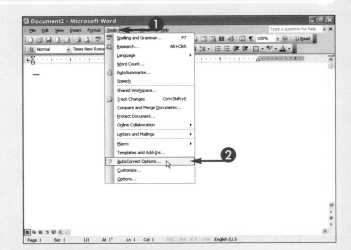

The AutoCorrect dialog box opens with the AutoCorrect tab displayed.

③ Type the common misspelling in the Replace text field.

Be sure to type the word exactly as you normally misspell it.

④ Type the correct spelling in the With text box.

⑤ Click **Add**.

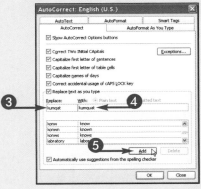

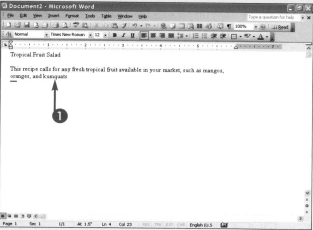

● AutoCorrect adds the word to the list.

The next time you misspell the word, AutoCorrect corrects it for you.

You can repeat Steps **3** to **5** to add more words to the list, as needed.

6 Click **Close** to exit the dialog box.

USE AUTOCORRECT

1 Click in the document and type the word you commonly misspell.

Within seconds after typing the word, AutoCorrect fixes the mistake.

Note: *If you type something you do not want corrected, press* **Ctrl** *+* **Z** *to undo AutoCorrect before you continue typing anything else.*

How do I remove or edit a word from the AutoCorrect list?

Open the AutoCorrect dialog box to the AutoCorrect tab. Click the word you want to remove and click **Delete**. To edit a word, select it from the list and make your change to the Replace or With text boxes. Click **OK** to exit the dialog box and apply your changes.

Can I customize how the AutoCorrect feature works?

Yes. You can also select or deselect options for AutoCorrect to be on the lookout for, such as typing two initial caps or capitalizing the first letter of a sentence. To control any of the AutoCorrect options, you must first open the AutoCorrect dialog box; click **Tools** and then **AutoCorrect Options**. Make any changes to the options. You can also turn the feature off. Deselect the **Replace text as you type** option (☑ changes to ☐). This turns the feature off. Click **OK** to exit the dialog box and apply your changes.

Track and Review Document Changes

If you work in an environment in which you share your Word documents with others, you can use the tracking and reviewing features to help you keep track of who adds changes to the file. For example, you can see what edits others have made, including formatting changes and text additions or deletions.

The tracking feature changes the color for each person's edits, making it easy to see who changed what in the document. When you review the document, you can choose to accept or reject the changes.

Track and Review Document Changes

TURN ON TRACKING

① Click **Tools**.

② Click **Track Changes**.

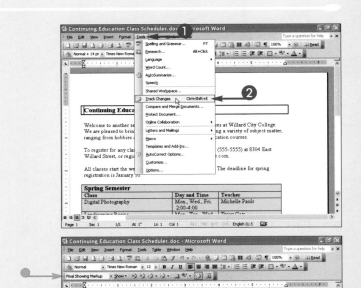

● The Reviewing toolbar appears and the tracking feature is turned on.

● Word bolds the TRK setting on the status bar.

③ Edit the document as needed.

Any changes you make appear underlined in color. Deleted text is marked with a strikethrough.

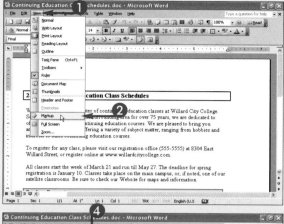

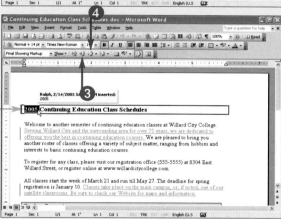

REVIEW CHANGES

① To make sure you can see the edits, click **View**.

② Click **Markup**.

Note: *If the Markup view is on already, clicking* **Markup** *toggles the view off again.*

If the Reviewing toolbar is not displayed, click **View**, **Toolbars**, and then **Reviewing**.

③ Click the **Next** button (⏩) on the Reviewing toolbar.

Word displays the next edit.

● To view details about the author, move the mouse pointer over the edit.

④ Click **Accept Change** (✅) to add the change to the final document.

To reject the change, click the **Reject Change** button (❎).

When you complete the review, click the **Track Changes** button (📝) to turn the feature off.

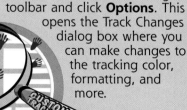

How can I customize the markup options?

To customize what color appears for your edits, click the **Show** ▾ on the Reviewing toolbar and click **Options**. This opens the Track Changes dialog box where you can make changes to the tracking color, formatting, and more.

What does the Reviewing pane do?

You can use the Reviewing pane as another tool for viewing changes to a document. The pane shows each person's edits, including the user's name and the time any edits and any comments were added. To view the pane, click the **Reviewing Pane** button (📄) on the Reviewing toolbar. To close the pane, click the button again.

E-mail a Document

You may need to log on to your Internet account before sending an e-mail message from Word.

You can e-mail a document without leaving the Word window. If you use Microsoft Outlook as your e-mail editor, you can tap into the program's features to insert e-mail addresses and send a Word document as an e-mail message.

E-mail a Document

① Click the **E-mail** button (📧) on the Standard toolbar.

● You can also click **File, Send To**, and then **Mail Recipient**.

② Type the recipient's e-mail address.

● You can click **To** to access the Outlook Address Book and retrieve an address.

   If typing more than one e-mail address, use a semicolon to separate them.

● You can replace the default subject title that Word uses with another title.

● Optionally, you can type a brief introduction about the message here.

③ Click **Send a Copy**.

   The message is sent.

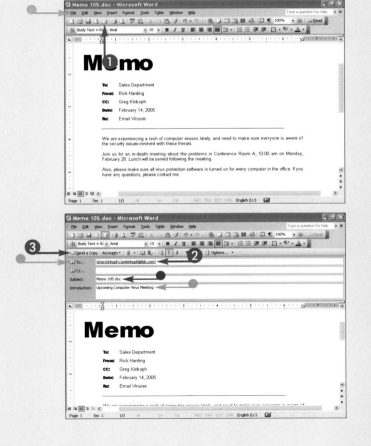

Change
Paper Size

You can change the size of your document page to print to a certain size of paper. For example, if you need to print your memo on legal size paper, you can use the Page Setup dialog box to switch to the Legal or Executive paper size. By default, Word sets the paper size as Letter size.

Change Paper Size

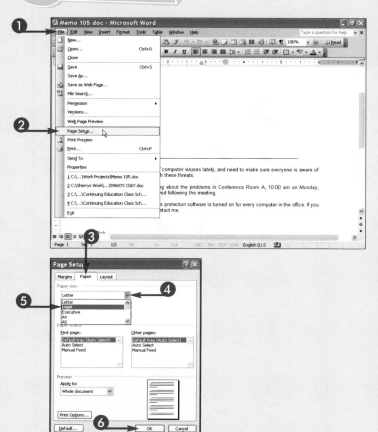

1 Click **File**.

2 Click **Page Setup**.

Note: To learn more about printing with Office, see Chapter 2.

The Page Setup dialog box appears.

3 Click the **Paper** tab.

4 Click the **Paper size** ⌄.

5 Click a paper size.

Note: You can also use the Page Setup dialog box to change the paper width and height settings to create a custom size.

Note: You can use the Page Setup dialog box to change paper source and page orientation.

6 Click **OK**.

Word applies the sizing to your document.

Print an Envelope

You can create instant envelopes in Word based on the information in a document. For example, when typing a letter, you can use the address from the document to create and print an envelope.

Print an Envelope

1 Click **Tools**.

2 Click **Letters and Mailings**.

3 Click **Envelopes and Labels**.

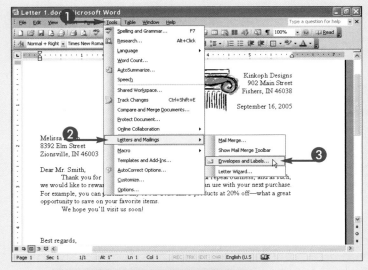

The Envelopes and Labels dialog box appears.

4 Click the **Envelopes** tab if it is not already displayed.

5 If needed, type the return address.

Word does not display a return address to accommodate preprinted envelopes.

6 Click **Options**.

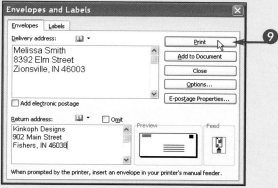

The Envelope Options dialog box appears.

7 Click the **Envelope size** ⊡ to choose an envelope size.

● You can change the font or positioning of addresses, if needed.

8 Click **OK**.

9 Click **Print**.

Word sends your envelope text to the printer.

Depending on your printer setup, the Feed area indicates how to feed the envelope into the printer.

Note: *See your printer documentation to learn how to print envelopes.*

Can I save the envelope information for later use?
Yes. You can save the delivery and return address information along with the document to use at a later time. Click **Add to Document** in the Envelopes and Labels dialog box. The next time you open the file and the dialog box, the information is already entered and ready to go.

How do I print labels?
You can use the same Envelopes and Labels dialog box to print labels. Click the **Labels** tab to view label options. You can create address labels, and print multiple copies or a single label. You can choose to print the return address or the delivery address on your labels. You can also choose a label type by clicking **Options** and selecting a label size from the Label Options dialog box.

Part III

Excel

Excel is a powerful spreadsheet program you can use to enter and organize data, and perform a wide variety of number crunching tasks. Excel is the second most widely used program in the Office suite, behind Word. You can use Excel strictly as a program for manipulating numerical data, or you can use it as a database program to organize and track large quantities of data. You can use Excel's charting capabilities to present your data to others in visual, easy-to-understand graphs.

In this part, you learn how to enter data into worksheets and format the data to make it easy to read. You also learn how to tap into the power of Excel's formulas and functions to perform mathematical calculations and analysis.

Enter Cell Data

Data can be text, such as row or column labels, or numbers, which are called *values* in Excel. Values also include formulas. Excel automatically left-aligns text data in a cell and right-aligns values. By default, Excel also considers numerical dates and times you enter as values, and assigns right alignment.

You can enter data into any cell within the Excel worksheet. When you click a cell, it immediately becomes the active cell in the worksheet, and any data you type appears within the active cell. You can type data directly into the cell, or you can enter data using the Formula bar.

Enter Cell Data

TYPE INTO A CELL

1 Click the cell you want to use.

The active cell always appears highlighted with a darker border than the other cells.

● To add data to another worksheet in your workbook, simply click the worksheet tab to display the worksheet.

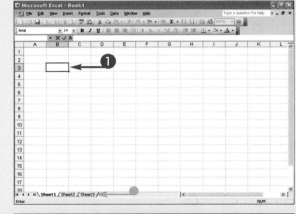

2 Type your data.

● The data appears both in the cell and in the Formula bar.

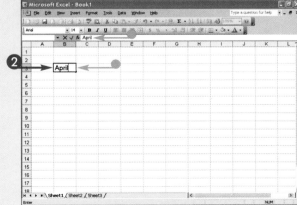

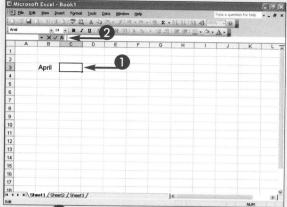

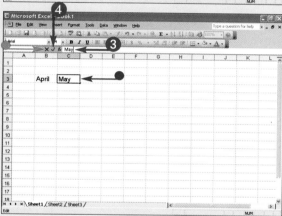

TYPE DATA IN THE FORMULA BAR

1 Click the cell you want to use.

2 Click in the Formula bar.

3 Type your data.

● The data appears both in the Formula bar and in the cell.

4 Click ☑ or press **Enter** to enter the data.

● To cancel an entry, click ☒.

What if the data I type is too long to fit in my cell?

Long text entries appear truncated when you enter data into adjoining cells. You can remedy this by resizing the column to fit the data, or by turning on the cell's text wrap feature, which wraps the text to fit in the cell and remain visible. Text wrapping will cause the cell depth to increase. To learn how to resize columns, see the section "Resize Columns and Rows." To learn how to turn on the text wrap feature, see the section "Turn On Text Wrapping."

When I start typing in a cell, Excel tries to fill in the text for me. Why?

Excel's AutoComplete feature is automatic. If you repeat an entry from anywhere in the same column, AutoComplete attempts to complete the entry for you based on the first few letters you type. If the AutoComplete entry is correct, press **Enter** and Excel fills in the text for you. If not, just keep typing the text you want to insert into the cell. The AutoComplete feature is just one of many Excel tools to help you speed up your data entry tasks.

Select Cells

You can select cells in Excel to perform editing, mathematical, and formatting tasks. Selecting a single cell is simple: You just click the cell. To select a group of cells, called a *range*, you can use your mouse or keyboard. For example, you might apply formatting to a range of cells rather than format each cell individually.

You can learn more about working with ranges in Chapter 10.

Select Cells

SELECT A RANGE

1️⃣ Click the first cell in the range of cells you want to select.

2️⃣ Click and drag across the cells you want to include in the range.

The ⌖ changes to ✛.

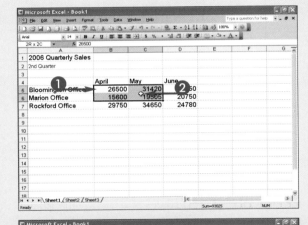

3️⃣ Release the mouse button.

● The cells are selected.

● To select all the cells in the worksheet, click here.

You can select multiple noncontiguous cells by pressing and holding **Ctrl** while clicking cells.

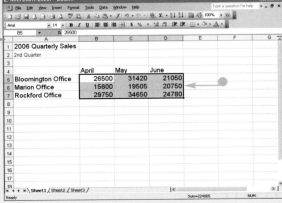

108

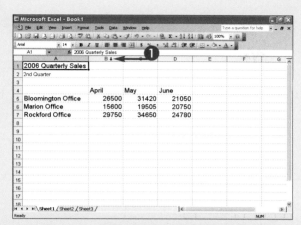

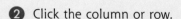

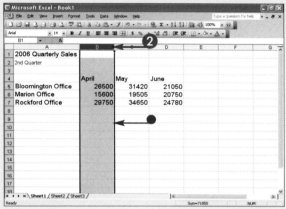

SELECT A COLUMN OR ROW

1 Move the mouse over the header of the column or row you want to select.

The ⌖ changes to ⬇.

2 Click the column or row.

● Excel selects the entire column or row.

To select multiple columns or rows, click and drag across the column or row headings.

You can select multiple noncontiguous columns or rows by pressing and holding **Ctrl** while clicking column or row headings.

How do I select data inside a cell?
To select a word or number inside a cell, you can click in front of the text in the Formula bar, and then drag over the characters or numbers you want to select. You can also select data directly in a cell. If a cell contains several words, you can double-click a word to select the word.

How do I use my keyboard to select cells?
You can use the arrow keys to navigate to the first cell in the range. Next, press and hold **Shift** while using an arrow key to select the range, such as ⬇ and ➡. Excel selects any cells you move over using the keyboard navigation keys.

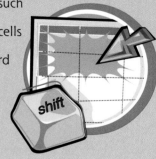

Faster Data Entry with AutoFill

When you make a cell active in the worksheet, a small fill handle appears in the lower-right corner of the selector. You can use the fill handle to create an AutoFill series.

You can use Excel's AutoFill feature to help you automate data entry tasks. You can use AutoFill to add duplicate entries or a data series to your worksheet cells, such as labels for Monday, Tuesday, Wednesday, and so on. You can create your own custom data lists as well as utilize built-in lists of common entries such as days of the week, months, and number series.

Faster Data Entry with AutoFill

AUTOFILL A TEXT SERIES

① Type the first entry in the text series.

② Click and drag the cell's fill handle across or down the number of cells you want to fill.

You can also use AutoFill to copy the same text to every cell you drag over.

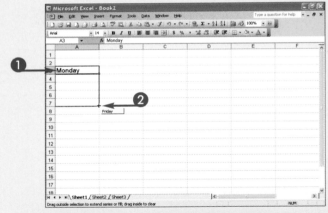

③ Release the mouse button.

● AutoFill fills in the text series.

● An AutoFill smart tag may appear offering additional options you can assign to the data.

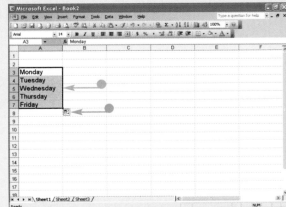

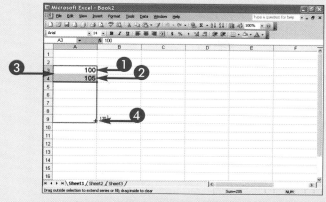

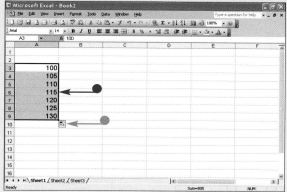

AUTOFILL A NUMBER SERIES

1 Type the first entry in the number series.

2 In an adjacent cell, type the next entry in the number series.

3 Select both cells.

Note: *See the previous section, "Select Cells," to learn more.*

4 Click and drag the fill handle across or down the number of cells you want to fill.

5 Release the mouse button.

● AutoFill fills in the number series.

● An AutoFill smart tag may appear offering additional options you can assign to the data.

How do I create a custom list?

To add your own custom list to AutoFill's list library, first create the custom list in your worksheet cells. Then follow these steps:

1 Select the cells containing the list you want to save.

2 Click **Tools**.

3 Click **Options**.

The Options dialog box appears.

● The list you selected in Step **1** is shown here.

4 Click the **Custom Lists** tab.

5 Click **Import**.

● Excel adds the series to the custom lists.

6 Click **OK**.

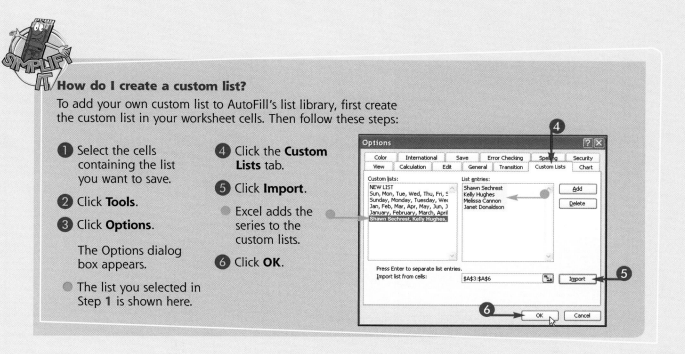

Add Columns and Rows

You can add columns and rows to your worksheets to add more data. For example, you may need to add a column in the middle of several existing columns to add data you left out the first time you created the workbook.

Add Columns and Rows

ADD A COLUMN

① Click the heading of the column to the right of where you want to insert a new column.

Note: See the section "Select Cells," earlier in this chapter, to learn how to select columns and rows.

② Right-click the selected column.

③ Click **Insert**.

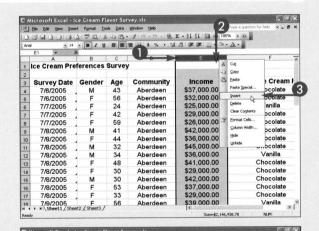

- Excel adds a column.

- A smart tag may appear when you insert a column, which you can click to view a list of options you can assign.

- You can click **Insert** and then **Columns** to add columns.

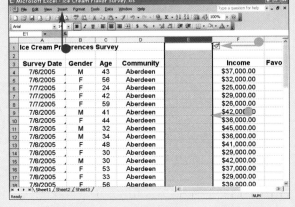

ADD A ROW

1 Click the heading of the row below where you want to insert a new row.

Note: *See the section "Select Cells," earlier in this chapter, to learn how to select columns and rows.*

2 Right-click the selected row.

3 Click **Insert**.

● Excel adds a row.

● A smart tag icon may appear, which you can click to view a list of options you can assign.

● You can also click **Insert** and then **Rows** to add rows.

Can I insert a multiple number of columns and rows?

Yes. First, select two or more columns and rows in the worksheet and then activate the **Insert** command. Excel adds the same number of new columns and rows as the number you originally selected. You can also click **Insert** and then **Columns** or **Rows** to insert multiple columns or rows into your worksheet.

Can I insert columns or rows using the Insert dialog box?

Yes. If you click a cell and activate the **Insert** command, the Insert dialog box appears. You can select the **Entire Row** or **Entire Column** options (○ changes to ●). When you click **OK** to exit the dialog box, Excel immediately adds a single row or column below or to the right of the active cell. You can also right-click a cell to activate the command.

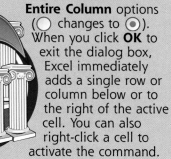

Delete Columns and Rows

You can remove columns or rows you no longer need in the worksheet. For example, you may want to remove a row of out-of-date data. When you delete an entire column or row, Excel also deletes any existing data within the selected cells. Excel also moves over the other columns and rows to fill the space left by the deletion.

Delete Columns and Rows

DELETE A COLUMN

① Click the heading of the column you want to delete.

Note: See the section "Select Cells," earlier in this chapter, to learn how to select columns and rows.

② Right-click the selected column.

③ Click **Delete**.

Note: If you press Delete *, Excel deletes the column's contents instead of the entire column.*

Excel deletes the column.

● You can also click **Edit** and then click **Delete** to remove a column or row.

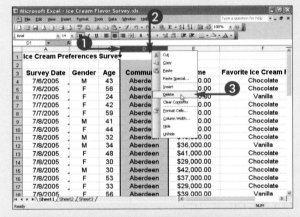

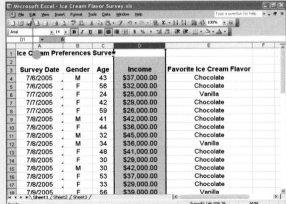

DELETE A ROW

① Click the heading of the row you want to delete.

Note: See the section "Select Cells," earlier in this chapter, to learn how to select columns and rows.

② Right-click the selected row.

③ Click **Delete**.

Note: If you press **Delete**, Excel deletes the row's contents instead of the entire row.

Excel deletes the row.

● You can also click **Edit** and then click **Delete** to remove a row.

How do I delete an entire worksheet from my workbook?

To remove a worksheet, right-click the worksheet tab and then click **Delete** from the shortcut menu. If the sheet contains any existing data, Excel prompts you to confirm the deletion by clicking **Delete**. To learn more about adding and deleting worksheets from a workbook file, see Chapter 9.

I accidentally deleted a column I need. How do I reinsert it?

If you click the **Undo** button (⬇) on the Standard toolbar immediately after deleting a row or column, you can undo the action. Excel reinserts the row or column, including any data it contained. You can also click **Edit** and then **Undo**.

Resize Columns and Rows

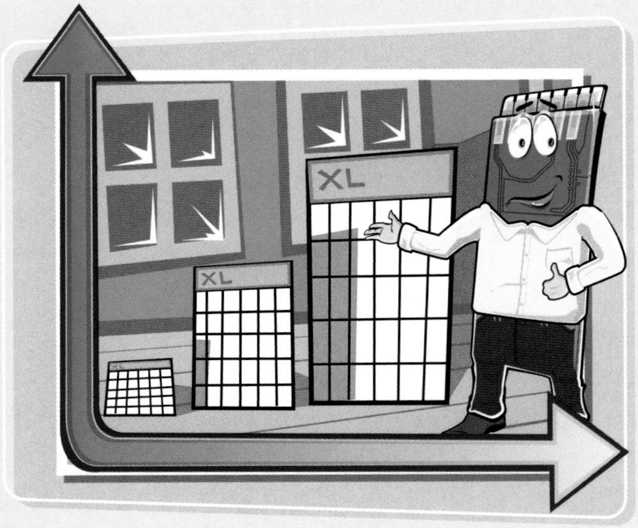

You can resize your worksheet's columns and rows to accommodate text or make the worksheet more aesthetically appealing.

Resize Columns and Rows

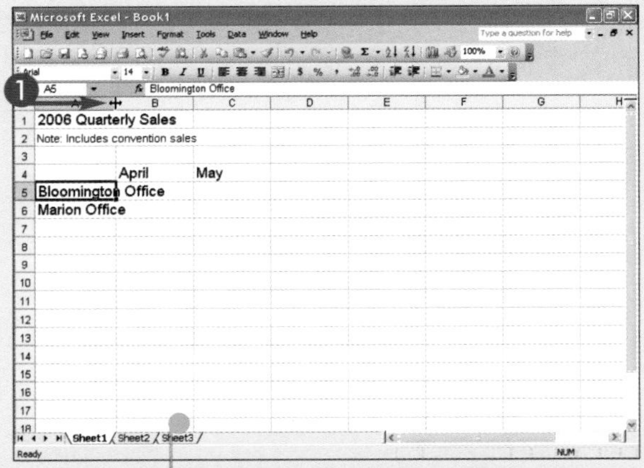

1. Move the mouse pointer over the heading of the border of the column or row you want to resize.

   The ⇖ changes to ✛.

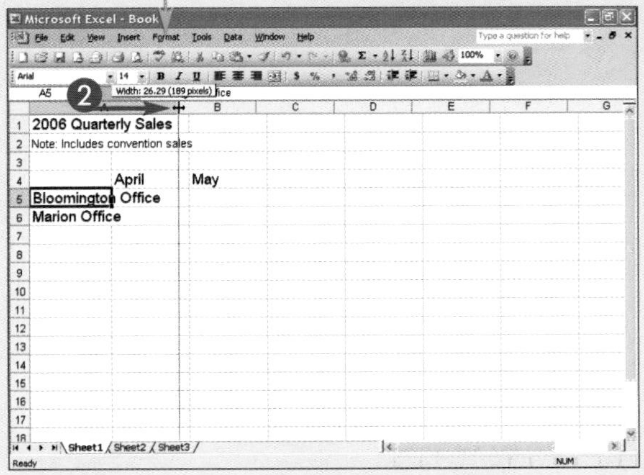

2. Click and drag the border to the desired size.

   A dotted line marks the new border of the column or row as you drag.

3. Release the mouse button and the column or row is resized.

- You can also click **Format**, **Column**, and then **AutoFit Selection** to quickly resize a highlighted column to fit existing text.

Turn On Text Wrapping

By default, long lines of text you type into a cell remain on one line. You can turn on the cell's text-wrapping option to make text wrap to the next line and fit into the cell without truncating the text. Text wrapping makes the row size taller to fit the number of lines that wrap.

Turn On Text Wrapping

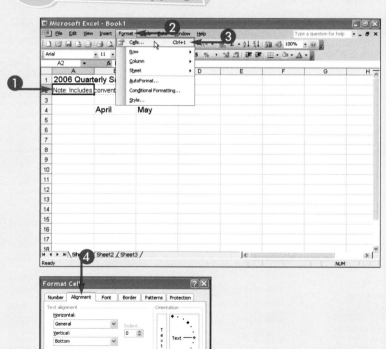

① Click the cell you want to edit.

Note: *You can also apply text wrapping to multiple cells. See the section "Select Cells," earlier in this chapter, to learn how to select multiple cells for a task.*

② Click **Format**.

③ Click **Cells**.

You can also right-click in the cell and click **Format Cells**.

The Format Cells dialog box appears.

④ Click the **Alignment** tab.

⑤ Select the **Wrap text** option (☐ changes to ☑).

⑥ Click **OK**.

Excel applies text wrapping to the cell.

Note: *See the previous section, "Resize Columns and Rows," to learn how to adjust cell depth and width to accommodate your text.*

117

Center Data Across Columns

You can center a title or heading across a range of cells in your worksheet. For example, you may want to include a title across multiple columns of labels. You can use the Merge and Center command to quickly create a merged cell to hold the title text.

Center Data Across Columns

① Select the cell containing the text you want to center and the cells you want to center across.

Note: See the section "Select Cells," earlier in this chapter, to learn how to select columns and rows.

② Click the **Merge and Center** button (⊞) on the Formatting toolbar.

● Excel merges the cells and centers the text.

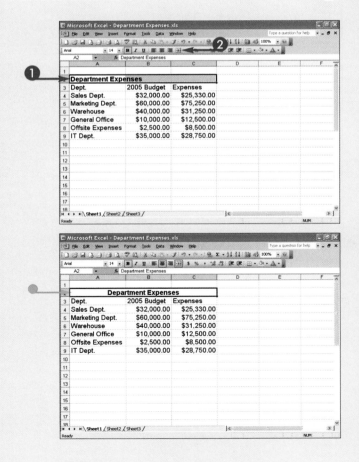

Freeze a Column or Row

You can freeze a column or row to keep the labels in view as you scroll through larger worksheets. The area you freeze is nonscrollable, while the unfrozen areas of the worksheet are still scrollable.

Freeze a Column or Row

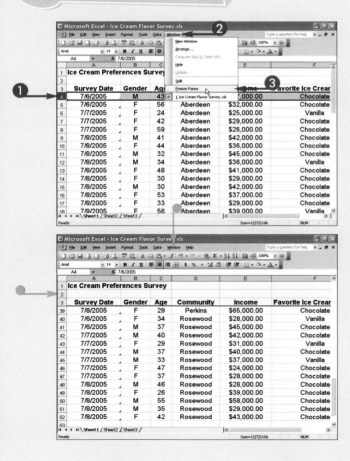

① Click to the right of the column or below the row you want to freeze.

Note: *To freeze only a row or column, click the row or column heading rather than a cell.*

② Click **Window**.

③ Click **Freeze Panes**.

● Excel freezes the areas above where you applied the Freeze Panes command.

The area below the panes is scrollable.

● To unlock the columns and rows, click **Window** and then **Unfreeze Panes**.

119

Remove
Data or Cells

You can delete Excel data you no longer need. When you decide to delete data, you can choose whether you want to remove the data and keep the cell or delete the cells entirely. When you delete a cell's contents, only the data is removed. When you delete a cell, Excel removes the cell as well as its contents. The existing cells in your worksheet shift over to fill any gap in the worksheet structure.

Remove Data or Cells

DELETE DATA

1 Click the cell or select the cells containing the data you want to remove.

Note: *See the section "Select Cells," earlier in this chapter, to learn how to select cells.*

2 Press **Delete**.

Excel deletes the data from the cell.

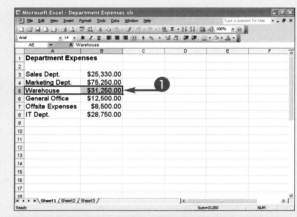

DELETE CELLS

1 Click the cell or select the cells you want to remove.

Note: *See the section "Select Cells," earlier in this chapter, to learn how to select cells.*

2 Right-click over the cell or range.

3 Click **Delete**.

You can also click **Edit** and then **Delete**.

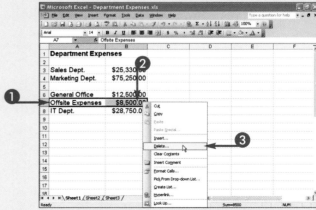

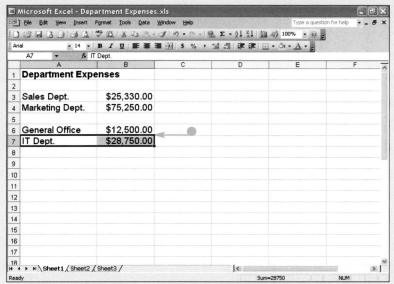

The Delete dialog box appears.

④ Select a deletion option (○ changes to ⊙).

You can also open another file to copy to.

⑤ Click **OK**.

● Excel removes the cells and their content from the worksheet.

Other cells shift over to fill the void of any cells you remove from a worksheet.

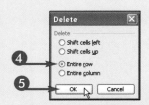

Can I remove a cell's formatting without removing the content?

Yes. You can use the Clear command to remove formatting, contents, or comments from your worksheet cells. To activate the command, follow these steps. Select the cell or cells you want to edit. Click **Edit** and then click **Clear**. A submenu appears. Click **Formats** to remove all the formatting in the cell. Click **Contents** to remove all the cell's data. Click **Contents** to remove all the cell's data. Click **Comments** to remove any comments assigned to the cell. To remove all formatting, contents, and comments at the same time, click **All**.

Assign Worksheet Names

You can name your Excel worksheets to help identify their content. For example, if your workbook contains four sheets, each detailing a different sales quarter, you can give each sheet a unique name, such as Quarter 1, Quarter 2, and so on.

Assign Worksheet Names

1 Double-click the sheet tab you want to rename.

The current name is highlighted.

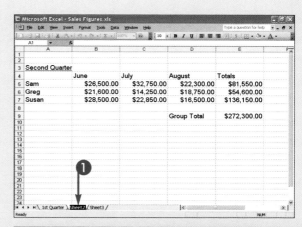

2 Type a new name for the worksheet.

3 Press **Enter**.

Excel assigns the new worksheet name.

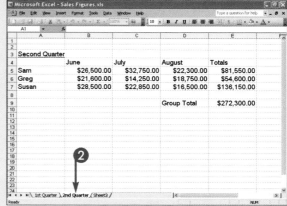

Delete a Worksheet

You can delete a worksheet you no longer need in your workbook. Always be sure to check the sheet's contents before deleting to avoid removing any important data. As soon as you delete a worksheet, it is permanently removed from the workbook file.

Delete a Worksheet

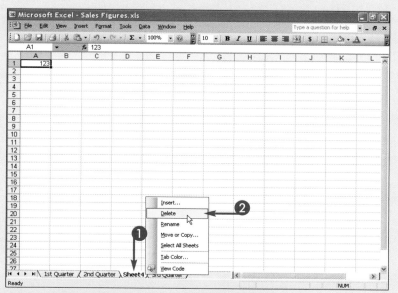

① Right-click the worksheet tab.

② Click **Delete**.

If the worksheet is blank, Excel deletes it immediately.

If the worksheet contains any data, Excel prompts you to confirm the deletion.

③ Click **Delete**.

The worksheet is deleted.

Add a Worksheet

Depending on which worksheet is active, Excel adds a new worksheet immediately before the active worksheet. You can move worksheets to reposition their order; see the next section, "Move a Worksheet," to learn more.

You can add a worksheet to your workbook to create another sheet in which to enter data. By default, every Excel workbook opens with three sheets. You can add more sheets as you need them.

Add a Worksheet

1 Click **Insert**.

2 Click **Worksheet**.

You can also right-click a sheet tab and click **Insert** to open the Insert dialog box, where you can choose to insert a worksheet.

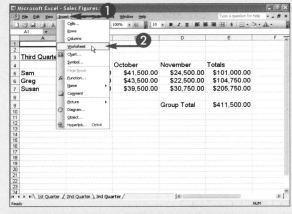

● Excel adds a new worksheet and a default worksheet name.

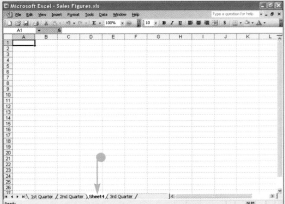

Move a
Worksheet

You can move a
worksheet within a workbook
to rearrange the sheet order.
For example, you may want to
position the sheet you use the
most as the first sheet in
the workbook.

Move a Worksheet

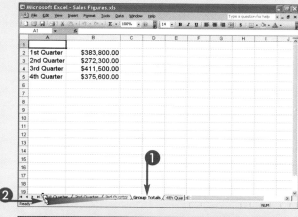

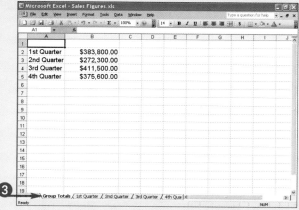

❶ Click the tab of the worksheet you want
to move.

❷ Drag the sheet to a new position in the
list of sheets.

The ⛾ changes to ⛾.

A small black triangle icon keeps track
of the sheet's location in the group while
you drag.

Note: *You can also use the Move or Copy
command on the Edit menu to move or copy
worksheets with the help of a dialog box.*

❸ Release the mouse button.

The worksheet is moved.

Copy a Worksheet

You can copy a worksheet within a workbook. For example, you may want to copy a sheet to use as a starting point for new, yet similar, data.

Copy a Worksheet

① Click the worksheet tab you want to copy.

② Press **Ctrl**.

The ⌖ changes to 🔏.

③ Drag the sheet to a new position in the list of sheets where you want the copy to appear.

● A small black triangle icon keeps track of the sheet's location in the group while you drag.

Note: *You can also use the Move or Copy command on the Edit menu to move or copy worksheets with the help of a dialog box.*

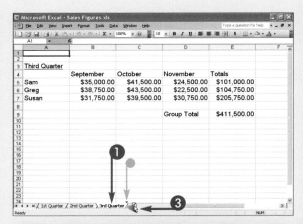

④ Release the mouse button.

● The worksheet is copied as a new sheet in the workbook and given a default name indicating it is a copy of another sheet.

Note: *Excel sequentially names sheet copies with a number, starting with (2), after the sheet name.*

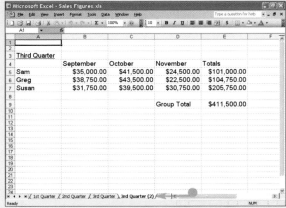

Format the Worksheet Tab Color

You can add color to your worksheet tabs to help distinguish one sheet from another. The color you add to a tab appears in the background, behind the worksheet tab name. By default, all worksheet tabs are white unless you assign another color.

Format the Worksheet Tab Color

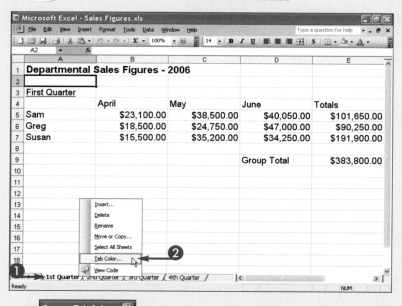

① Right-click the worksheet tab you want to format.

② Click **Tab Color**.

The Format Tab Color dialog box appears.

③ Click a color.

④ Click **OK**.

Excel assigns the color to the tab.

To see the new tab color, click another worksheet tab.

Note: You can set the tab color to white to return it to the default state.

Find and Replace Data

You can use Excel's Find tool to search through your worksheet for a particular number, formula, word, or phrase. You can use the Replace tool to replace instances of text or numbers with other data. For example, you may need to sort through a long worksheet replacing a reference with another name.

Find and Replace Data

FIND DATA

① Click **Edit**.

② Click **Find**.

The Find and Replace dialog box appears with the Find tab displayed.

③ Type the data you want to find.

④ Click **Find Next**.

- Excel searches the worksheet and finds the first occurrence of the specified data.

  You can click **Find Next** again to search for the next occurrence.

⑤ When finished, click **Close** or **Cancel** to close the dialog box.

Note: *Excel may display a prompt box when the last occurrence is found. Click* **OK**.

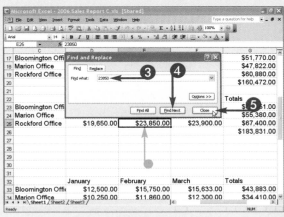

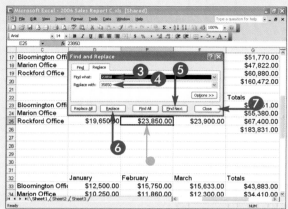

REPLACE DATA

1 Click **Edit**.

2 Click **Replace**.

The Find and Replace dialog box appears with the Replace tab displayed.

3 Type the data you want to find.

4 Type the replacement data.

5 Click **Find Next**.

● Excel locates the first occurrence of the data.

6 Click **Replace** to replace the occurrence.

You can click **Replace All** to replace every occurrence in the worksheet.

7 When finished, click **Close**.

Note: *Excel may display a prompt box when the last occurrence is found. Click **OK**.*

Where can I find detailed search options?

You can click **Options** in the Find and Replace dialog box to reveal additional search options you can apply. For example, you can search by rows or columns, matching data, and more. You can also search for specific formatting or special characters using **Format** options. To hide the additional search options, click **Options** again.

How can I search for and delete data?

To search for a particular word, number, or phrase using the Find and Replace dialog box and remove the data completely from the worksheet, start by typing the text in the **Find what** field. Leave the **Replace with** field empty. When you activate the search, Excel looks for the data, and replaces it without adding new data to the worksheet.

Sort Data

You can sort your Excel data to reorganize the information. This technique is particularly useful when using Excel to create database tables — lists of related data. For example, you might want to sort a client table to list the names alphabetically. An ascending sort lists records from A to Z, and a descending sort lists records from Z to A.

Sort Data

PEFORM A QUICK SORT

① Click in the field name, or heading, you want to sort.

② Click the **Sort Ascending** (🔼) or **Sort Descending** (🔽) button on the Formatting toolbar.

● Excel sorts the records based on the field you specified.

Note: If you do not want the records sorted permanently, click 🔄 to return the list to its original state.

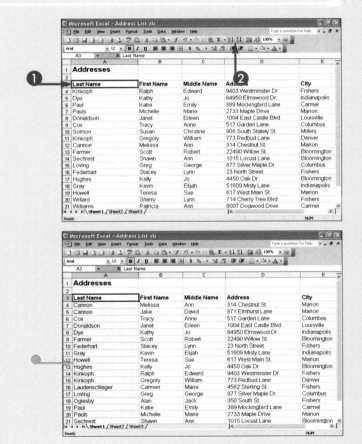

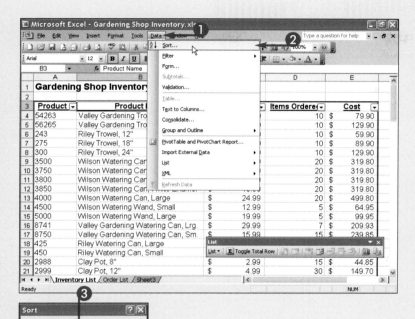

SORT WITH THE SORT DIALOG BOX

1 Click **Data**.

2 Click **Sort**.

The Sort dialog box appears.

3 Click the first **Sort by** ☑ and select the primary field to sort by.

4 Select an option to sort the field in ascending or descending order (○ changes to ◉).

To specify additional fields for the sort, repeat Steps **3** and **4** to select other sort fields.

5 Click **OK**.

Excel sorts the data.

What are database tables and how do I use them in Excel?

A database is a collection of related information, such as an address book. You can create a variety of database lists in Excel to manage sales contacts, inventory, household valuables, and more. An entire database list of information is called a *table*. You use *fields* to break down your list into manageable pieces. Fields are typically the columns you use to define each part of your list, such as name, address, and phone number. You use rows to enter each database entry for your list of data. Database entries are called *records*.

Can I sort data in rows?

Yes. If the listed data is across a row instead of down a column, you can activate the **Sort Left to Right** option. Open the Sort dialog box as shown in this section and click **Options**. The Sort Options dialog box appears. Then select the **Sort left to right** option (○ changes to ◉).

Filter Data with AutoFilter

When using Excel as a database, you can use a filter to view only portions of your data. Unlike a sort, which sorts the entire table, a filter selects certain records to display based on your criteria, while hiding records that do not match the criteria.

See the previous section to learn how to sort data in Excel.

Filter Data with AutoFilter

① Select the field labels for the data you want to sort.

② Click **Data**.

③ Click **Filter**.

④ Click **AutoFilter**.

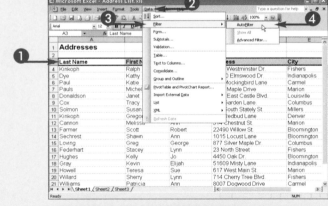

● Excel adds drop-down arrow buttons (▾) to your field labels.

⑤ Click ▾.

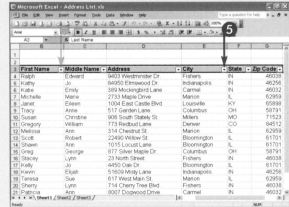

132

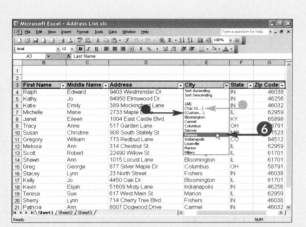

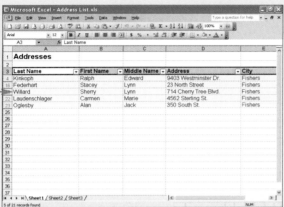

6 Click a filter type.

You can filter the table based on a particular field.

● To display the ten most-repeated items for this field, click **Top 10**.

● To customize your filter, you can click **Custom**.

● Excel filters the table.

To view all the records again, display the filter list and click **All**.

What is a Top 10 list?
AutoFilter lists a Top 10 option for every field. You can use the option to quickly filter for the top or bottom ten items in your table. For example, you might want to view the top ten salespeople or the bottom ten sellers from your product list. To activate the command, click **Top 10** in the filter list to display the Top 10 AutoFilter dialog box, and then select the filtering options you want to apply.

In what ways can I customize a filter?
You can click **Custom** in the Filter drop-down list to open the Custom AutoFilter dialog box. Here you can further customize the filter by selecting operators and values to apply on the filtered data. To learn more about customizing AutoFilters, see Excel's Help files.

Insert a Comment

You can add comments to your worksheets to make a note to yourself about a particular cell's contents, or as a note for other users to see. For example, if you share your workbooks with other users, you can add comments to leave feedback about the data without typing directly in the worksheet. Excel displays comments in a balloon.

Insert a Comment

ADD A COMMENT

① Click the cell to which you want to add a comment.

② Click **Insert**.

③ Click **Comment**.

You can also right-click on the cell and click **Insert Comment**.

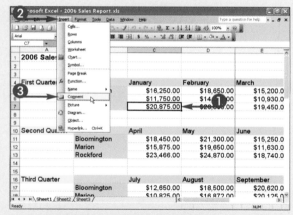

A comment balloon appears.

④ Type your comment text.

⑤ Click anywhere outside the comment balloon to deselect the comment.

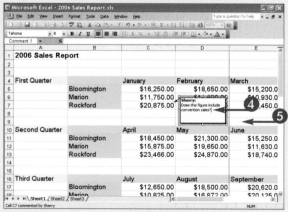

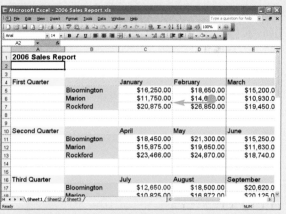

- Cells that contain comments display a tiny red triangle in the corner.

VIEW A COMMENT

1 Position the mouse pointer over the upper-right corner of the cell.

- The comment balloon appears displaying the comment.

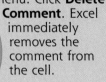

How do I remove a comment?

You can remove comments you no longer want to associate with a cell. Right-click over the cell containing the comment to display a shortcut menu. Click **Delete Comment**. Excel immediately removes the comment from the cell.

How do I respond to another user's comment?

If the worksheet's tracking features are turned on, you can add a comment to another user's comment. Excel's tracking features enable you to see the edits each user makes to the workbook. After all the edits are completed, you can decide which edits to accept or reject to create a final file. To turn on workbook tracking, click **Tools**, **Track Changes**, and then **Highlight Changes**. See the next section, "Track and Review Workbook Changes," to learn more.

Track and Review Workbook Changes

The tracking feature changes the color for each person's edits, making it easy to see who changed what in the workbook. When you review the workbook, you can choose to accept or reject the changes.

If you work in an environment in which you share your Excel workbooks with others, you can use the tracking and reviewing features to help you keep track of who adds changes to the file. For example, you can see what edits others have made, including formatting changes and data additions or deletions.

Track and Review Workbook Changes

TURN ON TRACKING

1. Click **Tools**.
2. Click **Track Changes**.
3. Click **Highlight Changes**.

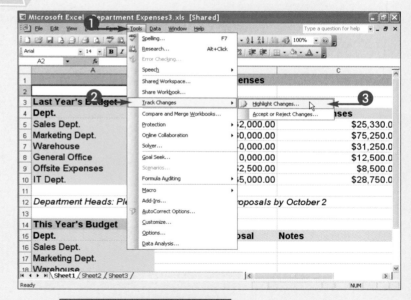

The Highlight Changes dialog box appears.

4. Select the **Track changes while editing** option (☐ changes to ☑).

This option automatically creates a shared workbook file if you have not already activated the share workbook feature.

● You can select an option to choose when, who, or where you track changes (☐ changes to ☑).

● Leave this option selected to view changes in the file.

5. Click **OK**.

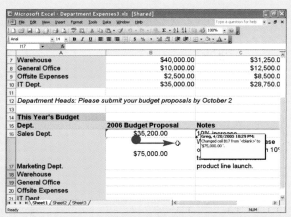

Excel's tracking feature is activated.

Excel highlights any changes in the worksheet.

- To view details about a change and the author, move ⬧ over the highlighted cell.

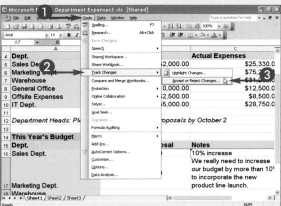

REVIEW CHANGES

1 Click **Tools**.

2 Click **Track Changes**.

3 Click **Accept or Reject Changes**.

Is there a way to view all the changes at the same time when reviewing a workbook?
Yes. When you display the Highlight Changes dialog box (click **Tools** and then **Highlight Changes**), you can select the **List changes on a new sheet** option (☐ changes to ☑). This opens a special History sheet in the workbook for viewing each edit. The History sheet breaks out the details of each edit, including the date, time, and author. You can use the filters to change the list of edits. When you save the workbook, the History sheet is deleted.

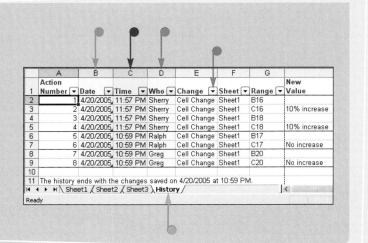

continued 137

Track and Review Workbook Changes *(continued)*

When you activate the reviewing process, Excel goes through each change in the worksheet and allows you to accept or reject the edit. When the review is complete, you can turn the tracking feature off.

Track and Review Workbook Changes *(continued)*

The Select Changes to Accept or Reject dialog box appears.

④ Select options for which changes you want to view (☐ changes to ☑).

⑤ Click **OK**.

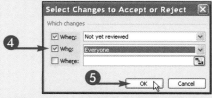

The Accept or Reject Changes dialog box appears.

● Excel highlights the first change in the worksheet.

⑥ Specify an action for each edit.

● Click **Accept** to add the change to the final worksheet.

● To reject the change, click **Reject**.

● Click here to accept or reject all the changes at the same time.

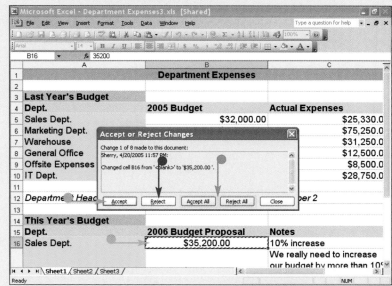

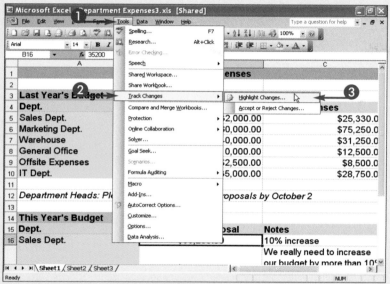

TURN OFF TRACKING

① Click **Tools**.

② Click **Track Changes**.

③ Click **Highlight Changes**.

The Highlight Changes dialog box appears.

④ Deselect the **Track changes while editing** option (☑ changes to ☐).

⑤ Click **OK**.

Excel's tracking feature is turned off.

Are there certain edits Excel does not track or highlight?

Excel's tracking feature does not keep track of changes in sheet names, inserted or deleted sheets, or hidden rows or columns. In addition, some of Excel's features do not work with shared workbooks, such as grouping data, recording and assigning macros, or inserting pictures or hyperlinks. For a complete list of changes and features supported with shared workbooks, see Excel's Help files.

Can I remove a user from a shared workbook?

Yes. You can open the Share Workbook dialog box and view which users are using the file. Click **Tools** and then **Shared Workbook** to open the dialog box. You can then remove a user by clicking his or her name and clicking **Remove User**.

Understanding Formulas

You can use formulas to perform all kinds of calculations on your Excel data. You can build formulas using mathematical operators, values, and cell references. For example, you can add the contents of a column of monthly sales totals to determine the cumulative sales total. If you are new to writing formulas, this section explains all the basics required to build your own formulas in Excel.

Formula Structure

Ordinarily, when you write a mathematical formula, you write the values and the operators, followed by an equal sign, such as $2 + 2 =$. In Excel, formula structure works a bit differently. All Excel formulas begin with an equal sign (=), such as $= 2 + 2$. The equal sign immediately tells Excel to recognize any subsequent data as a formula rather than as a regular cell entry.

Referencing Cells

Although you can enter specific values in your Excel formulas, you can also easily reference data in specific cells. For example, you can add two cells together or multiply the contents of one cell by a value. Every cell in a worksheet has a unique address, also called a cell reference. By default, cells are identified by the specific column letter and then by row number, so cell D5 identifies the fifth cell down in column D. To help make your worksheets easier to use, you can also assign your own unique names to cells. For example, if a cell contains a figure totaling weekly sales, you might name the cell Sales.

Cell Ranges

A group of related cells in a worksheet is called a range. Cell ranges are identified by their anchor points in the upper-left corner of the range and the lower-right corner. The range reference includes both anchor points separated by a colon. For example, the range name A1:B3 includes cells A1, A2, A3, B1, B2, and B3. You can also assign unique names to your ranges to make it easier to identify their contents. Range names must start with a letter or underscore, and can include uppercase and lowercase letters. Spaces are not allowed in range names.

Operator Precedence

Excel performs a series of operations from left to right in the following order, which gives some operators precedence over others:

Operator Precedence	
First	All operations enclosed in parentheses
Second	Exponential equations
Third	Multiplication and division
Fourth	Addition and subtraction

When you are creating equations, the order of operations determines the results. For example, if you want to determine the average of values in A2, B2, and C2, and you enter the equation $=A2+B2+C2/3$, you will calculate the wrong answer. This is because Excel divides the value in cell C2 by 3 and then adds that result to $A2+B2$. Following operator precedence, division takes precedence over addition. The correct way to write the formula is $=(A2+B2+C2)/3$. By enclosing the values in parentheses, Excel adds the cell values first before dividing them by 3.

Mathematical Operators

You can use mathematical operators in Excel to build formulas. Basic operators include the following:

Mathematical Operators	
Operator	*Operation*
+	Addition
-	Subtraction
*	Multiplication
/	Division
%	Percentage
^	Exponentiation
=	Equal to
<	Less than
≤	Less than or equal to
>	Greater than
≥	Greater than or equal to
< >	Not equal to

Reference Operators

You can use Excel's reference operators to control how a formula groups cells and ranges to perform calculations. For example, if your formula needs to include the cell range D2:D10 and cell E10, you can instruct Excel to evaluate all the data contained in these cells using a reference operator. Your formula might look like this: $=SUM(D2:D10,E10)$.

Reference Operators		
Operator	*Example*	*Operation*
:	$=SUM(D3:E12)$	Range operator. Evaluates the reference as a single reference, including all the cells in the range from both corners of the reference.
,	$=SUM(D3:E12,F3)$	Union operator. Evaluates the two references as a single reference.
[space]	$=SUM(D3: D20 D10:E15)$	Intersect operator. Evaluates the cells common to both references.
[space]	$=SUM(Totals Sales)$	Intersect operator. Evaluatesthe intersecting cell(s) of the column labeled Totals and the row labeled Sales.

Create Formulas

You can create a formula in the Formula bar at the top of the worksheet. Formula results appear in the cell in which you assign a formula.

You can write a formula to perform a calculation on data in your worksheet cells. All formulas begin with an equal sign (=) in Excel. You can reference values in cells by entering the cell name, also called a cell reference. For example, if you want to add the contents of cells C3 and C4 together, your formula looks like this: =C3+C4.

Create Formulas

① Click in the cell to which you want to assign a formula.

② Type **=**.

● Excel displays the formula in the Formula bar and in the active cell.

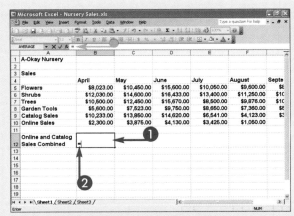

③ Click in the first cell you want to reference in the formula.

● Excel inserts the cell reference into the formula.

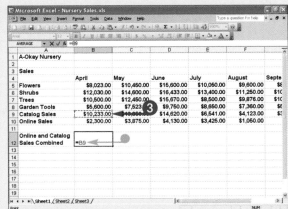

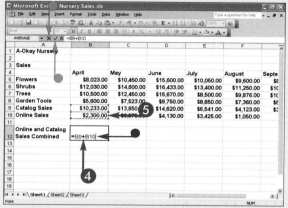

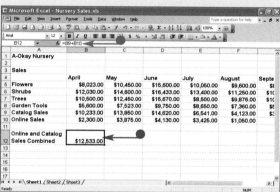

④ Type an operator for the formula.

Note: See the section "Understanding Formulas," later in this chapter, to learn more about mathematical operators.

⑤ Click in the next cell you want to reference in the formula.

● Excel inserts the cell reference into the formula.

⑥ Press **Enter**.

● You can also click ☑ on the Formula bar to accept the formula.

● You can click ☒ to cancel the formula.

● The formula results appear in the cell.

To view the formula in the Formula bar, simply click in the cell.

● The Formula bar displays any formula assigned to the active cell.

Note: If you change any of the values in the cells referenced in your formula, the formula results automatically update to reflect the changes.

How do I edit a formula?

To edit a formula, simply click in the cell containing the formula and make any corrections in the Formula bar. You can also double-click in the cell to make edits directly to the formula within the cell rather than the Formula bar. You can use the keyboard arrow keys to move the cursor to the place you want to edit in the data, or simply click the cursor in place. You can press **Backspace** and **Delete** to make changes to the formula and type new values or references as needed. When finished with the edits, press **Enter** or click ☑ on the Formula bar.

What happens if I see an error message in my formula?

If you see an error message, such as #DIV/0!, double-check your formula references, making sure you referenced the correct cells. Also make sure you did not attempt to divide by 0, which always produces an error. To learn more about fixing formula errors, see the section "Audit a Worksheet for Errors," later in this chapter.

Define a Range Name

You can assign distinctive names to the cells and ranges of cells you work with in a worksheet, making it easier to identify the cell's contents. A *range* is simply a rectangular group of related cells, or a range can consist of a single cell. Naming ranges can also help you when deciphering formulas. A range name, such as Sales_Totals, is much easier to recognize than a generic reference, such as B24:C24.

Define a Range Name

ASSIGN A RANGE NAME

① Select the range you want to name.

② Click inside the **Name** box on the Formula bar.

③ Type a name for the range.

④ Press Enter.

Excel assigns the name to the cells.

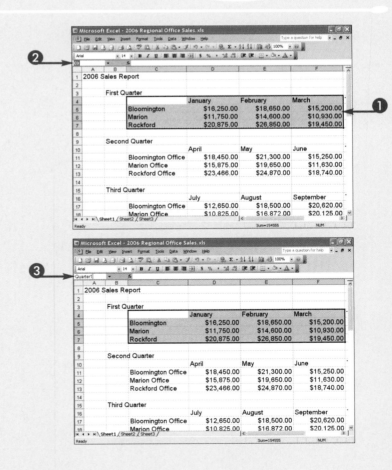

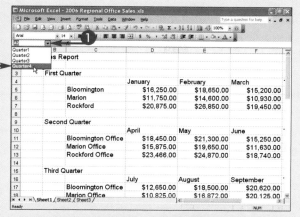

GO TO A RANGE

1 Click the **Name** ⬚.

2 Click the range name you want to move to.

● Excel immediately activates the cells.

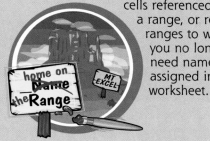

Are there any rules for naming ranges?
Yes. Range names must start with a letter or an underscore (_). After that, you can use any character, uppercase or lowercase, or any punctuation or keyboard symbols, with the exception of a hyphen or space. No hyphens or spaces are allowed in range names. Instead, substitute a period or underscore for spaces and hyphens.

How do I edit a range name?
You can use the Define Name dialog box to make changes to your range names. To display the dialog box, click **Insert**, **Name**, and then **Define**. You can edit existing range names, change the cells referenced by a range, or remove ranges to which you no longer need names assigned in the worksheet.

Reference Ranges in Formulas

You can reference an entire group of cells in a formula by referencing the range name. This can speed up the time it takes to build a formula in a worksheet, and range names are much easier to remember than the default range names Excel assigns.

Reference Ranges in Formulas

1. Click in the cell to which you want to assign a formula.

2. Start or create the formula you want to apply.

   Note: See the section "Create Formulas," earlier in this chapter, to learn more.

3. When you are ready to insert a range into the formula, select the range in the worksheet.

   Excel automatically inserts the range name.

4. Continue creating the formula as needed.

5. Press **Enter**.

   ● You can also click ☑ on the Formula bar to complete the formula.

   The formula results appear in the cell.

   ● You can also click **Insert**, **Name**, and then **Paste** to open the Paste Name dialog box and select which range you want to use in the formula.

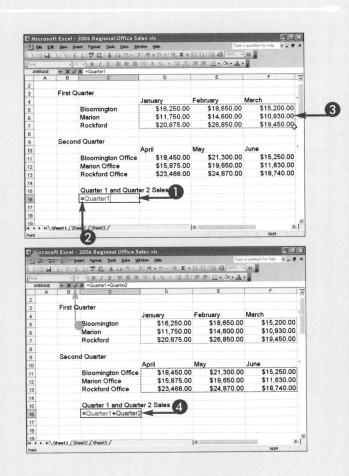

Reference Cells from Other Worksheets

You can reference cells in other worksheets in your Excel formulas. When referencing data from other worksheets, you must specify the sheet name followed by an exclamation mark and then by the cell address, such as Sheet2!D12. If the sheet has a specific name, such as Sales, you must use the name along with an exclamation mark, followed by the cell or range reference (Sales!D12). If the sheet name includes spaces, enclose the reference in single quote marks, such as 'Sales Totals!D12'.

See Chapter 9 to learn more about naming Excel worksheets.

Reference Cells from Other Worksheets

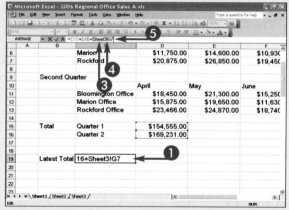

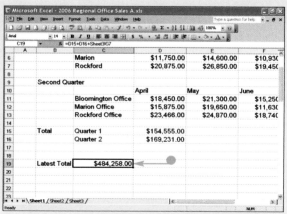

① Click the cell to which you want to assign a formula.

② Create the formula you want to apply.

Note: See the section "Create Formulas," earlier in this chapter, to learn more.

③ When you are ready to insert a cell or range from another sheet into the formula, type the sheet name.

④ Type an exclamation mark.

⑤ Type the cell address or range.

You can continue creating the formula as needed.

⑥ When finished, press Enter.

You can also click ☑ on the Formula bar to complete the formula.

● The formula results appear in the cell.

Apply Absolute and Relative Cell References

By default, Excel treats the cells you include in formulas as relative locations rather than set locations in the worksheet. This is called *relative cell referencing*. For example, when you copy a formula to a new location, the formula automatically adjusts using relative cell addresses. If you want to address a particular cell location no matter where the formula appears, you can assign an *absolute cell reference*. Absolute references are preceded with a $ sign in the formula, such as = D2 + E2.

Apply Absolute and Relative Cell References

ASSIGN ABSOLUTE REFERENCES

1 Click in the cell containing the formula you want to change.

2 Select the cell reference.

3 Press **F4**.

Note: You can also type dollar signs to make a reference absolute.

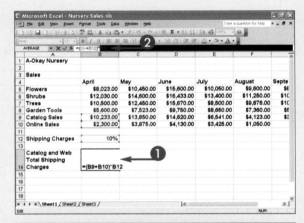

● Excel enters dollar signs ($) before each part of the cell reference, making the cell reference absolute.

Note: You can continue pressing **F4** to cycle through mixed, relative, and absolute references.

4 Press **Enter** or click ✓.

Excel assigns the changes to the formula.

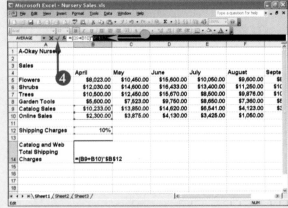

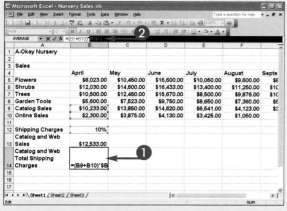

ASSIGN RELATIVE REFERENCES

1 Click in the cell containing the formula you want to change.

2 Select the cell reference.

3 Press **F4** to cycle to relative addressing.

Note: You can press **F4** multiple times to cycle through mixed, relative, and absolute references.

Note: You can also type dollar signs to make a reference absolute.

4 Press **Enter** or click **fx**.

● Excel assigns the changes to the formula.

When would I use absolute cell references?
You can use absolute referencing to always refer to the same cell in the worksheet. For example, perhaps your worksheet contains several columns of pricing information that refers to one discount rate disclosed in cell G10. When you create a formula based on the discount rate, you want to make sure the formula always refers to cell G10, even if the formula is moved or copied to another cell. By making cell G10 absolute instead of relative, you can always count on an accurate value for the success of your formula.

When would I use mixed cell references?
You can use mixed referencing to reference the same row or column, but different relative cells within, such as $C6, which keeps the column from changing while the row remains relative. If the mixed reference is C$6, the column is relative but the row is absolute. You can press **F4** while writing a formula to cycle through absolute, mixed, and relative cell referencing, or you can type the dollar signs ($) as needed.

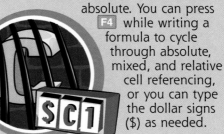

Understanding Functions

If you are looking for a speedier way to enter formulas, you can tap into a wide variety of built-in formulas, called *functions*. Functions are ready-made formulas that perform a series of operations on a specified range of values. Excel offers more than 300 functions you can use to perform mathematical calculations on your worksheet data.

Function Elements

Because functions are formulas, all functions must start with an equal sign (=). Functions are also distinct in that each one has a name. For example, the function that sums data is called the SUM function, while the function for averaging values is AVERAGE. You can type functions directly into your worksheet cells or use the Formula bar. You can also use the Insert Function dialog box to help construct functions. This dialog box offers help in selecting and applying functions to your data.

Constructing Arguments

Functions typically use arguments to indicate the cell addresses upon which you want the function to calculate. Arguments are enclosed in parentheses. When applying a function to individual cells in the worksheet, you can use a comma to separate the cell addresses, such as =SUM(A5,B5,C5). When applying a function to a range of cells, you can use a colon to designate the first and last cells in the range, such as =SUM(B5:E12). If your range has a name, you can insert the name, such as =SUM(Sales).

Types of Functions

Excel groups functions into ten categories and each category can include a variety of functions:

Types of Functions	
Category	**Description**
Database & List Management	You can use the database functions to count, add, and filter database items.
Date & Time	Includes functions for calculating dates, times, and minutes.
Engineering	This category offers all kinds of functions for engineering calculations.
Financial	Includes functions for calculating loans, principal, interest, yield, and depreciation.
Information	Includes functions for testing your data.
Logical	Includes functions for logical conjectures, such as if-then statements.
Lookup & Reference	Use these functions to locate references or specific values in your worksheets.
Mathematical & Trigonometric	Includes a wide variety of functions for calculations of all types.
Statistical	This category includes functions for calculating averages, probabilities, rankings, trends, and more.
Text	Use these text-based functions to search and replace data and other text tasks.

Common Functions

The table below lists some of the more popular Excel functions you might use with your own spreadsheet work.

Common Functions			
Function	**Category**	**Description**	**Syntax**
SUM	Math & Trig	Adds up values	=SUM(number1,number2,...)
INT	Math & Trig	Rounds down to the nearest integer	=INT(number)
ROUND	Math & Trig	Rounds a number specified by the number of digits	=ROUND(number,number_digits)
ROUNDDOWN	Math & Trig	Rounds a number down	=ROUNDDOWN(number,number_digits)
COUNT	Statistical	Returns a count of text or numbers in a range	=COUNT(value1,value2,...)
AVERAGE	Statistical	Averages a series of arguments	=AVERAGE(number1,number2,...)
MIN	Statistical	Returns the smallest value in a series	=MIN(number1,number2,...)
MAX	Statistical	Returns the largest value in a series	=MAX(number1,number2,...)
MEDIAN	Statistical	Returns the middle value in a series	=MEDIAN(number1,number2,...)
PMT	Financial	Finds the periodic payment for a fixed loan	=PMT(interest_rate,number_of_periods, present_value,future_value,type)
RATE	Financial	Returns an interest rate	=RATE(number_of_periods,payment, present_value,future_value,type,guess)
TODAY	Date & Time	Returns the current date	=TODAY()
IF	Logical	Returns one of two results you specify based on whether the value is TRUE or FALSE	=IF(logical_text,value_if_true, value_if_false)
AND	Logical	Returns TRUE if all the arguments are true, FALSE if any are false	=AND(logical1,logical2,...)
OR	Logical	Returns TRUE if any argument is true or FALSE if all arguments are false	=OR(logical1,logical2,...)

Apply a Function

You can use functions to speed up your Excel calculations. You can use the Insert Function dialog box to look for a particular function from among Excel's ten function categories.

Apply a Function

① Click in the cell to which you want to assign a function.

② Click the **Insert Function** (fx) button on the Formula bar.

● You can also click **Insert** and then **Function**.

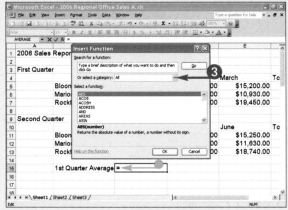

● Excel inserts an equal sign automatically to denote a formula and displays the Insert Function dialog box.

③ Click the **Category** .

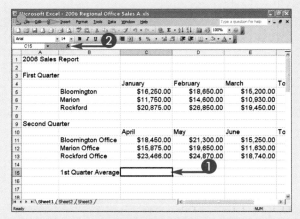

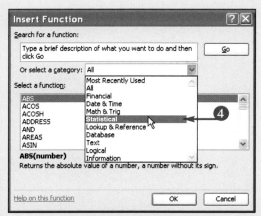

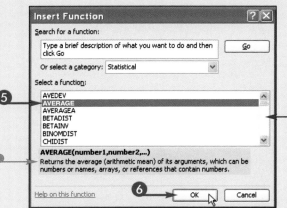

④ Click a category.

Excel's built-in functions are grouped into ten categories.

Note: *See the previous section, "Understanding Functions," to learn more about function categories.*

● A list of functions appears here.

⑤ Click the function you want to apply.

● A description of the function you select appears here.

⑥ Click **OK**.

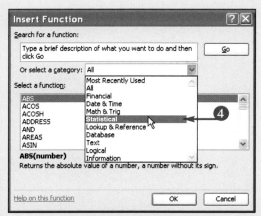

What kind of results can I expect with Excel functions?

Most of the time, the functions you create will produce number results. Because functions use different types of arguments, however, some functions produce different types of results.

Excel Functions	
Result	***Description***
Number	Number results can include any integer or decimal number.
Time and date	When applying time and date functions, you can expect time and date results.
Logical values	Logical arguments produce results such as TRUE, FALSE, YES, NO, 1, 0.
Text	Any text results always appear surrounded by quote marks.
Arrays	An array is a column or table of cells that are treated as a single value, and array formulas operate on multiple cells.
Cell references	Some function results display references to other cells rather than actual values.
Error values	If a function uses error values as arguments, the results appear as error values as well. Error values are not the same as error messages.

continued

Apply a Function *(continued)*

After selecting a function, you can then apply the function to a cell or range of cells in your worksheet. You can use the Function Arguments dialog box to help you construct all the necessary components of a function. The dialog box can help you determine what values you need to enter to build the formula.

Apply a Function *(continued)*

The Function Arguments dialog box appears.

⑦ Depending on the function's arguments, select the desired cells for each argument required by the function.

You can select a cell or range of cells directly in the worksheet, and Excel automatically adds the references to the argument.

● You can also type a range or cell address directly into the argument text box.

● The dialog box displays additional information about the function here.

⑧ If needed, continue adding the necessary cell references to complete all of the function's arguments.

⑨ When finished constructing the arguments, click **OK**.

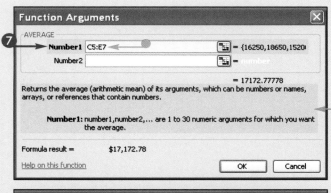

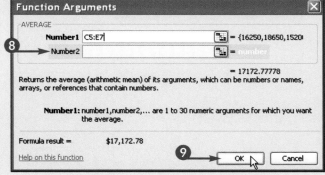

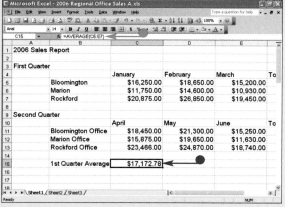

- Excel displays the function results in the cell.

- The function appears in the Formula bar.

EDIT A FUNCTION

1 Click the cell containing the function you want to edit.

2 Click the **Insert Function** button (f_x) on the Formula bar.

- Excel displays the Function Arguments dialog box, and you can make changes to the cell references or values as needed.

How can I find help with a particular function?

If you click the **Help on this function** link in either the Insert Function or Function Arguments dialog boxes, you can access Excel's help files to find out more about the function. The function help includes an example of the function in action and tips about how to use the function.

The Function Arguments dialog box covers the cells I need to select. How do I move the dialog box out of the way?

You can click the **Collapse** button (⬚) at the end of the argument text box to minimize the dialog box. You can then select any cells needed, and click the **Expand** button (⬚) to maximize the dialog box again. You can also click and drag the dialog box by its title bar to move it around the screen.

Total Cells with AutoSum

One of the most popular functions available in Excel is the AutoSum function. AutoSum automatically totals the contents of cells. For example, you can quickly total a column of sales figures. AutoSum works by guessing which surrounding cells you want to total, or you can specify exactly which cells to sum.

Total Cells with AutoSum

APPLY AUTOSUM

1 Click in the cell where you want to insert a sum total.

2 Click the **AutoSum** (Σ) button on the Standard toolbar.

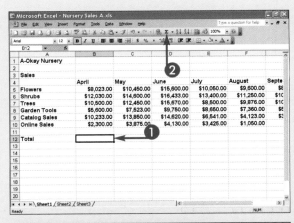

● AutoSum immediately attempts to total the adjacent cells.

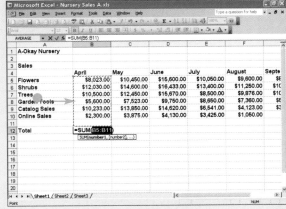

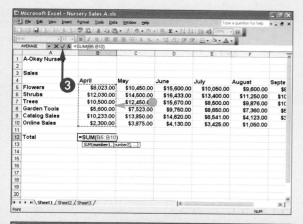

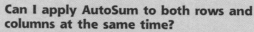

- To sum another range of cells instead of AutoSum's guess, select the cells you want to include in the sum.

3 Press **Enter** or click ☑.

- Excel totals the selected cells.

Can I total cells without applying a function?

Yes. You can use the AutoCalculate feature to quickly sum cells or apply results from several other popular functions without having to insert a formula or function. You can select a group of cells you want to total and Excel immediately adds all the cell contents and displays a total in the status bar at the bottom of the program window. To change the calculation type, right-click over the total on the status bar and click another function. To sum noncontiguous cells, press and hold **Ctrl** while clicking cells.

Can I apply AutoSum to both rows and columns at the same time?

Yes. Simply select both the row and column of data you want to sum, along with a blank row and column to hold the results. When you apply the AutoSum function, Excel sums the row and column and displays the results in the blank row and column.

Audit a Worksheet for Errors

When dealing with larger worksheets in Excel, it is not always easy to figure out the source of a formula error when scrolling through the many cells. To help you with errors that arise, you can utilize Excel's Formula Auditing toolbar, which includes several tools for examining and correcting formula errors. The Error Checking feature looks through your worksheet for errors and helps you find solutions.

Audit a Worksheet for Errors

APPLY ERROR CHECKING

1. Click **Tools**.
2. Click **Formula Auditing**.
3. Click **Show Formula Auditing Toolbar**.

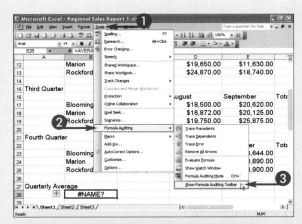

The Formula Auditing toolbar appears.

4. Click the **Error Checking** button (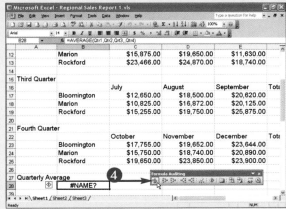).

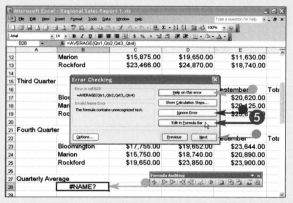

- Excel displays the Error Checking dialog box and highlights the first cell containing an error.

5 To fix the error, click **Edit in Formula Bar**.

- To find help with an error, click here to open the Help files.

- To ignore the error, click **Ignore Error**.

- You can click **Previous** and **Next** to scroll through all of the errors on the sheet.

6 Make edits to the cell references in the Formula bar.

7 Click **Resume**.

8 When the error check is complete, click **OK**.

What kind of error messages does Excel display for formula errors?
The following table explains the different types of error values that can appear in cells when an error occurs:

Formula Errors		
Error Message	**Problem**	**Solution**
######	The cell is not wide enough to contain the value	Increase the column width
#DIV/0!	Dividing by zero	Edit the cell reference or value of the denominator
#N/A	Value is not available	Check to make sure the formula references the correct value
#NAME?	Does not recognize text in a formula	Make sure the name referenced is correct
#NULL!	Specify two areas that do not intersect	Check for an incorrect range operator or correct intersection problem
#NUM!	Invalid numeric value	Check the function for an unacceptable argument
#REF!	Invalid cell reference	Correct cell references
#VALUE!	Wrong type of argument or operand	Double-check arguments and operands

continued

Audit a Worksheet for Errors *(continued)*

Auditing tools can trace the path of your formula components and check each cell reference that contributes to the formula. When tracing the relationships between cells, you can display tracer lines to find *precedents*, cells referred to in a formula, or *dependents*, cells that contain the formula results.

Audit a Worksheet for Errors *(continued)*

TRACE PRECEDENTS

① Click in the cell containing the formula results or content you want to trace.

② Display the Formula Auditing toolbar.

   Note: *See the previous page to learn how to display the Auditing toolbar.*

③ Click the **Trace Precedents** button (⬚).

● To trace dependents instead, click the **Trace Dependents** button (⬚).

● Excel displays trace lines from the current cell to the cells referenced in the formula.

   You can make changes to the cell contents or changes to the formula to make any corrections.

● In this example, the trace lines show that the wrong total cell is referenced.

● You can click **Remove Precedent Arrows** (⬚) to turn off the trace lines.

● To turn off dependent trace lines, click the **Remove Dependent Arrows** button (⬚).

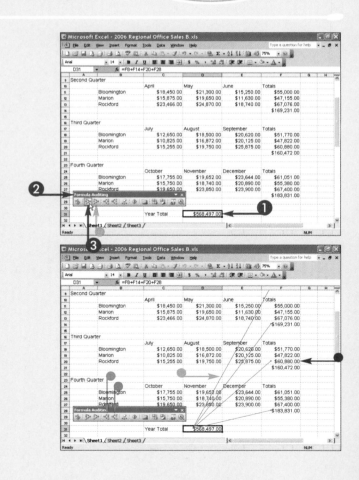

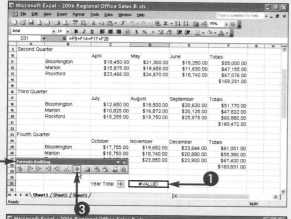

TRACE ERRORS

1 Click in the cell containing the error you want to trace.

2 Display the Formula Auditing toolbar.

Note: *See the previous page to learn how to display the toolbar.*

3 Click the **Trace Error** button (⊕).

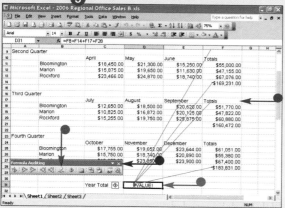

● Excel displays trace lines from the current cell to any cells referenced in the formula.

You can make changes to the cell contents or changes to the formula to correct the error.

● In this example, the text cell is referenced in the formula instead of a numeric value.

● You can click **Remove All Arrows** (⬚) to turn off the trace lines.

● You can click ✖ to hide the toolbar.

How do I use the Smart Tag to fix formula errors?

Excel displays a Smart Tag icon (◈) any time you encounter an error. You can click the Smart Tag to view a menu of options, including options for correcting the error. For example, you can click the **Help on this error** menu command to find out more about the error message.

help on
this error

What does the Evaluate Formula button do?

You can click the **Evaluate Formula** button (◉) on the Formula Auditing toolbar to check over your formula or function step by step. When you click the cell containing the formula you want to evaluate, and click ◉, Excel opens the Evaluate Formula dialog box and you can evaluate each portion of the formula to check it for correct references and values.

Change Number Formats

You can use number formatting to control the appearance of numerical data in your worksheet. For example, if you have a column of prices, you can apply currency formatting to the data to format the numbers with dollar signs and decimal points. Excel offers 12 different number categories, or styles, from which to choose.

Change Number Formats

1. Select the cell, range, or data you want to format.

   Note: See Chapter 8 to learn how to select cells; see Chapter 10 to learn about ranges.

2. Click **Format**.

3. Click **Cells**.

   Note: You can apply number formatting to single cells, ranges, columns, rows, or an entire worksheet.

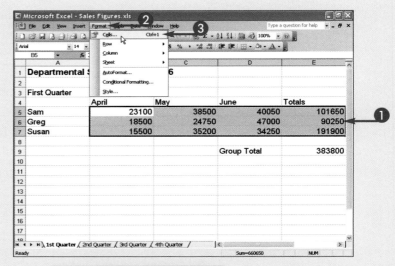

The Format Cells dialog box appears.

4. Click the **Number** tab.

5. Click a number category.

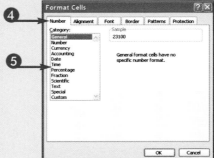

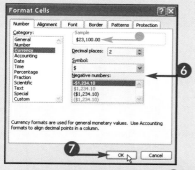

6 Specify any additional options, if desired.

● The Sample area displays a sample of the selected number style and options.

7 Click **OK**.

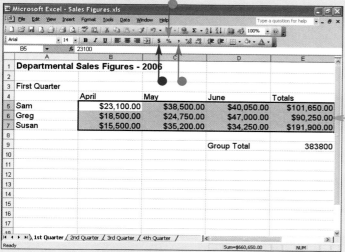

● Excel applies the number formatting to the numerical data in the cell or range.

● To quickly apply dollar signs to your data, click the **Currency Style** button ($) on the Formatting toolbar.

● To quickly apply percent signs to your data, click the **Percent Style** button (%).

● To quickly apply commas to your number data, click the **Comma Style** button (,).

What sort of number formats can I apply to my numeric data?
Each number format style is designed for a specific use.

Number Formats	
Style	**Description**
General	The default category; no specific formatting is applied
Number	General number display with two default decimal points
Currency	Adds dollar signs and decimals to display monetary values
Accounting	Lines up currency symbols and decimal points in a column
Date; Time	Use to display date and time values, respectively
Percentage	Multiplies cell value by 100 and displays percent sign
Fraction	Displays value as a specified fraction
Scientific	Uses scientific or exponential notation
Text	Treats values as text
Special	Works with list and database values
Custom	Enables you to create your own custom format

Change the Font and Size

The font controls the design appearance of letters and numbers, while the font size controls the height of the characters, measured in points. By default, Excel assigns Arial as the font and 10-point as the font size for every new workbook you create.

You can control the font you use for your worksheet data, along with the size of the data text. For example, you may want to make the worksheet title larger than the rest of the data, or you may want to resize the font for the entire worksheet to a more legible size to make the data easier to read.

Change the Font and Size

CHANGE THE FONT

1. Select the cell or data you want to format.

   Note: See Chapter 8 to learn how to select cells.

2. Click the **Font** ⏷.

   You can use the scroll arrows and scroll bar to scroll through all the available fonts.

   You can also begin typing a font name to choose a font.

3. Click a font.

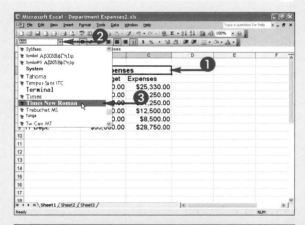

● Excel immediately applies the font.

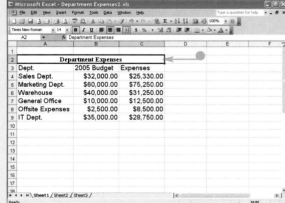

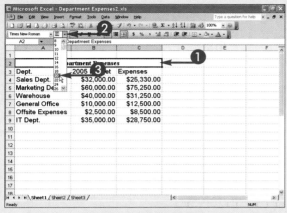

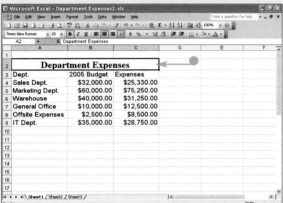

CHANGE THE FONT SIZE

① Select the cell or data you want to format.

Note: See Chapter 8 to learn how to select cells.

② Click the **Font Size** ⊡.

③ Click a size.

● Excel immediately applies the new size to the selected cell or data.

Is there a way to apply numerous formatting options all at once?

You can use the Format Cells dialog box to apply a new font, size, or any of the basic formatting controls, such as bold, italics, and underlining. Follow these steps to display the dialog box:

① Click **Format**.

② Click **Cells**.

The Format Cells dialog box opens.

③ Click the **Font** tab.

You can use the various options within the Font tab to control the font, size, and style of the data.

④ Click **OK** to save your changes.

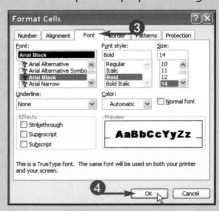

Increase or Decrease Decimals

You can control the number of decimals that appear with numeric data using the Increase Decimal and Decrease Decimal commands. For example, you may want to increase the number of decimals shown in a cell, or reduce the number of decimals in a formula result.

Increase or Decrease Decimals

① Select the cell or range you want to format.

Note: See Chapter 8 to learn how to select cells; see Chapter 10 to learn about ranges.

② Click a decimal button.

You can click **Increase Decimal** (⊞) to increase the number of decimals.

You can click **Decrease Decimal** (⊞) to decrease the number of decimals.

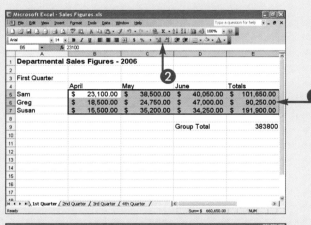

● Excel adjusts the number of decimals that appear in the cell or cells.

In this example, only one decimal is removed.

● You can click ⊞ again to remove another decimal.

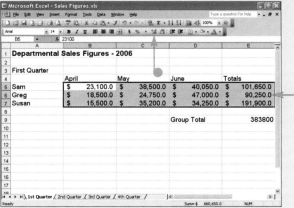

Change Data Color

When adding color to worksheets, always consider the color's effect on the legibility of your data both in print and on-screen. You want your worksheet to appear easy to read, not jarring and distracting to the eye.

You can change the color of your data, whether the data is numeric or text. For example, you might choose a brighter color for any cell data you want to bring attention to, or select a different color for the column headers in your worksheet.

Change Data Color

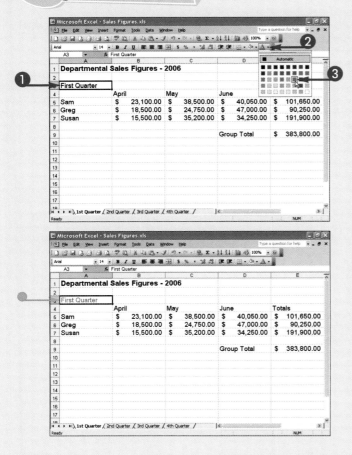

① Select the cell, range, or data you want to format.

Note: *See Chapter 8 to learn how to select cells; see Chapter 10 to learn about ranges.*

② Click the **Font Color** ⬝.

To apply the current color shown, simply click the **Font Color** button (⬛).

③ Click a color from the palette.

● Excel applies the color to the data.

Adjust the Cell Alignment

You can control the alignment of data within your worksheet cells. By default, Excel automatically aligns text data to the left and number data to the right of each cell. Data is also aligned vertically to sit at the bottom of the cell. You can change horizontal and vertical alignments to improve the appearance of your worksheet data.

Adjust the Cell Alignment

SET HORIZONTAL ALIGNMENT

1 Select the cells you want to format.

Note: See Chapter 8 to learn how to select cells.

2 Click an alignment button on the Formatting toolbar.

You can click the **Align Left** button (☰) to align data to the left.

You can click the **Center** button (☰) to center align the data.

You can click the **Align Right** button (☰) to align data to the right.

● Excel immediately applies the alignment to your cells.

In this example, the cell data is now centered.

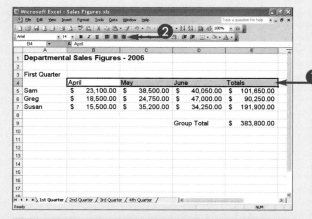

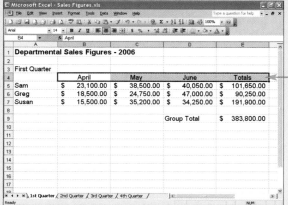

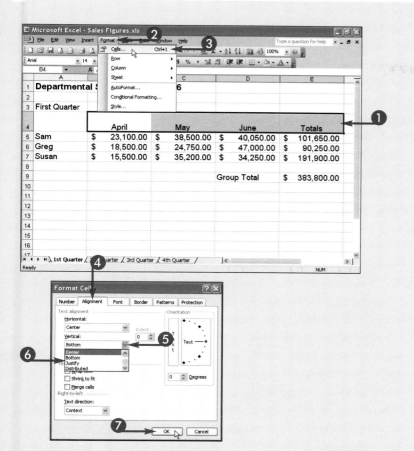

SET VERTICAL ALIGNMENT

① Select the cells you want to format.

Note: See Chapter 8 to learn how to select cells.

② Click **Format**.

③ Click **Cells**.

The Format Cells dialog box appears.

④ Click the **Alignment** tab.

⑤ Click the **Vertical** ⊡.

⑥ Click a vertical alignment.

⑦ Click **OK**.

Excel applies the vertical alignment to the cells.

How do I set indents for my cell text?

You can use the Increase Indent and Decrease Indent commands to add indents to lines of text in your worksheet. To indent text, click the **Increase Indent** button (⊞) on the Formatting toolbar. To decrease an indent, click the **Decrease Indent** button (⊞).

Can I justify my text to create left and right margins in a cell?

Yes. To justify cell text, you must open the Format Cells dialog box and display the **Alignment** tab, as outlined in the steps in this section. You can then click the **Horizontal** ⊡ and click **Justify** to assign justification to your cell text.

Control
Text Wrap

By default, any text you type into a cell stays on one line. For longer text entries, this means the text may appear to span several columns. To make the text stay in one cell and wrap to fit the cell width, you can activate the text-wrapping feature using the Format Cells dialog box. Wrapping cell text increases the depth of the worksheet row containing the cell.

Control Text Wrap

1. Select the cells you want to format.

   Note: See Chapter 8 to learn how to select cells.

2. Click **Format**.

3. Click **Cells**.

The Format Cells dialog box appears.

4. Click the **Alignment** tab.

5. Select the **Wrap text** option (☐ changes to ☑).

6. Click **OK**.

● Excel applies text wrapping to the cell or cells.

   Note: To force a line break in a cell, press Alt + Enter.

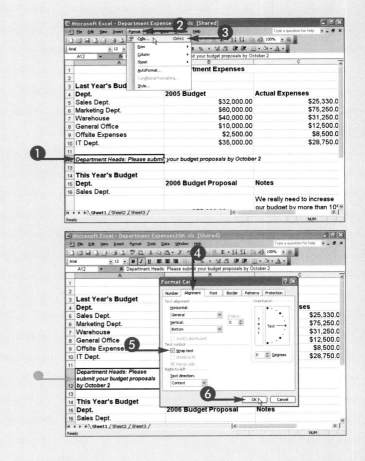

Copy Cell Formatting

You can use the Format Painter feature to copy formatting to other cells in your worksheet. For example, perhaps you have applied a variety of formatting options to a range of cells to create a certain look. When you want to re-create the same look elsewhere in the worksheet, you do not have to repeat the same steps you applied to assign the original formatting. Instead, you can paint the formatting to the other cells in one action.

Copy Cell Formatting

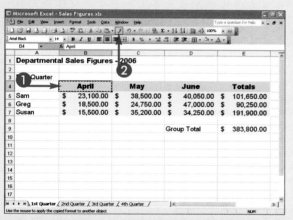

① Select the cell or range containing the formatting you want to copy.

Note: *See Chapter 8 to learn how to select cells.*

② Click the **Format Painter** button () on the Standard toolbar.

Excel surrounds the cell or range with a blinking border.

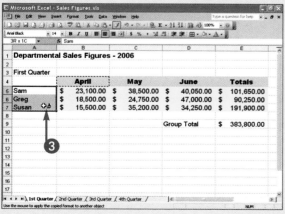

③ Click and drag over the cells to which you want to copy the formatting.

Excel immediately copies the formatting to the new cells.

Note: *To copy the same formatting multiple times, double-click* 🖊.

Note: *You can press* Esc *to cancel the Format Painter at any time.*

Add Borders

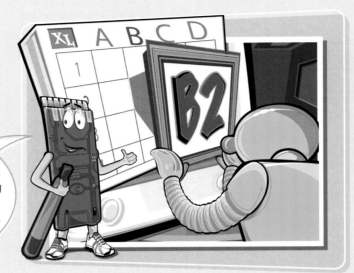

You can add borders to your worksheet cells to help define the contents or more clearly separate the data from surrounding cells. By default, Excel displays a grid format to help you enter data, but the borders defining the grid do not print.

You can add borders to all four sides of a cell, or choose to add borders to just one or two sides. Any borders you add to the sheet print along with the worksheet data.

Add Borders

ADD QUICK BORDERS

① Select the cells you want to format.

   Note: *See Chapter 8 to learn how to select cells.*

② Click the **Borders** button ▪.

   To apply the current border selection shown, simply click the **Borders** button (▦).

③ Click a border style.

● Excel immediately assigns the borders to the cell.

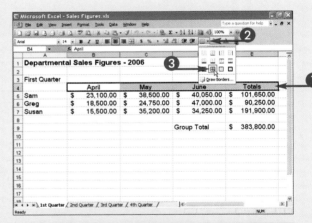

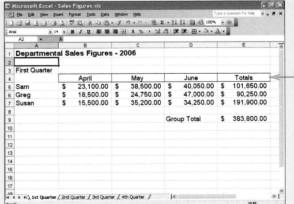

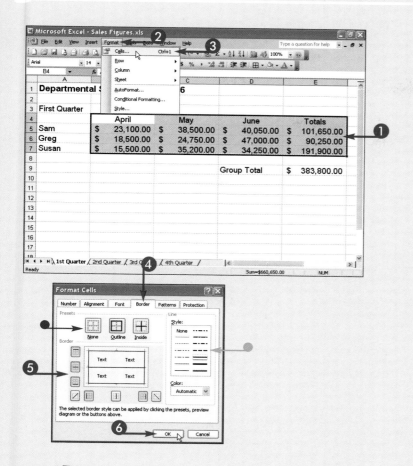

CREATE CUSTOM BORDERS

1 Select the cells you want to format.

Note: See Chapter 8 to learn how to select cells.

2 Click **Format**.

3 Click **Cells**.

The Format Cells dialog box appears.

4 Click the **Border** tab.

5 Click the type of border you want to assign.

You can click multiple border buttons to create a custom border.

● To set a particular line style to the border, click a style here.

● You can also click a preset style to assign.

6 Click **OK**.

Excel assigns the border.

Can I turn the worksheet gridlines on or off?
Yes. By default, Excel displays gridlines to help you differentiate between cells as you build your worksheets. You can turn gridlines off to view how your data will look when printed. Click **Tools** and then click **Options**. Click the **View** tab and deselect the **Gridlines** option (☑ changes to ☐) to turn gridlines off. Excel does not print gridlines unless you specify.

What does the Draw Borders command do?
When you click ▾, the drop-down list displays the **Draw Borders** command at the bottom of the list. When you activate the command, the Borders toolbar appears and you can draw your own borders around worksheet cells. You can control exactly which sides of a cell use borders, and you can erase borders you no longer need. The toolbar also includes buttons for controlling the line thickness and color of your borders.

Format Data with AutoFormat

You can use Excel's AutoFormat feature to apply preset formatting styles to your worksheet data. AutoFormat offers 16 different preset styles from which you can choose, and each one creates a different look for your worksheet.

The AutoFormat feature is a great way to quickly apply professional-looking formatting to your worksheet data. If you apply an AutoFormat you do not like, you can try another until you find just the right look for your worksheet.

Format Data with AutoFormat

① Select the cells you want to format.

Note: See Chapter 8 to learn how to select cells.

② Click **Format**.

③ Click **AutoFormat**.

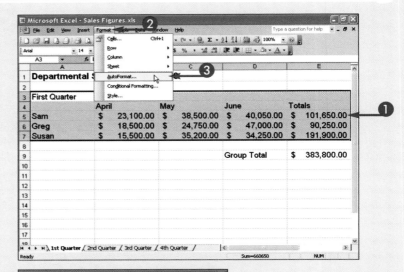

The AutoFormat dialog box appears.

● You can use the scroll arrows to view all the available styles.

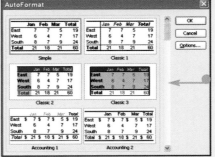

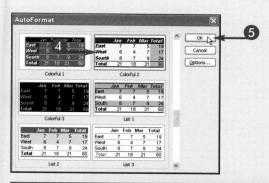

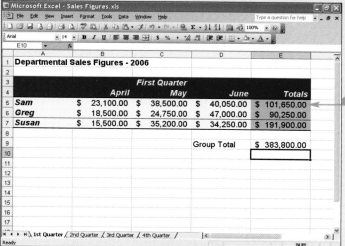

4 Click a style.

5 Click **OK**.

● Excel applies the formatting to the selected data.

Can I customize an AutoFormat style?

Yes. If you like some aspects of a style, but want to change others, you can customize the style. Follow these steps:

❶ Display the AutoFormat dialog box and select the style you want to customize.

❷ Click **Options**.

The AutoFormat dialog box expands to show format options you can add to or subtract from the formatting style.

❸ Click to select or deselect the formats you want to change for the style.

❹ Click **OK** to apply any changes.

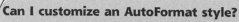

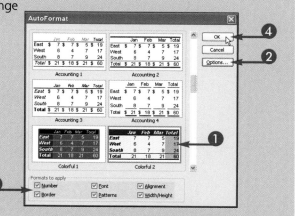

Create a Chart with Chart Wizard

You can use the Chart Wizard to quickly assemble and create all kinds of charts in Excel. The wizard walks you through each step for creating the chart, including selecting the chart type, data range, and specifying a location for the chart. You can determine exactly which type of chart works best for your data.

Create a Chart with Chart Wizard

❶ Select the range of data you want to chart.

Note: See Chapter 8 to learn how to select cells; see Chapter 10 to learn about ranges.

Include any headings and labels, but do not include subtotals or totals.

❷ Click the **Chart Wizard** button (📊).

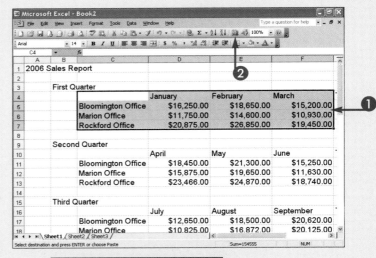

The first Chart Wizard screen opens.

❸ Click a chart type.

❹ Click a sub-type.

● You can click and hold here to view a sample of your data as depicted in the chart type you select.

❺ Click **Next**.

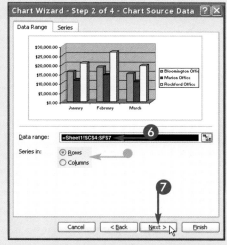

The second Chart Wizard screen appears.

6 Verify the data range.

If the data range is incorrect, you can select the correct range on the worksheet.

● You can change the orientation for the data series by choosing one of these options (○ changes to ●). Rows treats each row of data as a data series, while Columns treats each selected column as a data series.

7 Click **Next**.

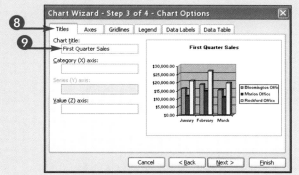

The third Chart Wizard screen appears.

8 Click the **Titles** tab.

Note: *Depending on the chart type you select, the available wizard tabs may vary.*

9 Type a title for your chart.

Note: *To learn how to add other titles to your chart, see the section "Change the Axes Titles," later in this chapter.*

Can I select noncontiguous data to include in a chart?

Yes. The data you select for a chart does not have to be adjacent to each other. To select noncontiguous cells and ranges, select the first range and then press and hold **Ctrl** while selecting additional ranges to include.

How do I create a custom chart?

You can click the **Custom Types** tab on the first Chart Wizard screen to customize your chart. Excel offers a variety of chart backgrounds and color selections to help you create a customized chart to your liking.

continued

Create a Chart with Chart Wizard *(continued)*

You can choose to insert your chart on the current worksheet or place it on a new sheet in your workbook. After you complete the Chart Wizard, Excel adds the chart to the designated location and displays a Chart toolbar you can use to fine-tune your chart.

Create a Chart with Chart Wizard *(continued)*

⑩ Click the **Legend** tab.

⑪ Select a location option for the legend (◯ changes to ◉).

⑫ Click **Next**.

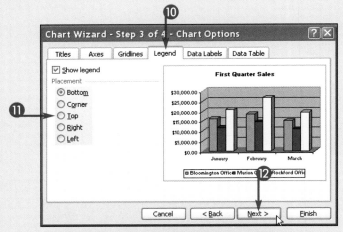

⑬ Select a placement option for the chart (◯ changes to ◉).

● To create the chart on a new sheet in your workbook file, select this option and give the sheet a title.

● To embed the chart in the current sheet, select this option.

Note: *Embedded charts are treated like objects in Excel, which means you can move, resize, and edit the chart as a separate element from your worksheet data.*

⑭ Click **Finish**.

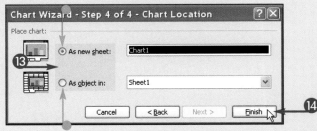

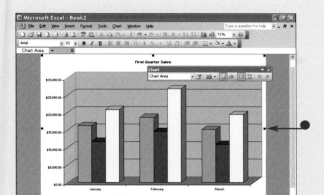

Excel creates the chart and displays it in the designated sheet.

● In this example, the chart appears on its own sheet in the workbook.

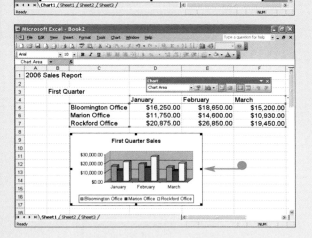

● In this example, the chart is embedded into the current sheet.

When embedding a chart, you may need to make room for it in the worksheet, or you can move it to another location on the sheet.

Note: *See the next section, "Move and Resize Charts," to learn how to move a chart.*

How do I create an organizational chart in Excel?

You can add an organizational chart to track hierarchy of an organization or method. When you insert an organization chart, Excel starts you with four shapes to which you can add your own text. You can add additional shapes and branches to the chart as needed. To create an organizational chart, click **Insert**, **Picture**, and then **Organization Chart**. Excel adds a basic organization chart to your worksheet and displays the Drawing toolbar and the Organization Chart toolbar. Click in one of the chart shapes and type your text.

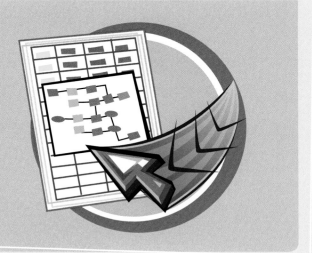

Move and Resize Charts

You can move and resize an embedded chart on your worksheet. For example, you may want to reposition the chart at the bottom of the worksheet or resize it to make the chart easier to read.

You cannot move or resize charts you create on their own sheets.

Move and Resize Charts

MOVE A CHART

1 Click an empty area of the chart.

● Excel selects the chart and surrounds it with handles.

2 Move the ⬚ over an empty area of the chart.

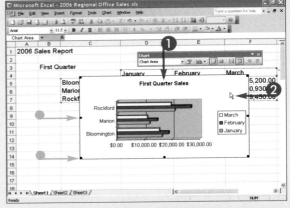

3 Click and drag the chart to a new location on the worksheet.

● A dotted border represents the chart as you move it on the worksheet.

Excel moves the chart.

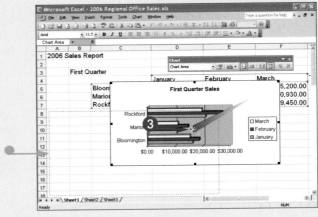

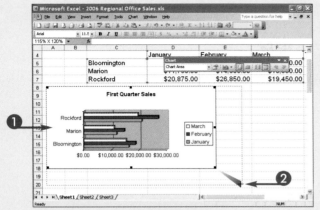

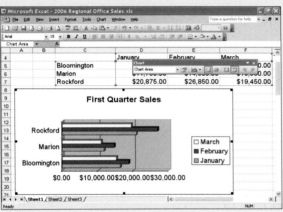

RESIZE A CHART

① Click an empty area of the chart.

Excel selects the chart and surrounds it with handles.

② Click and drag a handle to resize the chart.

Excel resizes the chart.

How do I delete a chart I no longer want?

To remove an embedded chart, simply select the chart and press **Delete**. Excel immediately removes the chart from the worksheet. If your chart appears on its own worksheet, you can right-click over the sheet name and click **Delete**. Excel asks you to confirm the deletion; click **Delete**.

How can I proportionately resize a chart?

You can press and hold **Shift** while dragging any of the corner selection handles of a selected chart to resize the chart proportionately. Dragging outwardly makes the chart proportionately bigger, while dragging inwardly makes the chart proportionately smaller.

Change the Chart Type

You can change the chart type at any time to present your data in a different way. For example, you might want to change a bar chart to a line chart. You can use the Chart toolbar to quickly change the chart type.

① Click an empty area of the chart to select the chart.

The Chart toolbar appears.

- ● If the Chart toolbar does not appear, click **View**, **Toolbars**, and then **Chart** to display the toolbar.

② Click the Chart Type button (🔲) on the Chart toolbar.

③ Click a new chart type.

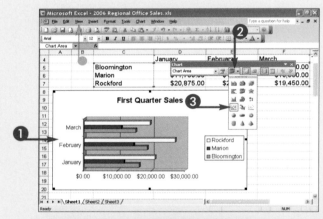

- ● Excel applies the type to the existing chart.

- ● You can also click **Chart** and then **Chart Type** to reopen the Chart dialog box and change the chart type.

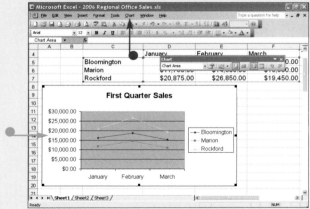

Change the Axes Titles

Axes are used to show the scale of all the values in a chart. The x-axis is the horizontal value display in a chart, and the y-axis is the vertical value display.

You can change the titles of the x- or y-axis on your chart. For example, you may prefer to give the axes more descriptive titles, or if your titles are too long, you may want to shorten the title text. You can change chart title information using the Chart Options dialog box.

Change the Axes Titles

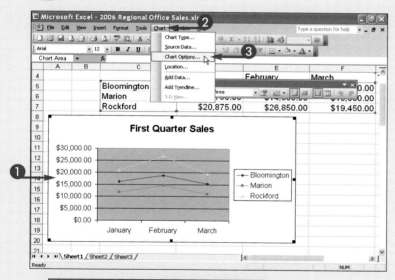

1 Select the chart you want to edit.

2 Click **Chart**.

3 Click **Chart Options**.

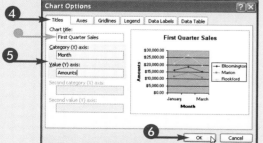

The Chart Options dialog box appears.

4 Click the **Titles** tab.

5 Type a title for the x- or y-axis you want to edit.

● You can type a title for your chart using this text box.

6 Click **OK**.

Excel applies the new titles to the chart.

183

Format Chart Objects

You can change the formatting for any of the elements, called *objects* in Excel, contained within a chart. For example, you can change the background color or pattern for the plot area, or change the color of a data series on the chart.

Format Chart Objects

1 Select the chart.

The Chart toolbar appears.

- If the Chart toolbar does not appear, click **View**, **Toolbars**, and then **Chart** to display the toolbar.

2 Click the **Chart Objects** ⬝ on the Chart toolbar.

3 Click the chart object you want to edit.

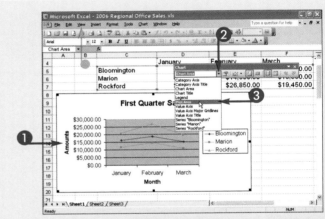

- Excel selects the object in the chart.

4 Click the **Format** button (⬚) on the Chart toolbar.

Depending on the chart object you want to edit, the Format button may use a different name.

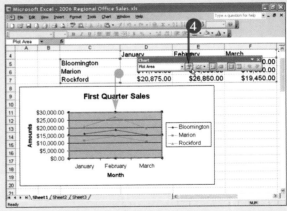

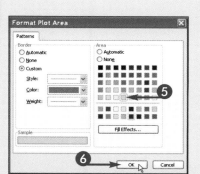

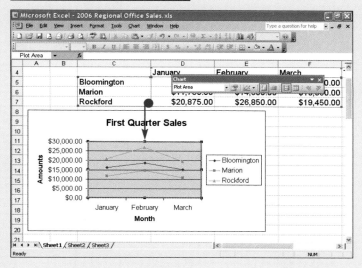

The Format Plot Area dialog box for the chart object appears.

⑤ Make any changes to the chart object as needed.

In this example, a new fill color is applied.

Depending on the chart object you edit, the dialog box may offer different tabs of formatting options you can apply.

⑥ When finished with your edits, click **OK**.

● Excel applies any changes to the chart.

In this example, a new fill color is added to the plot area.

How do I change the font for my chart text?

You can double-click any chart element to open the Format dialog box and quickly make any edits. For example, if you double-click chart text, the Format dialog box for the element opens and you can click the **Font** tab to make changes to the font, font size, color, and style.

How do I print my chart?

To print only the chart, first select the chart on the worksheet, click **File**, and then click **Print**. The Print dialog box appears. Make sure the **Selected Chart** option is selected (○ changes to ⊙) and then click **OK** to print the chart. If the chart is on its own sheet, you can just click 🖶 to print the sheet.

Add Chart Objects

You can add additional objects to your charts, such as including data labels, adding gridlines, or a legend. The Chart Options dialog box lists a variety of chart objects you can turn on or off in your chart.

Add Chart Objects

① Select the chart you want to edit.

② Click **Chart**.

③ Click **Chart Options**.

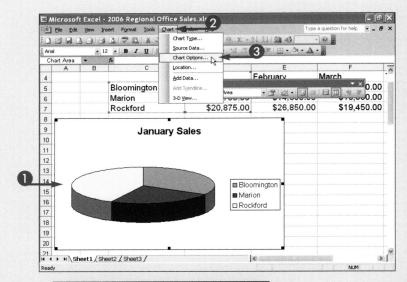

The Chart Options dialog box appears.

④ Click the tab for the type of object you want to add.

⑤ Designate any new elements you want to include (☐ changes to ☑).

The preview area shows what the new objects will look like on the chart.

⑥ Click **OK**.

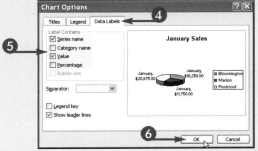

Change the Chart Data

Whenever you make changes to the data referenced in your chart, the chart data is automatically updated. For example, if you change a value, the chart updates to reflect the new value. If you need to add more data to the chart, you can easily update the source cells.

Change the Chart Data

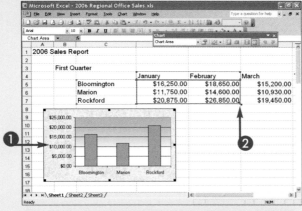

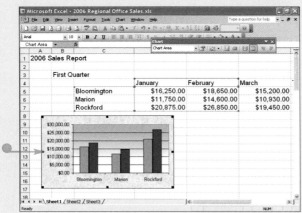

① Select the chart you want to edit.

Excel surrounds the chart with selection handles and marks the source data in the worksheet with a colored border.

② Click and drag the corner handle of the source range to add or subtract cells.

● Excel updates the chart with any changes.

Part IV

PowerPoint

PowerPoint is a presentation program you can use to convey all kinds of messages to an audience. By presenting your information in slide format, you can walk the audience through each point you want to make. You can use PowerPoint to create slide shows to present ideas to clients, explain a concept or procedure to employees, teach a class about a new subject, or present your family photos.

In this part, you learn how to create slide shows, add text and artwork, create speaker notes, and package your show on a CD-ROM. You also learn how to add special effects to make your slide show lively and engaging to watch.

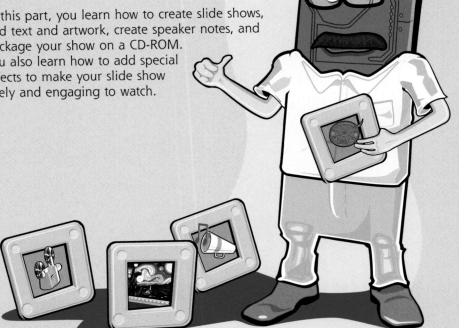

Create a Presentation with the AutoContent Wizard

You can use PowerPoint's AutoContent Wizard to help you create a new presentation. The wizard walks you through each of the steps necessary to design and build a slide show. With the wizard, you can specify a type of presentation from a library of premade designs.

Create a Presentation with the AutoContent Wizard

① From the Getting Started task pane, click the **Create a new presentation** link.

Note: See Chapter 1 to learn how to view and work with task panes.

You can also click **File** and then **New** to open the New Presentation task pane.

The New Presentation task pane appears.

② Click the **From AutoContent wizard** link.

The AutoContent Wizard appears.

③ Click **Next**.

The Presentation Type screen opens.

④ Click a category.

● To view all of the presentation types, click **All**.

⑤ Click the type of presentation you want to build.

⑥ Click **Next**.

What types of presentations does the AutoContent Wizard offer?
The AutoContent Wizard offers five categories, and each category includes a selection of presentation types. The All category lists every presentation type. The other four categories list category-specific presentations.

Category	Presentations
General	Generic, Recommending a Strategy, Communicating Bad News, Training, Brainstorming Session, Certificate
Corporate	Business Plan, Financial Overview, Company Meeting, Employee Orientation, Group Home Page, Company Handbook
Project	Project Overview, Reporting Progress or Status, Project Post-Mortem
Sales/Marketing	Selling a Product or Service, Marketing Plan, Product/Services Overview

Create a Presentation with the AutoContent Wizard *(continued)*

When building a presentation with the AutoContent Wizard, you can specify how you want to deliver your presentation: as a slide show, overheads, or 35mm slides. When you finish all the wizard steps, you can begin to add your own text to the presentation.

After you create a slide show, you can save it. See Chapter 2 to learn how to save Microsoft Office files.

Create a Presentation with the AutoContent Wizard *(continued)*

⑦ Select an output option that best describes how you want to give your presentation (○ changes to ◉).

⑧ Click **Next**.

● You can cancel the wizard at any time by clicking **Cancel**.

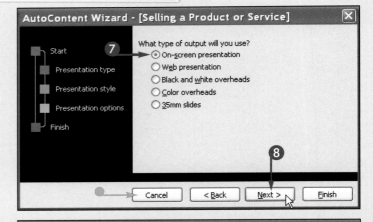

⑨ Type a title for your presentation.

● Optionally, click any footer options you want to appear at the bottom of each slide (☐ changes to ☑).

⑩ Click **Next**.

The final AutoContent Wizard screen appears.

⓫ Click **Finish**.

- PowerPoint creates the presentation and displays it in Normal view.

- An outline of each slide appears here.

  Note: See the section "Change PowerPoint Views," later in this chapter, to learn more about PowerPoint's views.

- You can add your own text to the new slide show, as shown here.

  Note: See Chapter 14 to learn how to add and format slide text.

What if I do not see a presentation type that meets my needs?

You can pick a presentation type closest to the type of presentation you want to create and modify the slides to tailor the presentation for your own purposes. You can also download additional presentation templates from the Microsoft Office Web site. To access the site, click the **Templates on Office Online** link in the New Presentation task pane.

What sort of footer text can I add to my slides?

Footer text appears in the bottom of every slide in the presentation. By default, the AutoContent Wizard includes the date and slide number unless you deselect the options in the wizard screens. You can include your department name, contact person's name, or overall presentation topic as footer text in your slides. The AutoContent Wizard includes a Footer text box you can use to add your own footer text.

Start a Presentation with a Design Template

You can create a slide show presentation using any of PowerPoint's predesigned templates. PowerPoint's design templates can give your slide show a common look and feel by providing a basic color scheme and preset formatting. It is up to you to fill in the slide content.

Start a Presentation with a Design Template

① From the Getting Started task pane, click the **Create a new presentation** link.

● If the task pane is not open, you can click **View** and then **Task Pane**.

Note: See Chapter 1 to learn how to work with task panes.

The New Presentation task pane appears.

● You can also click **File** and then **New** to open the New Presentation task pane.

② Click the **From design template** link.

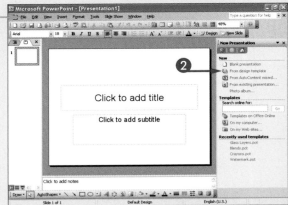

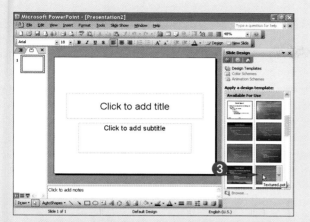

The Slide Design task pane opens.

3 Click the design template you want to apply.

You can use the scroll bar to view all the available templates.

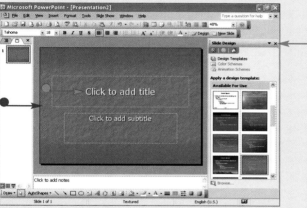

● PowerPoint creates a slide based on the template you chose.

● You can add your own text to the new slide.

● You can click ☒ to close the task pane.

Note: *See Chapter 14 to learn how to add and format slide text. See Chapter 2 to learn how to save files.*

Where can I find more design templates to use with my presentations?
You can click the **Additional Design Templates** link in the Slide Design task pane. PowerPoint prompts you to insert the CD-ROM you used to install the program and installs any additional design templates. You can also find more presentation templates on the Web. Click the **Design Templates on Microsoft Office Online** link in the Slide Design task pane.

Can I customize a design template and save the changes?
Yes. You can customize any presentation and save it as a template to use over and over again. To save a presentation as a template, open the Save As dialog box and assign the template a unique name. Before saving the file, click the **Save as type** ☑ and click **Design Template**. PowerPoint automatically assigns the POT file extension that designates the file as a template file.

Build a Blank Presentation

By default, PowerPoint starts a blank slide for you whenever you start the program. You can use the slide as the first slide in your presentation and add more slides as you go along. See Chapter 14 to learn more about working with slides.

You can create a blank presentation, containing just one slide and add your own slide show elements and formatting. This technique allows you the freedom to set your own color schemes and design touches. You can use PowerPoint's layouts to quickly assign a layout to any blank slide.

Build a Blank Presentation

① From the Getting Started task pane, click the **Create a new presentation** link.

Note: *See Chapter 1 to learn how to work with task panes.*

● You can also click **File** and then **New** to open the New Presentation task pane.

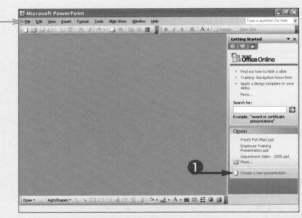

The New Presentation task pane appears.

② Click the **Blank presentation** link.

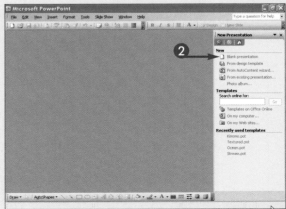

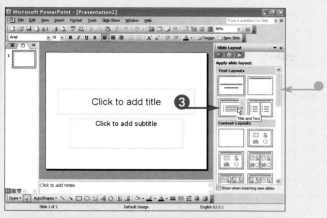

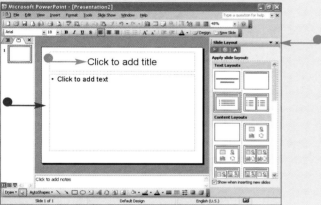

The Slide Layout task pane appears.

③ Click the layout you want to apply.

● You can use the scroll bar to view all the available layouts.

● PowerPoint creates a slide based on the layout you chose.

● You can add your own text to the new slide.

Note: *See Chapter 14 to learn how to add and format slide text. See Chapter 2 to learn how to save files.*

● You can click ⊠ to close the task pane.

How do I add a color scheme to my blank presentation?

Follow these steps to add a PowerPoint color scheme to your blank slide:

① Right-click the blank slide.

② Click **Slide Design**.

The Slide Design task pane appears.

③ Click the **Color Schemes** link.

④ Click the color scheme you want to apply.

PowerPoint immediately adds it to the slide.

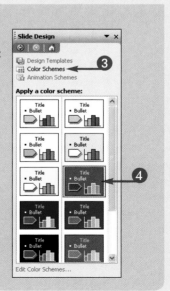

Change PowerPoint Views

You can use PowerPoint's views to change how your presentation appears on-screen. The PowerPoint view modes can help you with the various presentation elements you want to edit. By default, PowerPoint displays your presentation in Normal view, which displays a single slide. You can switch to Outline view to see your presentation in an outline format, or Slide Sorter view to see all the slides at the same time.

Change PowerPoint Views

USE OUTLINE VIEW

1 Click the **Outline** tab.

PowerPoint displays the presentation in an outline format.

● You can click the outline text to edit it.

● You can click a slide to view the slide.

USE SLIDES VIEW

1 Click the **Slides** tab.

PowerPoint displays the current slide in the presentation.

● To view a particular slide, click the slide in the Slides tab.

● To close the tabs pane entirely and free up on-screen workspace, click ⊠.

Note: To redisplay the tabs pane, click ▤.

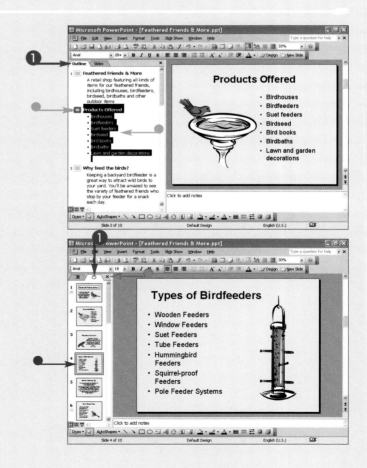

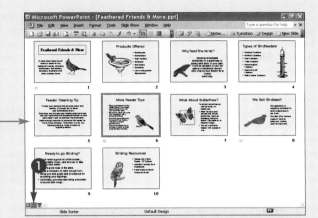

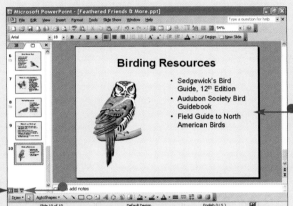

USE SLIDE SORTER VIEW

① Click the **Slide Sorter View** button (⊞).

● PowerPoint displays all the slides in the presentation.

Note: See Chapter 15 to learn more about using Slide Sorter view to prepare a presentation.

USE NORMAL VIEW

① Click the **Normal View** button (⊡).

● PowerPoint returns to the default view, displaying the current slide in the presentation.

● You can also click the **Slide Show View** button (⬚) to view your presentation as a slide show.

Note: To learn more about running a presentation with Slide Show view, see Chapter 16.

How do I zoom my view of a slide?

To zoom your magnification of a slide, you can use the **Zoom** ⊡ on the Standard toolbar. A click of the **Zoom** ⊡ displays a drop-down list of zoom percentages. Simply click a zoom level to change the magnification level of the slide. You can also use the Zoom dialog box to magnify your view; click **View** and then **Zoom** to display the dialog box.

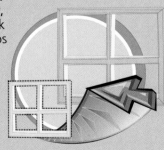

Can I resize the PowerPoint pane areas?

Yes. You can resize any of the panes shown in the PowerPoint program window, including the task pane and the tabs pane. Simply move the ⤢ over the pane's border, and then click and drag to resize the pane's width.

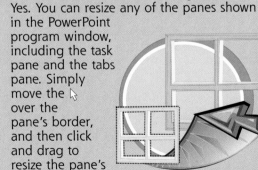

Understanding Slide Elements

PowerPoint slides are constructed of layouts. A layout controls the positioning of elements on the slide. You can use slide elements to control the type of content you place on a slide. When choosing from among PowerPoint's many slide layouts, it is helpful to know the different types of slide elements available.

Text Objects

Text objects, also called text boxes, are layout boxes that hold text. For example, your slide might include a text box for the title of the slide, or a second text box to contain a subheading or paragraph about the slide topic. Text objects allow you to communicate any text-related information you want to display on a slide.

Bulleted Text

Bulleted text boxes are a popular type of text object found in PowerPoint presentations. Bulleted text allows you to quickly present important information in a succinct manner, allowing your audience to focus on specific points. You can format bulleted text boxes with bullets or with numbers.

Clip Art

You can use clip art objects to present artwork on a slide. PowerPoint installs with a library of clip art you can use to illustrate your presentation. You can use the Clip Art task pane to search for specific types of clip art. You can also access additional clip art images on the Microsoft Office Web site.

Charts

You can use charts to present text and numeric data in a visual way. For example, you might create a chart to show changes over a period of time or to show monthly sales goals. When you select a chart object in PowerPoint, you can use a datasheet to create your chart data. A datasheet looks like a scaled-down Excel worksheet, with columns and rows for entering chart data.

Tables

Tables are another type of slide element you can use to present data in an organized fashion. Consisting of columns and rows, tables can help you present lists of data in an easy-to-read format.

Media Clips

Media clip objects allow you to place multimedia elements on a slide, such as a video or audio clip. For example, you might place a video clip on a slide to show footage of your latest product or use an audio clip to deliver an interview with the company president.

Content Objects

You can use PowerPoint's content objects to choose from a variety of content types. Content objects offer you a quick way to insert a table, chart, clip art, picture file, diagram, or media clip. With a content object, you control exactly which type of element you want to place on the slide.

Add and Edit Slide Text

When you apply one of PowerPoint's text layouts to a slide, the text box appears with placeholder text. You can replace the placeholder text with your own text.

Add and Edit Slide Text

ADD SLIDE TEXT

1 Click the text box to which you want to add text.

Note: *It is easiest to add slide text in Normal View mode. See Chapter 13 to learn more about PowerPoint's views.*

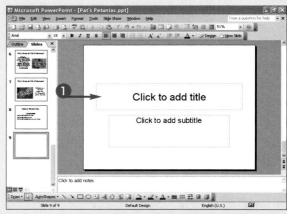

PowerPoint hides the placeholder text and displays a cursor.

2 Type the slide text you want to add.

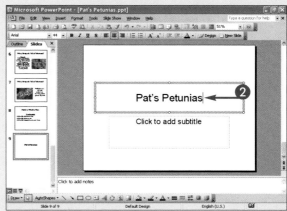

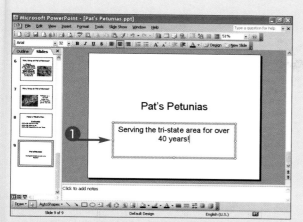

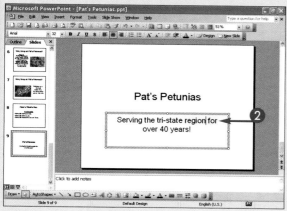

EDIT SLIDE TEXT

1 Click the text box you want to edit.

PowerPoint selects the object and adds a cursor to the text box.

2 Make any changes you want to the slide text.

You can use the keyboard arrow keys to move the cursor in the text, or you can click where you want to make a change.

How do I add slide text in Outline view?

You can use Outline mode to see your entire presentation in an outline format. To add text to slides in Outline mode, follow these steps:

1 Click the **Outline** tab.

2 Click the slide you want to edit.

3 Type the text you want to add or change.

PowerPoint immediately changes the text on the slide.

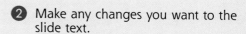

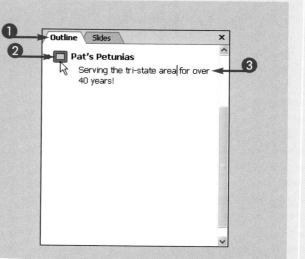

Change the Font and Size

By default, any slide layouts and slide designs you assign use a default font and size for the text. You can change the font and size to change the appearance of your slide text.

Change the Font and Size

CHANGE THE FONT

1. Click the text box you want to edit.

   To select a text box without selecting text within, click the text box border.

2. Click the **Font** ⏷ on the Formatting toolbar.

3. Click a font.

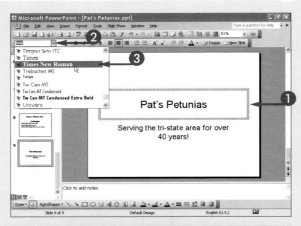

- PowerPoint immediately applies the new font to the text box.

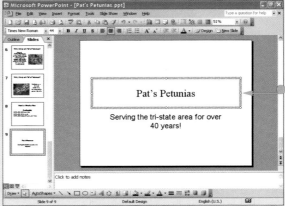

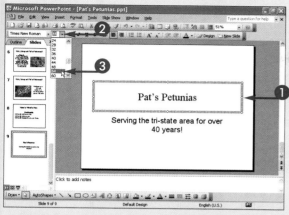

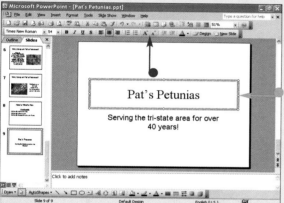

CHANGE THE SIZE

① Click the text box you want to edit.

To select a text box without selecting text within, click the text box border.

② Click the **Font Size** ⬇ on the Formatting toolbar.

③ Click a size.

● PowerPoint immediately applies the new font size to the text in the text box.

● For a quick size increase or decrease, you can click the **Increase Font Size** (Ａ) and **Decrease Font Size** (Ａ) buttons on the Formatting toolbar.

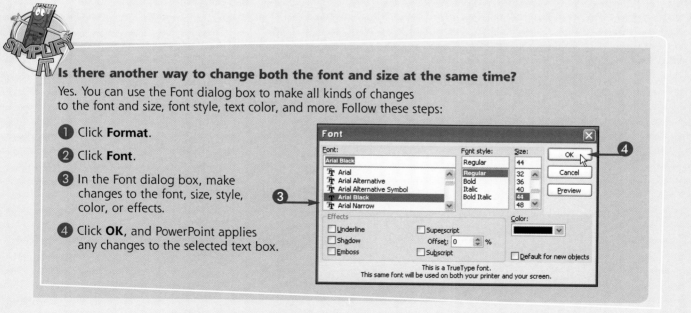

Is there another way to change both the font and size at the same time?

Yes. You can use the Font dialog box to make all kinds of changes to the font and size, font style, text color, and more. Follow these steps:

① Click **Format**.

② Click **Font**.

③ In the Font dialog box, make changes to the font, size, style, color, or effects.

④ Click **OK**, and PowerPoint applies any changes to the selected text box.

Change the Text Color

Refrain from using too many colors for your text. The presentation message can become difficult to follow when the various colors act as a distraction rather than an enhancement to your message.

You can change the color of your slide text to create a different look for a slide. For example, you may need to change the text color to make the text more legible against the slide background.

Change the Text Color

CHOOSE A COORDINATING COLOR

1 Click the text box you want to edit.

To select a text box without selecting text within, click the text box border.

2 Click the **Font Color** button (⬛) on the Formatting toolbar.

PowerPoint displays coordinating color schemes designed to go with the current slide design.

3 Click a color.

● PowerPoint applies the color to the text in the selected text box.

You can also format text within the text box, such as a single word or phrase.

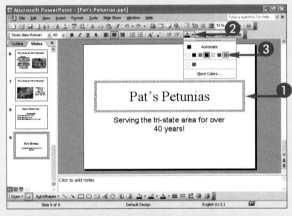

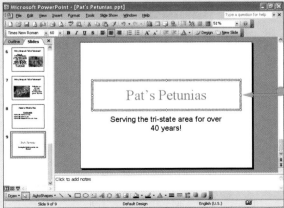

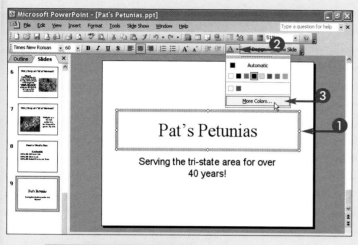

OPEN THE COLORS DIALOG BOX

1 Click the text box you want to edit.

You can also format text within the text box, such as a single word or phrase.

2 Click ⚟ on the Formatting toolbar.

3 Click **More Colors**.

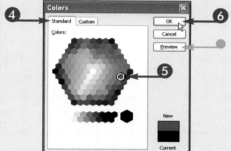

The Colors dialog box appears.

4 Click the **Standard** tab.

5 Click a color.

● You can click **Preview** to preview the color selection in the slide.

6 Click **OK**.

PowerPoint applies the color to the text in the selected text box.

How do I set a custom color?

You can use the Colors dialog box to create your own custom color to use with the slide text or other slide elements. To set a custom color, follow these steps:

1 Open the Colors dialog box, as shown in this section, and click the **Custom** tab.

2 Click the color you want to customize.

3 Drag the intensity arrow to adjust the color intensity.

● You can also adjust the color channel settings.

4 Click **OK**.

PowerPoint assigns the custom color.

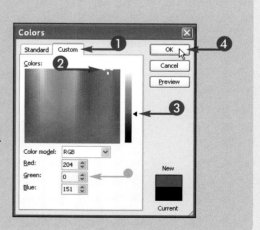

Change the Text Style

You can quickly change the appearance of text by changing the text style. You can choose from four different styles: Bold, Italic, Underline, and Shadow. You can assign a single style or use a combination of styles to create just the right look for your presentation text.

Change the Text Style

1 Select the text box or text you want to edit.

2 Click a style button.

Click the **Bold** button (**B**) to make the text bold.

Click the **Italic** button (**I**) to italicize the text.

Click the **Underline** button (**U**) to underline the text.

Click the **Shadow** button (**S**) to add a shadow effect to the text.

● PowerPoint assigns the formatting.

In this example, the title text is now bold.

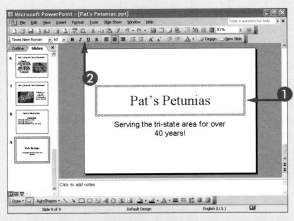

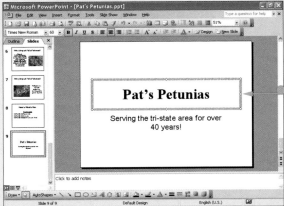

Change the Text Alignment

You can change the horizontal positioning of text in a text box by assigning a different alignment command. By default, PowerPoint centers the text in text objects found among the many slide layouts, with the exception of bulleted text, which uses left alignment by default.

Change the Text Alignment

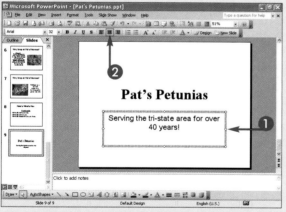

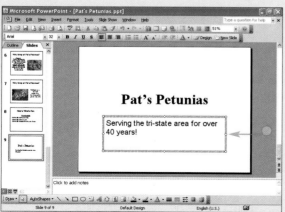

① Select the text or text box you want to edit.

② Click an alignment button.

Click the **Align Left** button (▤) to align the text to the left of the text box.

Click the **Center** button (▤) to align the text in the center of the text box.

Click the **Align Right** button (▤) to align the text to the right of the text box.

● PowerPoint assigns the formatting.

In this example, the text is now left-aligned.

Set Line Spacing

You can change the line spacing to create more or less space between lines of text. For example, you might want to increase line spacing so the text fills up more space in the text box, or to make text easier to read.

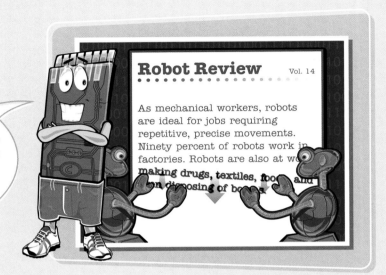

Set Line Spacing

① Select the text box or text you want to edit.

To select a text box without selecting text within, click the text box border.

② Click **Format**.

③ Click **Line Spacing**.

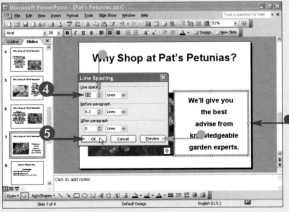

The Line Spacing dialog box appears.

④ Type the amount of spacing you want to set.

● You can also click 🔼 to set the line spacing.

● You can click here to preview the effect before applying the spacing to your text.

⑤ Click **OK**.

● PowerPoint assigns the line spacing.

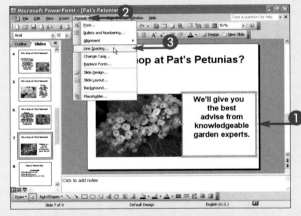

Insert Symbols

If your PowerPoint text calls for special symbols not found on the keyboard, you can look for the symbols in the Symbol dialog box. Different font libraries list different symbols. The Symbol and Wingdings fonts are two examples of font libraries of symbols and other special characters.

Insert Symbols

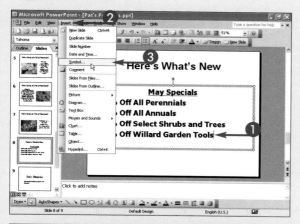

① Click in the text where you want to insert a symbol.

② Click **Insert**.

③ Click **Symbol**.

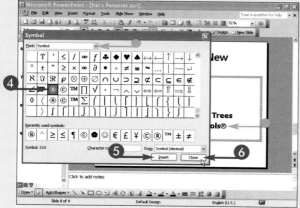

The Symbol dialog box appears.

④ Click the symbol you want to insert.

● You can click ☑ to change the font and view other symbols.

⑤ Click **Insert**.

● PowerPoint inserts the symbol and leaves the dialog box open for inserting more symbols.

⑥ Click **Close**.

The Symbol dialog box closes.

Change the Slide Layout

You can change a slide's layout at any time. For example, you may want to change a slide to include a bulleted text box or use one of PowerPoint's many content layouts.

If you assign a new slide layout to a slide with existing text, you may need to make a few adjustments to the text position and size to fit the new layout. For best results, assign a new layout before adding content to your slides.

Change the Slide Layout

① Display the slide you want to change.

② Click **Format**.

③ Click **Slide Layout**.

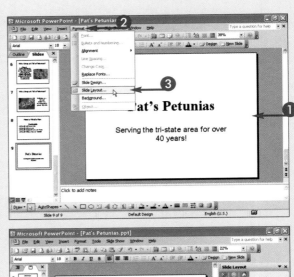

PowerPoint opens the Slide Layout task pane.

● You can use the scroll bar arrows to locate the layout you want to assign.

④ Click a layout.

● PowerPoint immediately assigns the layout to the slide.

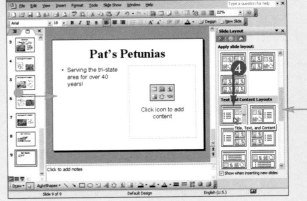

Add a New Text Object

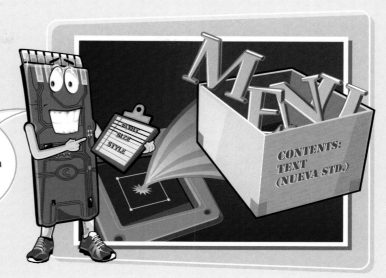

You can add new text boxes to a slide when you need to customize a layout. Text boxes are simply receptacles for text in a slide. With new text boxes, you can control the placement and size of the object.

Add a New Text Object

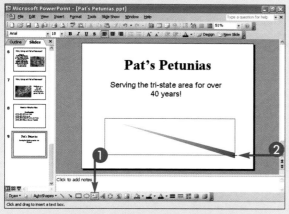

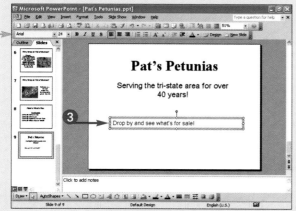

① Click the **Text Box** button (⊞) on the Drawing toolbar.

Note: See Chapter 1 to learn how to work with the Office toolbars.

② Click and drag where you want to place a text box on the slide.

③ Type the text you want to insert.

● You can use the Formatting toolbar buttons to change the font, size, alignment, and more.

You can click anywhere outside the text box to deselect the text object.

Note: To delete a slide object you no longer need, select the object and press **Delete**.

Add Clip Art to a Slide

You can add artwork to a slide by inserting clip art images. Clip art is premade art. Microsoft Office installs with a clip art collection that includes a variety of illustrations for a variety of topics. You can add clip art to a placeholder object or insert a new clip art object.

Add Clip Art to a Slide

FILL IN A CLIP ART PLACEHOLDER

1. Click the slide object you want to edit.

   If the slide layout has a clip art object, double-click the object.

   If the placeholder object is a content box, click the **Insert Clip Art** icon (📷).

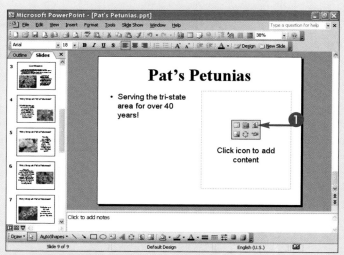

The Select Picture dialog box appears.

2. Type a keyword for the type of clip art you want to insert.

3. Click **Go**.

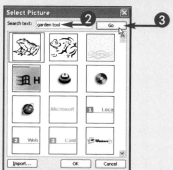

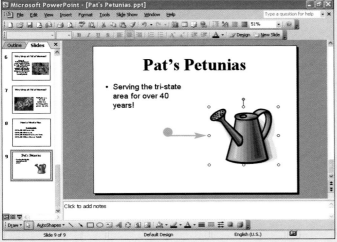

PowerPoint searches the clip art collection for possible matches.

④ Click the clip art you want to insert.

⑤ Click **OK**.

● PowerPoint inserts the clip art image.

Note: *You can move and resize clip art objects. See the sections "Move a Slide Object" and "Resize a Slide Object," later in this chapter, to learn more.*

How do I insert a photo or image file instead of clip art?

To insert a photograph, or other image file onto a slide, follow these steps:

① Click the **Insert Picture** tool (🖼) on the Drawing toolbar.

If using a content layout, click the **Insert Picture** icon (🖼) in the placeholder box.

② Navigate to the file you want to insert and select it.

③ Click **Insert**, and PowerPoint inserts the file.

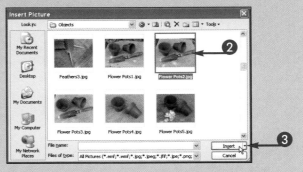

Add Clip Art to a Slide *(continued)*

You can use the Clip Art task pane to insert new clip art objects onto your slides. You can search for a specific type of clip art image to use by typing keywords into the task pane.

Add Clip Art to a Slide *(continued)*

ADD A NEW CLIP ART OBJECT

① Click the **Insert Clip Art** button (▣) on the Drawing toolbar.

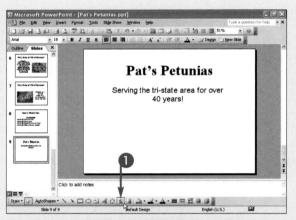

The Clip Art task pane opens.

② Type a keyword for the type of clip art you want to insert.

③ Click **Go**.

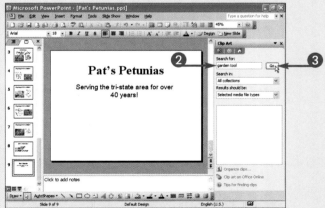

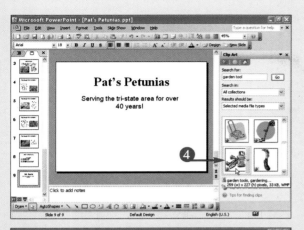

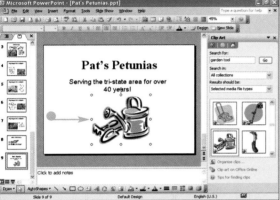

PowerPoint searches the clip art collection for possible matches.

④ Click the clip art you want to insert.

● PowerPoint inserts the clip art onto the slide.

Note: *You can move and resize clip art objects. See the sections "Move a Slide Object" and "Resize a Slide Object," later in this chapter, to learn more.*

Where can I find more clip art?
You can access more clip art on the Microsoft Office Web site. To do so, open the Clip Art task pane and click the **Clip art on Office Online** link at the bottom of the pane. Your Web browser opens to the Microsoft Clip Art page where you can conduct a search of available clip art and download the clips onto your computer.

How do I edit a clip art object?
You can double-click a clip art object to open the Format Picture dialog box. You can use the dialog box to add a border around the clip art, crop the image, resize the object, and more.

217

Add a Chart to a Slide

You can add a chart to a slide to turn numeric data into a visual element your audience can quickly interpret and understand. When you create a chart in PowerPoint, you use a datasheet, which looks very much like an Excel worksheet. You can type your own chart data and choose the type of chart you want to display.

Add a Chart to a Slide

❶ Click the slide object you want to edit.

If the slide layout has a chart object, double-click the object.

If the placeholder object is a content box, click the **Insert Chart** icon (⊞).

Note: To add a new chart object to the slide, click the **Insert** menu and then click **Chart**.

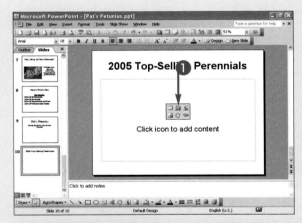

PowerPoint opens a datasheet window along with a default chart and displays chart tools in the Standard toolbar.

❷ Click the **Chart Type** button (▣).

❸ Click a chart type.

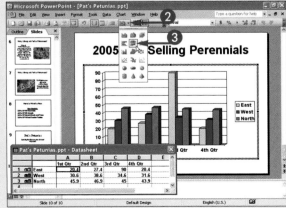

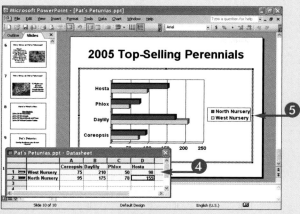

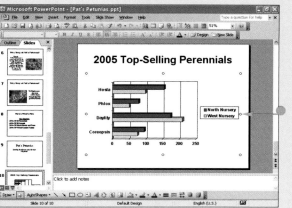

PowerPoint immediately displays a sample of the chart type.

④ Type the chart data you want to illustrate using the datasheet cells.

You can press `Tab` to move from cell to cell in the datasheet.

To create a larger datasheet window, click and drag the window corner or border.

⑤ When finished entering chart data, click anywhere outside of the chart area.

● PowerPoint displays the finished chart on the slide.

To edit the chart at any time, double-click the chart object.

Can I insert an Excel chart onto my PowerPoint slide?
Yes. You can use the **Copy** and **Paste** commands to copy an Excel chart and insert it onto a PowerPoint slide. You can also link and embed an Excel chart. To learn more about copying and pasting data between Microsoft Office programs, and linking and embedding data, see Chapter 2.

How do I edit a chart on my slide?
You can double-click the chart to open the datasheet window and the chart editing tools again. To add titles, control gridlines, and set a chart legend, you can open the Chart Options dialog box. Click the **Chart** menu and then click **Chart Options**. To remove a chart entirely, select the chart and press `Delete`.

Add a Table to a Slide

You can add tables to your slides to organize data in an orderly fashion. Tables use a column and row format to present information. For example, you might use a table to present a list of products or classes.

Add a Table to a Slide

① Click the slide object you want to edit.

● If the slide layout has a table object, double-click the object.

If the placeholder object is a content box, click the **Insert Table** icon (▦).

● To add a new table object to the slide, click the **Insert** menu and then click **Table**.

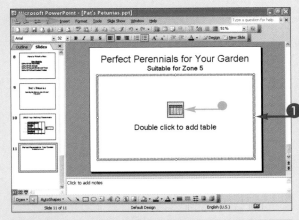

PowerPoint displays the Insert Table dialog box.

② Type the number of columns you want to appear in the table.

③ Type the number of rows you want to appear in the table.

④ Click **OK**.

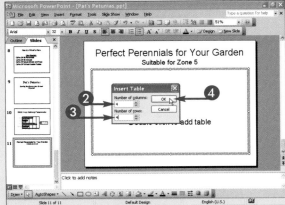

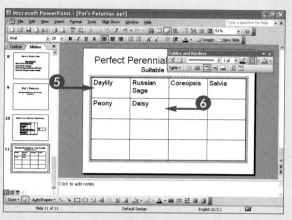

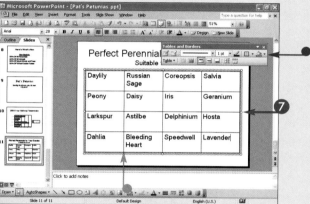

PowerPoint inserts the table onto the slide and displays the Tables and Borders toolbar.

⑤ Click inside the first table cell and type your data.

You can press **Tab** to move from one table cell to the next.

⑥ Continue entering additional table cell data to fill the table.

● You can use the toolbar buttons to merge table cells, split table cells, change alignment, add borders, and more.

● You can resize columns or rows by clicking and dragging the borders.

⑦ When finished entering table data, click anywhere outside of the table area.

PowerPoint displays the finished table on the slide.

How do I add a column or row to my table?

To add a column or row to a table, follow these steps:

❶ Select the row below or the column to the right of where you want to insert a new row or column.

❷ Right-click in the selected row or column.

❸ Click **Insert Rows** or **Insert Columns**.

PowerPoint immediately inserts a new row or column.

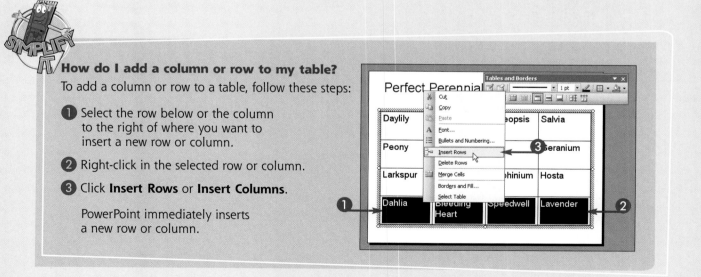

Move a Slide Object

You can move any slide element to reposition it in the slide. For example, you can move a text box to make room for a clip art box, or move a title to make the text fit better on a slide.

Move a Slide Object

① Click the slide object you want to move.

② Drag the object to a new location on the slide.

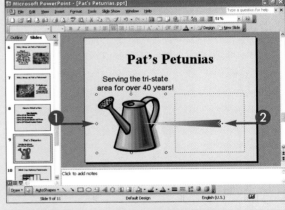

● PowerPoint immediately repositions the object.

Note: You can also resize slide elements. See the next section, "Resize a Slide Object," to learn more.

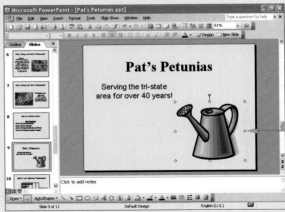

Resize a Slide Object

You can resize any slide element to make it larger or smaller on the slide. For example, you can resize a text box to make room for more text, or resize a clip art box to make the artwork larger.

Resize a Slide Object

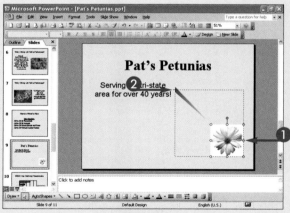

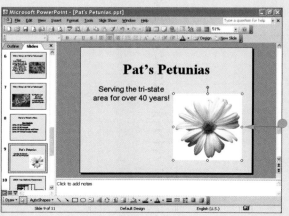

① Click the slide object you want to resize.

PowerPoint surrounds the object box with handles.

② Click and drag a handle.

Drag a corner handle to resize the object height and width.

Drag a side handle to resize the object only along the one side.

● PowerPoint immediately resizes the object.

Note: *You can also move slide elements. See the previous section, "Move a Slide Object," to learn more.*

Change the Slide Background Color

You can change the slide background and replace it with a solid color. You can choose from coordinating colors or choose a color from PowerPoint's full color palette. You can apply a background color to a single slide, or every slide in your presentation.

If the slide already has a design template applied, the template's design aspects remain in place and only the background color changes.

Change the Slide Background Color

① Click **Format**.

② Click **Background**.

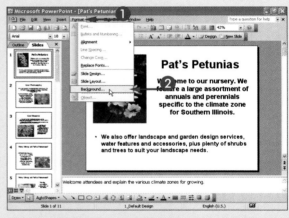

The Background dialog box appears.

③ Click the **Color** ☑.

④ Click a color.

● To choose a color other than the coordinating color choices, click **More Colors** to open the Colors dialog box and choose a color.

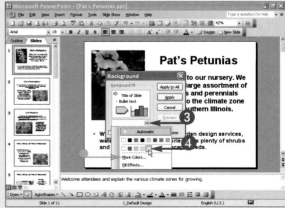

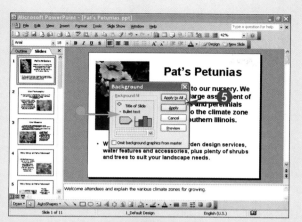

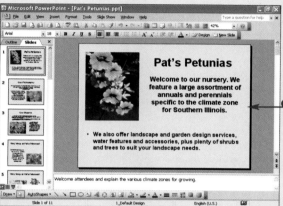

● A preview of the color appears here.

⑤ Specify how you want to apply the new color.

To apply the color only to the current slide, click **Apply**.

To apply the color to every slide in the presentation, click **Apply to All**.

● PowerPoint applies the background color.

How do I use an image as a slide background?

To use an image as a slide background, follow these steps:

① Open the Background dialog box, as shown in this section.

② Click the **Color** ☑ and click **Fill Effects**.

③ In the Fill Effects dialog box, click the **Picture** tab.

④ Click **Select Picture**.

⑤ In the Select Picture dialog box, double-click the picture file you want to assign.

⑥ Click **OK**.

You can now assign the picture to a single slide or to the entire presentation.

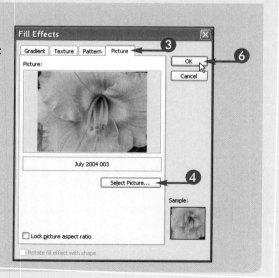

Add a New Slide

You can add new slides to your presentation at any time. You can add new slides at the end of the presentation or anywhere in-between existing slides. When you insert a new slide, PowerPoint automatically opens the Slide Layout task pane so you can choose a layout for the slide.

Add a New Slide

1 Click the slide you want to appear before the new slide.

2 Click the **New Slide** button (□).

You can also right-click over the slide in the Slides tab and choose **New Slide**.

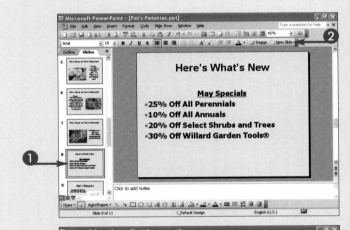

● PowerPoint inserts a new slide and opens the Slide Layout task pane so you can choose a layout.

Note: See the section "Change the Slide Layout," earlier in this chapter, to learn more about layout options.

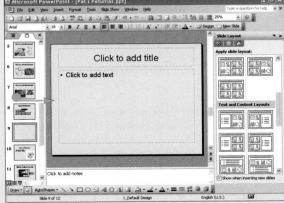

Delete
a Slide

> You can delete a slide you no longer need in a presentation. When you delete a slide, its removal is permanent.

Delete a Slide

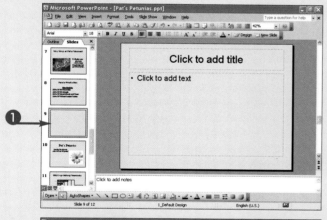

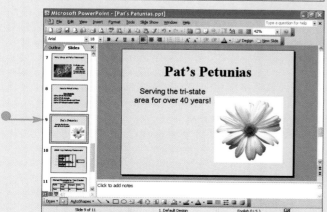

① Click the slide you want to delete in the Slides tab.

② Press **Delete**.

You can also right-click over the slide in the Slides tab and choose **Delete Slide**.

● PowerPoint removes the slide from the presentation and moves any subsequent slides up to replace the deleted slide.

Note: *If you make a mistake and delete the wrong slide, click* 🔄 *immediately to undo the deletion.*

Insert and Delete Slides

As you assemble your slide show, you can add more slides to a presentation, or you can remove slides you no longer want. PowerPoint makes it easy to insert new slides and delete existing slides using Slide Sorter view. Slide Sorter view shows all the slides in your presentation, making it easy to see where you need to add or remove slides.

INSERT A SLIDE

1 Click ⊞ to change to Slide Sorter view.

Note: See Chapter 13 to learn how to work with PowerPoint views.

PowerPoint displays Slide Sorter view.

2 Click the slide in front of where you want to insert a new slide.

3 Click the **New Slide** button (▣) on the Slide Sorter toolbar.

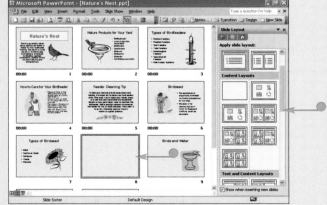

● PowerPoint adds a new slide and opens the Slide Layout task pane.

You can switch to Normal view to add a layout and content to the new slide.

Note: See Chapter 14 to learn how to work with slide content.

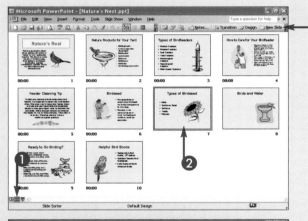

228

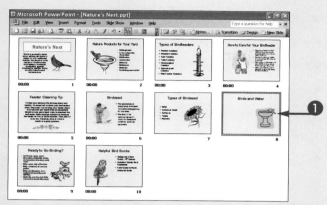

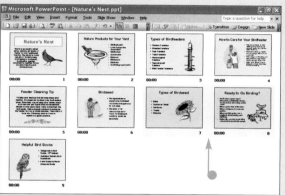

DELETE A SLIDE

1 In Slide Sorter view, click the slide you want to remove from the presentation.

Note: See the previous steps to learn how to switch to Slide Sorter view.

2 Press **Delete**.

● PowerPoint immediately deletes the slide.

Note: If you accidentally delete the wrong slide, click 🔄 to undo the mistake.

How do I add and subtract slides in Normal view?

In Normal view, you can quickly add slides using the Slides tab. Click where you want to insert a new slide in the Slides tab, and then click the **New Slide** button (🖼) on the Formatting toolbar. You can also click **Insert** and then **New Slide**. The Slide Layout pane immediately opens for you to choose a layout for the new slide. See Chapter 14 to learn more about slide layouts. To remove a slide in the Slides tab, click the slide and press **Delete**.

Can I add slides from another presentation?

Yes. Click where you want the new slides to appear in Slide Sorter view, click **Insert**, and then click **Slides from Files**. Use the Slide Finder dialog box to select the files you want to insert. You can also link the slides. If you link slides, however, you must be careful of making changes to the linked presentation or your links may be broken.

Reorganize Slides

You can reorganize the order of your slides using PowerPoint's Slide Sorter view. For example, you may want to move a slide to appear later in the presentation.

Reorganize Slides

① In Slide Sorter view, click the slide you want to move.

Note: See Chapter 13 to learn how to work with PowerPoint views.

② Drag the slide to a new location in the presentation.

To move multiple slides at the same time, press and hold **Ctrl** as you click each slide, and then drag the slides to a new location.

● PowerPoint moves the slide.

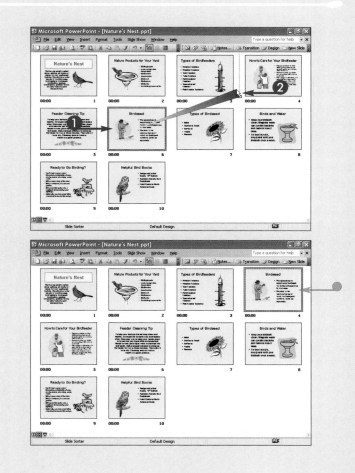

Create a Summary Slide

You can add a summary slide to the beginning of your presentation that sums all the titles of your slides as a bulleted list. Summary slides are helpful when you want to introduce all of your presentation topics before viewing each individual slide.

Create a Summary Slide

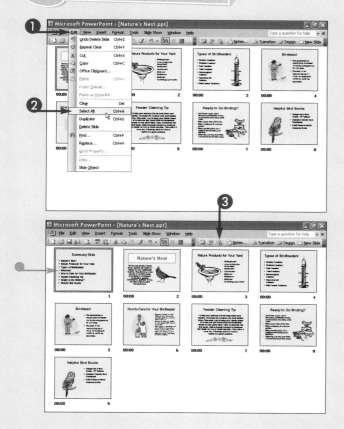

1 In Slide Sorter view, click **Edit**.

2 Click **Select All**.

Note: See Chapter 13 to learn how to work with PowerPoint views.

PowerPoint selects all the slides in the presentation.

3 Click the **Summary Slide** button (🖳).

● PowerPoint inserts a summary slide at the beginning of the presentation.

Note: Depending on the size of your presentation, PowerPoint may continue the summary to a second summary slide.

To view the summary, double-click the slide.

Define Slide Transitions

Use good judgment when assigning transitions. If you use too many different types of transitions, you may end up detracting from your presentation.

You can add transition effects to your slides to control how one slide segues to the next. Transition effects include fades, dissolves, and wipes. You can control the speed of the transition to appear fast or slow. You can also specify how PowerPoint advances the slides, either manually or automatically.

Define Slide Transitions

① In Slide Sorter view, click the slide you want to edit.

Note: See Chapter 13 to learn how to work with PowerPoint views.

② Click the **Transition** button (⊞) on the Formatting toolbar.

The transition affects how the current slide transitions into the next slide in your program.

● You can also click **Slide Show** and then **Slide Transition**.

If the task pane is already open, you can click ▼ and click **Slide Transition**.

The Slide Transition task pane opens.

● You can use the scroll bars to view all the available transition effects.

③ Click the transition you want to assign.

● PowerPoint immediately displays a preview of the transition effect.

● PowerPoint adds an animation icon below the slide.

● If the animation does not play, select the **AutoPreview** option in the task pane (☐ changes to ☑).

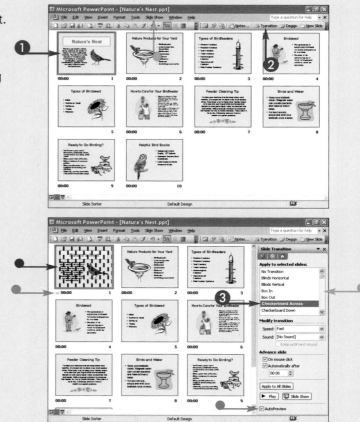

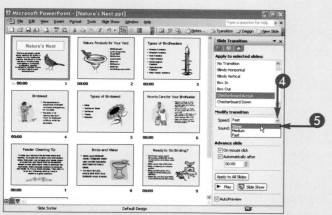

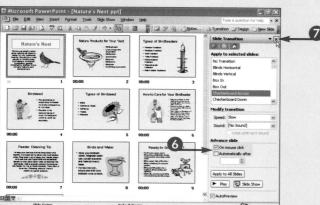

④ Click the **Speed** ▾.

⑤ Click a speed setting for the transition.

⑥ Select an advance option (☐ changes to ☑).

To use a mouse click to move to the next slide, select the **On mouse click** option (☐ changes to ☑).

To move to the next slide automatically, select the **Automatically after** option (☐ changes to ☑) and set a time.

⑦ Click ⊠.

The Slide Transition task pane closes.

Note: See Chapter 16 to learn how to run the slide show.

How do I remove a transition effect?
To remove a transition effect, reopen the Slide Design task pane to the transition effects. Click the **No Transition** option in the list box. PowerPoint removes the previous transition you assigned to the slide and returns the slide to the default state.

What does the sound option do?
You can assign sounds as transition effects with your slides. For example, you might assign the Applause sound effect for the first or last slide in a presentation. To assign a sound transition, click the **Sound** ▾ and select a sound. PowerPoint immediately previews the sound with the slide transition.

Add Animation Effects

Refrain from assigning too many animation effects or you risk overwhelming the audience. For best results, limit the effects to slides in which they make the most impact.

You can use PowerPoint's animation effects to add even more visual interest to your slide show presentations. PowerPoint's animation schemes include a variety of preset animations, such as spinning, zooming, and scrolling credits. When you assign an animation scheme, PowerPoint animates the text elements of the slide.

Add Animation Effects

① In Slide Sorter or Normal view, click the slide you want to edit.

Note: See Chapter 13 to learn how to work with PowerPoint views.

② Click the **Design** button (🖼) on the Formatting toolbar.

● You can also click **Slide Show** and then **Animation Schemes**.

The Slide Design task pane opens.

③ Click the **Animation Schemes** link.

● You can use the scroll bars to view all the available animation effects.

④ Click a scheme.

PowerPoint immediately previews the effect on the slide.

● To assign the effect to every slide in the presentation, click here.

⑤ When finished assigning animation effects, click ✖.

The task pane closes.

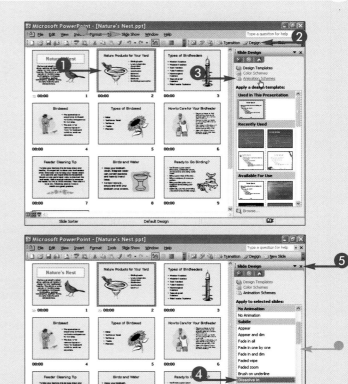

Animate Individual Slide Elements

You can assign animation effects to individual elements on a slide. For example, you may want the slide title to spin into view or make a clip art image fly onto the slide. You can assign customized animations using Normal view.

Animate Individual Slide Elements

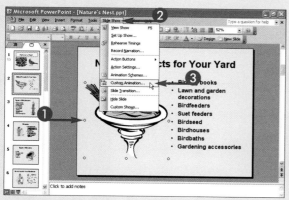

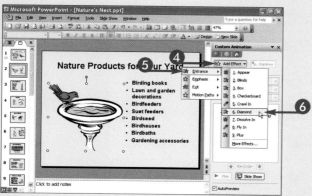

① In Normal view, click the slide element you want to animate.

Note: See Chapter 13 to learn how to work with PowerPoint views.

② Click **Slide Show**.

③ Click **Custom Animation**.

The Custom Animation task pane opens.

④ Click **Add Effect**.

⑤ Click an effect category.

⑥ Click an animation.

PowerPoint immediately assigns the animation to the slide element.

Rehearse a Presentation

You can time exactly how long each slide is displayed during a presentation using PowerPoint's Rehearse Timings feature. When rehearsing a presentation, rehearse what you want to say during each slide as well as allow the audience time to read the entire content of each slide. After you record the timings, PowerPoint saves the timings.

Rehearse a Presentation

① Click 🔳 to switch to Slide Sorter view.

② Click the **Rehearse Timings** button (🖳) on the Formatting toolbar.

● You can also click **SlideShow** and then **Rehearse Timings**.

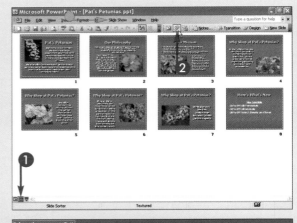

PowerPoint switches to Slide Show mode, displays the first slide, the Rehearsal toolbar, and starts a timer.

③ Rehearse what you want to say while the slide is displayed.

● If you need to pause the rehearsal, click the **Pause** button (⏸).

If you need to restart the timing, click the **Pause** button (⏸) again.

④ When finished with the first slide, click the **Next** button (➡).

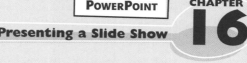

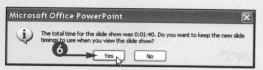

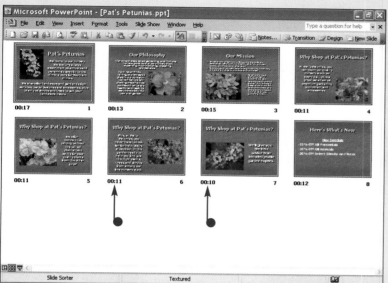

PowerPoint displays the next slide.

⑤ Repeat Steps **3** and **4** for each slide in your presentation.

⑥ When the slide show is complete, click **Yes**.

● PowerPoint saves the timings and displays them below each slide.

To edit a slide's timings, click the slide and open the Slide Transition task pane to change the timing setting.

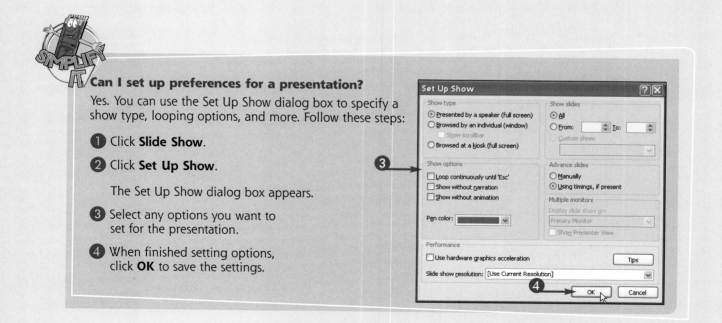

Can I set up preferences for a presentation?

Yes. You can use the Set Up Show dialog box to specify a show type, looping options, and more. Follow these steps:

❶ Click **Slide Show**.

❷ Click **Set Up Show**.

The Set Up Show dialog box appears.

❸ Select any options you want to set for the presentation.

❹ When finished setting options, click **OK** to save the settings.

Run a Slide Show

You can view a presentation using PowerPoint's Slide Show view. Slide Show view displays full-screen images of your slides. You can advance each slide manually, use a control bar containing navigation buttons, or instruct PowerPoint to advance the slides automatically for you.

Run a Slide Show

① Click 🖳 to switch to Slide Show view.

Note: See Chapter 13 to learn more about PowerPoint views.

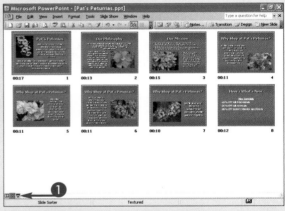

PowerPoint switches to Slide Show mode and displays the first slide.

When you move the mouse near the bottom-left corner, a small slide show control bar appears.

② Click anywhere on the slide to advance to the next slide or click the **Next** button.

● To return to a previous slide, click the **Previous** button.

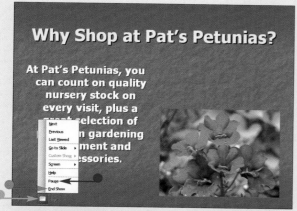

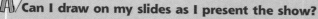

- To view a menu of slide show commands, click here.
- You can pause the show with this command.
- You can end the show early by activating this command.

  Note: *You can end a slide show at any time by pressing* **Esc**.

③ When the slide show is complete, click anywhere on-screen.

PowerPoint closes the presentation.

Can I draw on my slides as I present the show?

You can use PowerPoint's pointer options to draw directly on the screen using the mouse. You can choose from several pen tools and colors. Follow these steps:

① During the slide show, click ✏.

② Click a pen style.

⦿ You can click here to choose a pen color.

③ Draw where you want to mark on the slide.

To erase your markings, press **E** and drag across the markings.

At the end of the slide show, PowerPoint asks if you want to save any of your markings.

Create Speaker Notes

You can create speaker notes of your presentation. Speaker notes are notations you add to a slide that you can print out and use to help you give a presentation.

Create Speaker Notes

① In Normal view, click the slide to which you want to add notes.

Note: See Chapter 13 to learn more about PowerPoint views.

② Click in the Notes pane and type any notes you want to include.

You can repeat Step **2** for other slides to which you want to add notes.

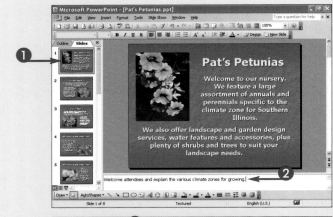

③ Click **View**.

④ Click **Notes Page**.

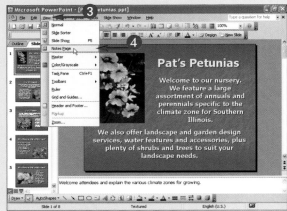

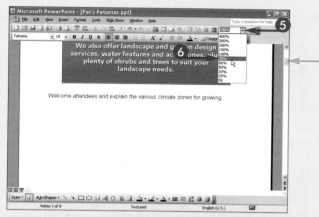

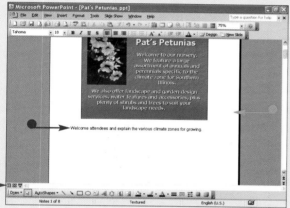

The Notes Page appears and displays the first page.

● You can use the scroll bars to scroll through the notes.

⑤ Click the **Zoom** ▾.

⑥ Click a magnification percentage.

● PowerPoint zooms your view of the page.

● You can edit and format your notes text as needed.

⑦ Click 🔳.

PowerPoint returns to Normal view.

How do I print my notes?

To print your speaker notes, follow these steps:

❶ Click **File**.

❷ Click **Print**.

The Print dialog box appears.

❸ Click the **Print what** ▾ and choose **Notes Pages**.

❹ Click **OK**.

PowerPoint prints the notes.

You can also print out your presentation as single slides or as handouts, which print multiple slides on a printed page. To learn more about printing Office files, see Chapter 2.

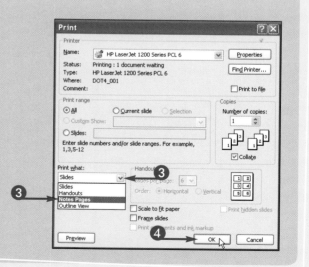

Package Your Presentation on a CD

PowerPoint can help you save your slide show to a CD to take with you for presentations on the go. With the Package for CD feature, PowerPoint bundles the presentation along with all the necessary clip art, multimedia elements, and other items needed to run your show.

The Package for CD feature only works with Windows XP.

Package Your Presentation on a CD

1. Click **File**.
2. Click **Package for CD**.

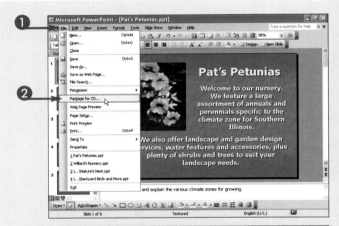

The Package for CD dialog box appears.

3. Type a name for the CD.
4. Click **Copy to CD**.

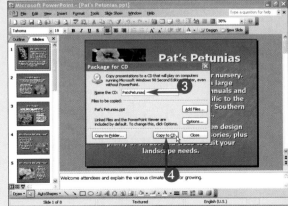

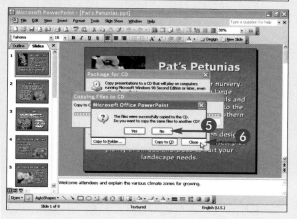

● PowerPoint copies the presentation files.

Depending on the size of the presentation, the copying process could take a few minutes.

⑤ When the copying process is complete, click **No**.

If you want to continue packing other presentations, you can click **Yes**.

⑥ Click **Close**.

The Package for CD dialog box closes.

What if I want to give the presentation to someone who does not have PowerPoint?
The Package for CD feature automatically includes a PowerPoint Viewer with the file in case the recipient does not have PowerPoint installed on his computer. The PowerPoint Viewer allows users to view slide shows without all the extra PowerPoint tools and features found in the full program.

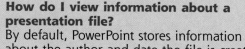

How do I view information about a presentation file?
By default, PowerPoint stores information about the author and date the file is created in the File Properties dialog box. To view the information, click **File** and then **Properties**. You can also use the dialog box to add more information, such as company name, subject, comments, and more.

Part V

Access

Access is a robust database program you can use to store and manage large quantities of data. You can use Access to manage anything from a home inventory to a giant warehouse of products. Whether you want to track a simply directory of contacts or a full range of shipping and receiving tasks, Access can help you organize your information into tables, speed up data entry with forms, and perform powerful analysis using filters and queries.

In this part, you learn how to build and maintain a database file; add tables; create; and analyze your data using filters, sort, and queries. You also learn how to generate reports to view specific types of data from your database.

Understanding Database Basics

Access is a popular database program you can use to catalog and manage large amounts of data. You can use Access to manage anything from a simple table of data, to large, multifaceted lists of information. If you are new to Access, take a moment and familiarize yourself with the basic terms associated with the program.

Defining Databases

Simply defined, a *database* is a collection of information. You use databases every day whether you are aware of it or not. Common databases include telephone directories or a television program schedule. Your own database examples might include a list of contacts, listing name, addresses, and phone numbers. Other examples of real-world databases include product inventories, client invoices, and employee payroll lists.

Tables

The heart of any Access database is a table. A table is a list of information organized into columns and rows. In the example of a client contact database, the table might list the names, addresses, phone numbers, company name, title, and e-mail addresses of your clients. You can have numerous tables in your Access database. For example, you might have one table listing client information and another table listing your company's product list.

Records and Fields

Every entry you make in an Access table is called a *record*.
Records always appear as rows in a database. You can organize the
information for each record in a separate column, called a *field*.
For example, in a client contact list, you might include fields for
first name, last name, company name, title, address, city, zip code,
phone number, and e-mail address. Field names appear at the
top of the table.

Forms

You can enter your database records directly into an Access
table, or you can simplify the process by using a *form*. Access
forms present your table fields in an easy-to-read, fill-in-the-blank
format. Forms allow you to enter records one at a time. Forms
are a great way to speed up data entry, particularly if other users
are adding information to your database list.

Reports and Queries

As soon as you create an Access database, you can begin
manipulating data. You can use the report feature to summarize
data in your tables and generate printouts of pertinent information,
such as your top ten salespeople and your top-selling products. You
can use queries to sort and filter your data. For example, you can
choose to view a select few of your table fields and filter them to
match certain criteria.

Planning a Database

The first step to building an Access database is deciding what sort
of data you want to store and manage. Think about what sort of
actions you want to perform on your data, and how you want it
organized. How many tables of data do you need? What types of
fields do you need for your records? What sort of reports and
queries do you hope to create? You might also take time to sketch
out on paper how you want the information grouped into tables
and how the tables are related. Taking time to plan the database
in advance can save you time when building the file.

Create a Blank Database

You can start a new, blank database and populate it with data. When you create a new database file, Access prompts you to assign a name to the file, and then displays the open database window.

To learn how to add data to a database, see Chapter 18.

Create a Blank Database

① Click the **Create a new file** link in the Getting Started task pane.

● You can also click **File** and then **New**.

Note: See Chapter 1 to learn more about using the Microsoft Office task panes.

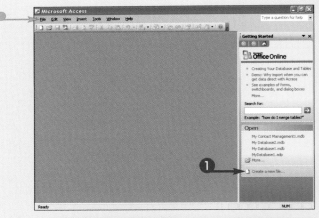

The New File task pane appears.

② Click the **Blank database** link.

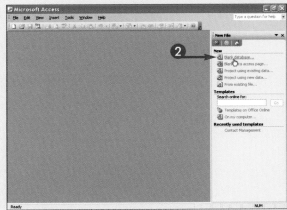

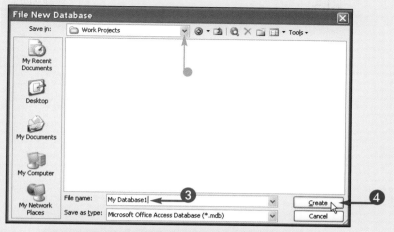

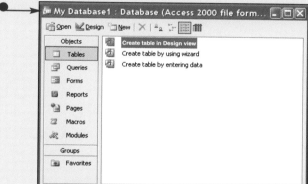

The File New Database dialog box appears.

● If needed, navigate to the folder or drive to which you want to store the file.

❸ Type a name for the database.

Access automatically assigns the .mdb (which stands for Microsoft Database) extension to all database files.

❹ Click **Create**.

● Access creates a new, blank database and displays the database window.

You can now create your own tables, enter records, and more.

Note: See Chapter 18 to learn how to populate a database with data.

What does the database window do?
The database window lists all the objects associated with your database, such as tables, forms, queries, and reports. You can use the window to open various objects. By default, the database window appears as a smaller window within the program window's workspace. You can maximize, minimize, restore, and close the database window just as you can any other window you work with on the computer using the window's control buttons.

How many databases can I open in Access?
Unlike other Microsoft Office programs, you can only work with one database file at a time in Access. When you open a new or existing database, Access closes any currently open database file.

Create a Database Based on a Template

You can build a new database based on any of the Access templates. When you create a new database using a template, the Database Wizard walks you through the necessary steps for building the database. You can control the structure of your database by determining which preset tables and fields are included in the file.

Create a Database Based on a Template

① Click the **Create a new file** link in the Getting Started task pane.

● You can also click **File** and then **New**.

Note: See Chapter 1 to learn more about using the Microsoft Office task panes.

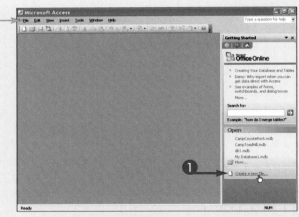

The New File task pane opens.

② Under the Templates heading, click the **On my computer** link.

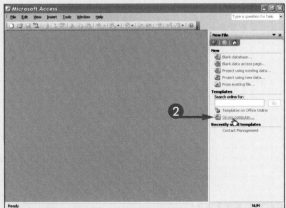

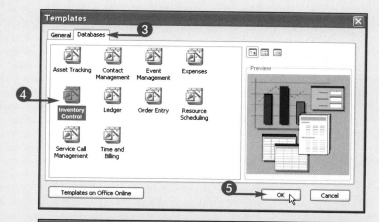

The Templates dialog box appears.

3 Click the **Databases** tab.

4 Click the template you want to use to create a database.

5 Click **OK**.

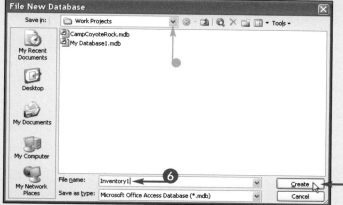

The File New Database dialog box appears.

● If needed, navigate to the folder or drive to which you want to store the file.

6 Type a name for the database.

7 Click **Create**.

What kind of templates can I use to build a database?
You can choose from ten different database templates in the Templates dialog box. The template names describe the type of database you can create using the template. Using the Database Wizard, you can customize each template to suit your own uses.

Where can I find more Access database templates?
You can download more Access templates from the Microsoft Office Web site.
Click **Templates on Office Online** in the Templates dialog box. This opens your browser window to the Web site where you can search for other database templates.

Create a Database Based on a Template *(continued)*

Most database templates offer several different types of tables you can create based on the type of template you choose. When building a database using the wizard, you can customize exactly which fields you want to include in the table. You can also customize the appearance of your database screen display and printed reports.

Create a Database Based on a Template *(continued)*

The Database Wizard opens.

8 Click **Next**.

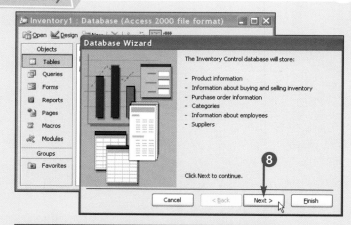

The next wizard screen offers options for defining the structure of your database.

9 Click the table you want to create.

10 Click to select or deselect the fields you want the table to contain.

11 Click **Next**.

The next wizard screen displays screen display backgrounds you can assign.

⑫ Click a background.

⑬ Click **Next**.

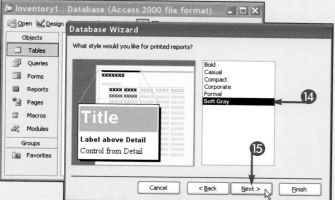

The next screen allows you to choose a style for your printed reports.

⑭ Click a report style.

⑮ Click **Next**.

How do I know which fields to keep or remove from my table?

To best determine which fields you need in your database, take time to do a little preplanning. Decide what kinds of information you want to track in your database and what sorts of reports and queries you want to generate to view your data. The Database Wizard lists necessary fields along with optional fields. For best results, use the suggested fields. You can always remove fields you do not use at a later time.

How are the database screen displays used in Access?

The screen displays are simply backgrounds that appear behind your database data in forms. Backgrounds can really spruce up your data entry process and make the database appear more professional.

continued

Create a Database Based on a Template *(continued)*

When the wizard steps are complete, Access creates the new database and table you chose. In addition, Access adds a Switchboard window you can use to quickly perform database tasks.

Create a Database Based on a Template *(continued)*

⑯ Type a title for your database.

You can use the same name as the filename, or create a new name.

⑰ Click **Next**.

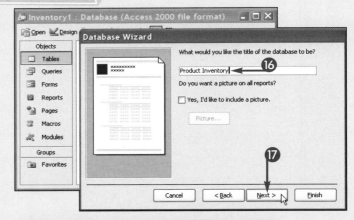

The final wizard screen appears.

⑱ Click **Finish**.

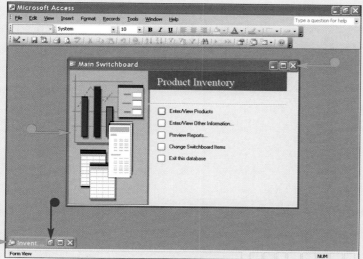

Access begins building the new database file.

The process may take a few moments depending on the type of database you chose.

● When the database is complete, Access displays the Switchboard and a minimized database window.

You can use the Switchboard window to quickly start new database tasks.

● You can click ⊠ to close the Switchboard window.

● Click 🗗 to display the database window.

Note: *See Chapter 18 to learn how to work with database objects using the database window.*

How do I include a picture with my database reports?
You can use the picture option in the Database Wizard to include artwork on your Access reports. For example, if you have a company logo, you can include it on all the reports you generate in Access, giving your printouts a more polished appearance. To include a picture file, select the **Yes, I'd like to include a picture** option (☐ changes to ☑) in the wizard, click **Picture**, and then navigate to the file you want to use.

What is the difference between the Switchboard window and the database window?
You can use either window to perform database tasks. If you are new to Access, you may find the Switchboard window easier to use because it lists all the common tasks for creating and managing database data and you can simply click a task to begin.

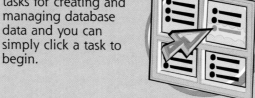

Create a Table

To learn more about starting a database file, see Chapter 17.

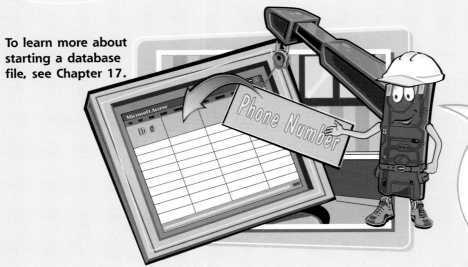

You can start building a database by entering data into a table. All Access data is stored in tables. You can have multiple tables in a single database. Tables consist of columns and rows that intersect to form *cells* for holding data. Each row is considered a *record* in a table. Use columns to hold *fields*, the individual units of information contained within a record.

Create a Table

1. In the database window, click the **Tables** object.

2. Double-click the **Create table by entering data** option.

   Note: See Chapter 17 to learn how to create a database file.

   To enter data into an existing table, double-click the table name in the database window.

   Access opens a new table in Datasheet view.

   Note: See the section "Change Table Views" to learn more about Datasheet view.

3. To create a field name, double-click the column header.

4. Type a name for the field.

5. Press Enter.

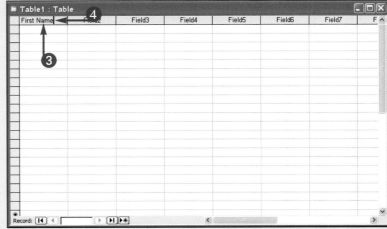

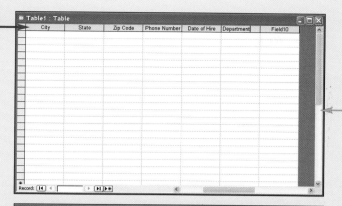

6 Repeat Steps **3** to **5** to create more fields for the table.

● You can resize columns by dragging the column border left or right.

● You can use the scroll bars to view different portions of the table.

7 To enter the first record, click inside the first field of the first row and type the data.

8 Press **Tab** or **Enter** .

9 Type the next field's data.

Repeat Steps **8** and **9** to complete the record.

When you reach the last field, you can press **Enter** to start a new record.

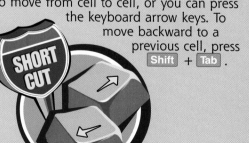

How do I navigate a table?

You can click in a cell to make the cell active, or you can use the keyboard keys to navigate around a table. You can press **Tab** to move from cell to cell, or you can press the keyboard arrow keys. To move backward to a previous cell, press **Shift** + **Tab** .

Is there an easy way to repeat an entry for a cell?

You can press **Ctrl** + ' to copy the contents of the cell directly above the active cell. For example, if you are copying the same state name in the State field, you can press **Ctrl** + ' and Access immediately fills in the same text for you. This shortcut only works in Datasheet view, not in Form view. See the section "Change Table Views" to learn more about Access views.

Create a
Table *(continued)*

When creating a new table, you can give the table a unique name and assign a primary key to identify records. After you save the table, you can reopen it to add more data or make changes to the existing data.

⑩ Continue filling the table with data.

⑪ When finished, click ☒.

Access prompts you to save the table changes.

⑫ Click **Yes**.

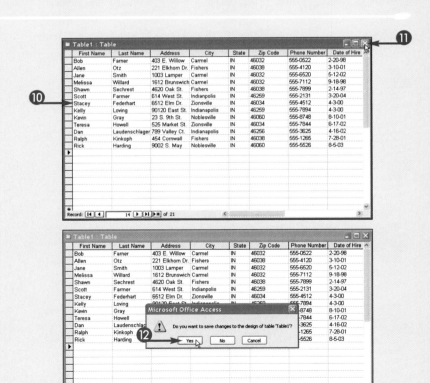

258

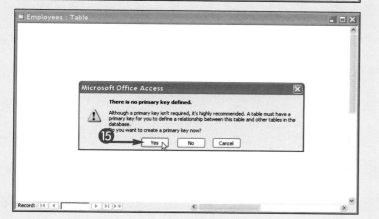

The Save As dialog box appears.

⑬ Type a name for the table.

⑭ Click **OK**.

Access prompts you to set a primary key.

⑮ Click **Yes**.

Access adds a primary key field, saves the data, and closes the table.

The table is now listed among the database objects in the database window.

What is a primary key?
A *primary key* uniquely identifies each record in a table. For many tables, the primary key is a numbering field that stores a unique number for each record as it is entered into the database. You can also designate another field as a primary key. When you save a new table, Access asks you if you want to create a primary key. If you click **Yes**, the AutoNumber feature creates a primary key for the table.

How do I edit a record?
You can keep adding more records to existing tables or edit existing records. To edit a record, reopen the table in Datasheet view and make changes to the data. When you close the table, Access automatically saves your changes. Unlike some of the other Office programs, you do not need to activate a Save command to save your database work.

Create a Table with a Wizard

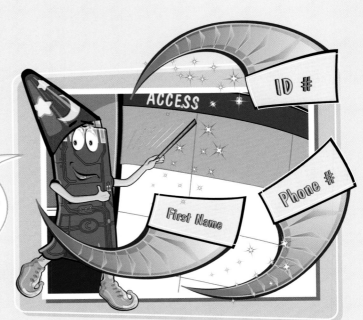

You can use an Access wizard to help you create and customize a table for your database. The wizard walks you through each of the necessary steps for creating a new table.

Create a Table with a Wizard

① In the database window, click the **Tables** object.

② Double-click the **Create table by using Wizard** option.

Note: See Chapter 17 to learn how to create a database file.

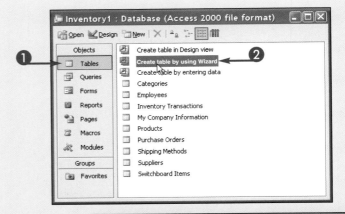

Access opens the Table Wizard dialog box.

③ Click a table type you want to create.

④ Click a field.

⑤ Click the **Add** button ([>]).

● To add all the sample fields, click the **Add All** button ([>>]).

● To remove a field from the list, click the **Subtract** button ([<]).

⑥ Click **Next**.

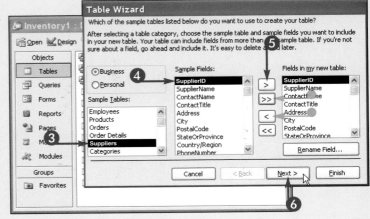

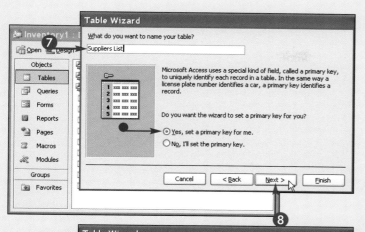

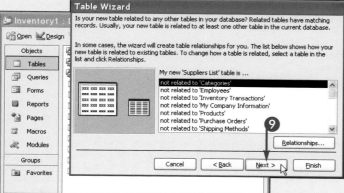

7 Type a name for the new table.

● Select this option to allow Access to set a primary key (○ changes to ⦿).

8 Click **Next**.

If the new table shares records with other tables in your database, you can change the relationships.

Note: *See the tip in this section for more about relationships.*

9 Click **Next**.

How can I customize my table using the wizard?

In the very first wizard dialog box that appears when creating a table, you can choose a specific type of table and the wizard displays common fields associated with such a table. You can pick and choose from among the fields from more than one type of table to assemble a table that includes just the right information for your database needs. If you find you added too many fields when creating the table, you can always remove a field later. See the section "Delete a Field," later in this chapter, to learn more.

Can I rename the fields?

Yes. You can rename fields in the Table Wizard dialog box by clicking the field and clicking **Rename Field**. If you have already created the table, simply double-click the field name, type a new name, and press Enter.

Create a Table with a Wizard *(continued)*

After you create a new table with the wizard, you can populate it with data. When you finish working with the table, you can close it and save your changes.

Create a Table with a Wizard *(continued)*

10 Select an option for working with the newly created table (⚪ changes to ⦿).

11 Click **Finish**.

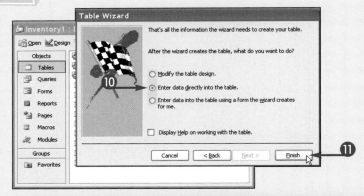

Access opens a new table.

12 Click in the first field you want to fill and type the table data.

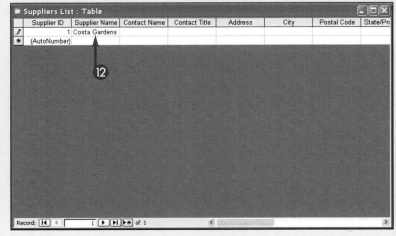

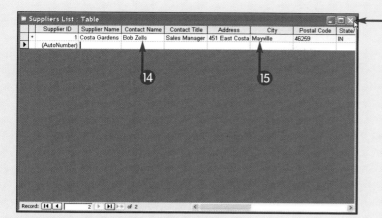

13 Press Tab .

14 Type the next field's data.

15 Continue filling in the record fields to complete the record.

When you reach the last field, you can press Enter to start a new record.

You can repeat Steps **13** to **15** to add more records to the table.

16 When you finish working with the table, click ✕.

Access closes the table and the table name appears in the database window.

● You can double-click the table name to reopen the table and add new records or make changes to the data.

Do my tables have to have relationships with other tables in the database?
Depending on how you want to use your database, it is quite common to have several tables that share records, creating relationships between tables. When creating a new table with the Table Wizard, the wizard can help create table relationships for you where needed. For example, an inventory database might include tables of products, customers, and orders, with the orders table sharing information from the products and customers tables. You can always change the relationships between your tables using the Relationships command found on the Tools menu.

How do I remove a table I no longer want?
Before attempting to remove a table, make sure it does not contain any important data you need. To delete the table, select it in the database window and press Delete . Access asks you to confirm the deletion before permanently removing the table and any data it holds.

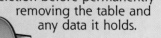

Change Table Views

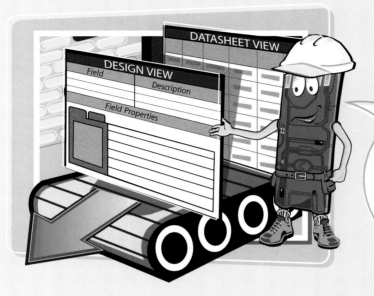

You can view your table data using two different view modes: Datasheet view and Design view. In Datasheet view, the table appears as an ordinary grid of intersecting columns and rows where you can enter data. In Design view, you can view the skeletal structure of your fields and their properties. You can use Design view to modify the design of the table.

Change Table Views

SWITCH TO DESIGN VIEW

① Click the **View** ▾.

② Click **Design View**.

Access displays the design of the table and shows the field properties.

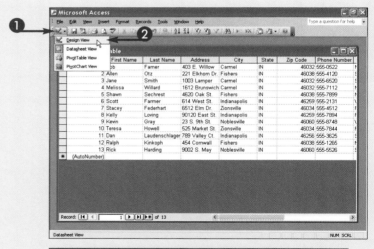

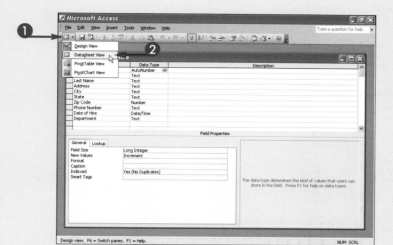

SWITCH TO DATASHEET VIEW

1 Click the **View** ▾.

2 Click **Datasheet View**.

Access displays the design of the table and shows the field properties.

What sort of modifications can I make in Design view?

You can add fields by typing new field names in the Field Name column. You can also change the field names or change the type of data allowed within a field, such as text or number data only. The Field Properties sheet at the bottom of Design view allows you to change the design of the field itself, specifying how many characters the field can contain, whether fields can be left blank in the record or not, and other properties.

What do the PivotTable and PivotChart views do?

If you create a PivotTable, you can use PivotTable view to summarize and analyze data by viewing different fields. You can use the PivotChart feature to create a graphical version of a PivotTable, and use the PivotChart view to see various graphical representations of the data. See the Access Help files to learn more about the PivotTable and PivotChart features.

Add a Field

You can add fields to your table to include more information in your records. For example, you may find you need to add a separate field to a Contacts table for mobile phone numbers.

Add a Field

① Open the table to which you want to add a field in Datasheet view.

Note: See the previous section, "Change Table Views," to learn more about the Access views.

② Right-click the column header to the right of where you want to insert a new field.

Access selects the entire column.

③ Click **Insert Column**.

You can also click the **Insert** menu and then **Column**.

Access adds a new column to the table.

④ Double-click the field name and type a new name for the field.

⑤ Press **Enter** .

The new field is ready to use.

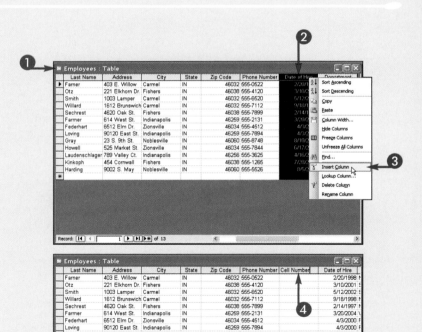

Delete a Field

You can delete a field you no longer need in a table. When you remove a field, Access permanently removes any data contained within the field for every record in the table.

Delete a Field

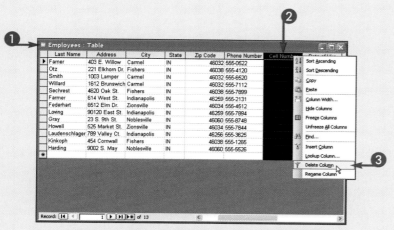

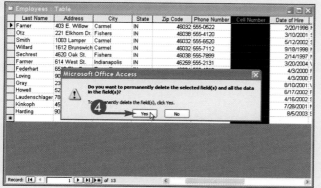

1 Open the table you want to edit in Datasheet view.

Note: See the section "Change Table Views," earlier in this chapter, to learn more about the Access views.

2 Right-click the column header of the field you want to remove.

Access selects the entire column.

3 Click **Delete Column**.

Access displays a prompt box.

4 Click **Yes**.

The field and any record content for the field are removed from the table.

Hide
a Field

You can hide a field in your table by hiding the entire column of data. You might hide a field to focus on other fields for a printout or hide a field from someone who might be using your computer.

Hide a Field

1 Click the field column header you want to hide.

Access selects the entire column.

2 Click **Format**.

3 Click **Hide Columns**.

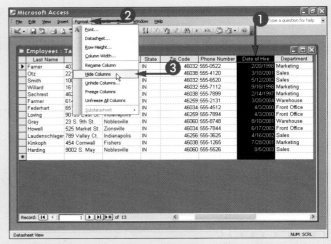

Access hides the column.

To view the column again, click the **Format** menu, click **Unhide Columns**, and then click the column you want to display again.

Note: *Access does not mark hidden fields, so you need to remember if you have previously hidden fields or activate the **Unhide Columns** command when in doubt.*

Move a Field

You can move a field in your table to rearrange how you view and enter record data. For example, you may want to move a field to appear before another field to suit the way you type your record data.

Move a Field

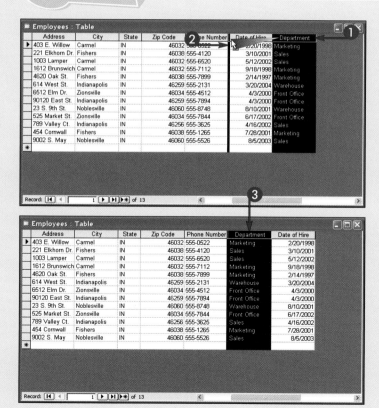

1. Click the field column header you want to move.

   Access selects the entire column.

2. Drag the column to a new position in the table.

   A bold vertical line marks the new location of the column as you drag.

3. Release the mouse button.

   Access moves the field to the new location.

Add a Record

You can add new records to your database table any time you need. Any new records you add are added to the end of the table.

Add a Record

1 Click the **New Record** button (▶) on the Standard toolbar.

● You can also click **Insert** and then **New Record**.

● You can also click the **New Record** button (▶*) on the navigation bar to add a new record.

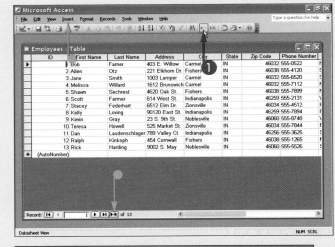

● Access immediately adds a new record at the bottom of the table.

You can fill in the record's fields as needed.

Note: *See the section "Create a Table," earlier in this chapter, to learn how to enter record data.*

● As your table grows longer, you can use the navigation buttons to move between records.

Delete a Record

You can remove a record from your database if it holds data you no longer need. Removing old records can reduce the overall file size of your database and make it easier to manage. When you delete a record, all the data within its fields is permanently removed.

Delete a Record

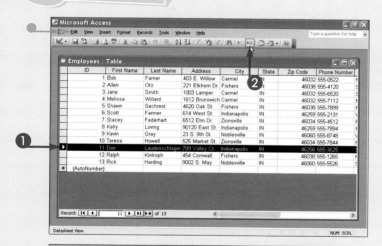

① Click to the left of the record you want to delete.

② Click the **Delete Record** button (⬛) on the Standard toolbar.

● You can also click **Edit** and then **Delete Record**.

Access displays a warning box about the deletion.

③ Click **Yes**.

Access permanently removes the record from the table.

Create a Form Using a Wizard

You can use the Access Form Wizard to help you create and customize a form for entering records into your database. The wizard walks you through each of the necessary steps for creating a form. You can choose exactly which fields the form contains.

Create a Form Using a Wizard

① In the database window, click the **Forms** object.

Note: See Chapter 17 to learn how to create a database file.

② Double-click the **Create form by using wizard** option.

- If the option is not available, click the **New** button (image) and double-click **Form Wizard**.

Access opens the Form Wizard dialog box.

③ Click the **Tables/Queries** ☑.

④ Click a table containing the fields on which you want to base the form.

Depending on the database template you used to create the file, you may see one or several tables from which to choose.

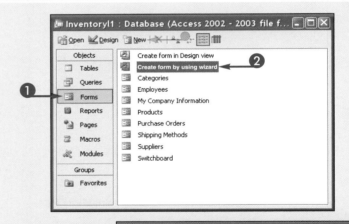

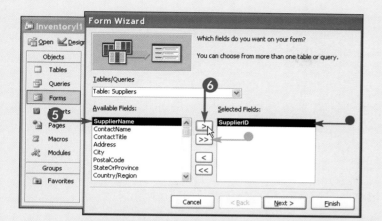

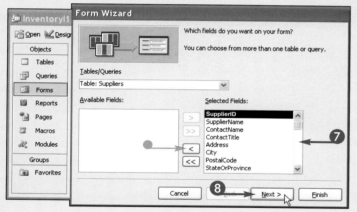

5 Click a field you want to include in the form.

6 Click the **Add** button (▷).

● To add all the sample fields, click the **Add All** button (▷▷).

● Access adds the field to the form.

7 Repeat Steps **5** and **6** to add more fields to the form.

● To remove a field from the list, click it and then click the **Subtract** button (◁).

8 Click **Next**.

Can I select fields from different tables for my form?

Yes. If you have more than one table in your database, you can choose fields from the different tables to use in a single form. Simply select a table from the **Tables/Queries** drop-down list in Step **3** and choose a different table.

Is there a way I can create a generic form?

You can click the **New** button (🔲) on the database window to open the New Form dialog box, and click a form option. For example, if you select the **AutoForm: Columnar** option, you can create a single column of fields in the form. If you select the **AutoForm: Tabular** option, you can create a form that looks like a table.

continued

273

Create a Form Using a Wizard (continued)

When creating a form, you can choose a layout, a design style, and assign a unique name to the form. After you create a new form with the wizard, you can begin entering records using the form.

Create a Form Using a Wizard (continued)

⑨ Select a layout option for the form (◯ changes to ◉).

⑩ Click **Next**.

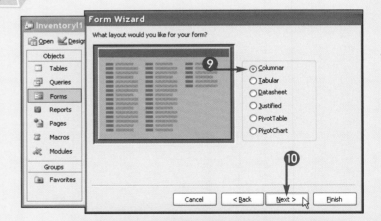

⑪ Click a style for the form.

⑫ Click **Next**.

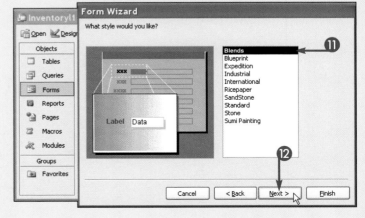

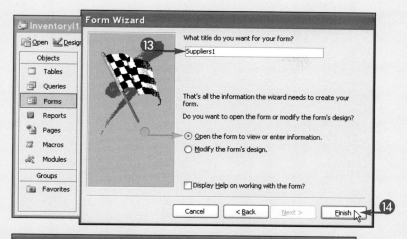

13 Type a name for the form.

● Select this option to view the form immediately (○ changes to ⊙).

14 Click **Finish**.

Access creates the new form.

The form name is added to the list of form objects in the database window.

Note: See the next section, "Add a Record," to learn how to use a form to add data to your database.

What kinds of layouts are available for my form?
You can choose from six different layouts. The table below explains the appearance of each format.

Form Layouts	
Format	**Appearance**
Columnar	Sets up your form fields in a column
Tabular	Presents your fields much like a table
Datasheet	Makes the form look just like a datasheet
Justified	Presents your fields so that they line up with both the left and right sides of the form
PivotTable and PivotChart	Presents your form in a graphical way to view and analyze data

Add a Record

You can use forms to quickly add records to your Access databases. Forms present your record fields in an easy-to-read format. The form window presents each field in your table as a box you can use to enter data.

Add a Record

① Click the **Forms** object in the database window.

② Double-click the form you want to use.

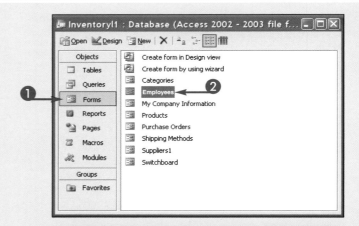

Access displays a blank record ready for filling out.

③ Click inside the first field and type the data.

④ Press **Tab**.

Access moves to the next field in the form.

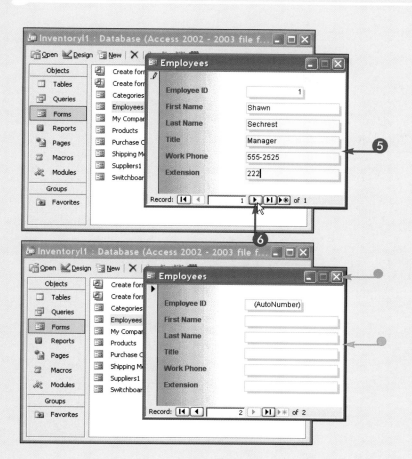

⑤ Repeat Steps **3** and **4** to fill in data for all the form fields in the record.

⑥ In the last field, press **Enter** or click the **Next Record** button (▶).

● Access displays another blank record ready for data.

Note: See the next section, "Navigate Records," to learn how to move among records using a form.

● To close the form window at any time, click ☒.

Are there other ways to insert a new record?
Yes. You can click the **Insert** menu and then **New Record** to open a new, blank record in your form. You can also click the **New Record** button (▶*) on the form window's navigation bar, or click the **New Record** button (▶) on the Standard toolbar.

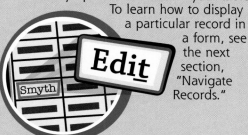

How do I edit a record?
You can reopen the form and navigate to the record you want to change and make your edits directly to the form data. You can then save your changes and Access automatically updates the data in your table. To learn how to display a particular record in a form, see the next section, "Navigate Records."

Navigate Records

You can navigate your table records using a form. The Form window includes a navigation bar for viewing different records in your database. You may find it easier to read a record using a form rather than reading it from a large table containing other records.

Navigate Records

① Open the form you want to view.

Note: See the section "Create a Form Using a Wizard," earlier in this chapter, to learn how to build a form.

● The Record Number box displays the number of the current record you are viewing.

② Click the **Previous Record** (◀) or **Next Record** (▶) buttons to move back or forward by one record.

● Access displays the previous or next record in the database.

● You can click the **First Record** (▶▮) or **Last Record** (▮◀) buttons to navigate to the beginning or end of the table.

● You can click the **New Record** button (▶＊) to start a new blank record.

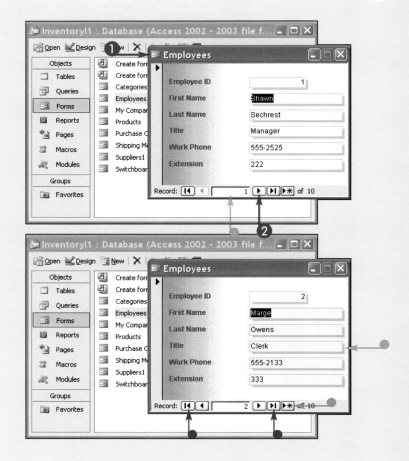

278

Delete a Record

You can remove records you no longer need using a form. Removing old records can reduce the overall file size of your database and make it easier to manage. When you delete a record, all the data within its fields is permanently removed.

Delete a Record

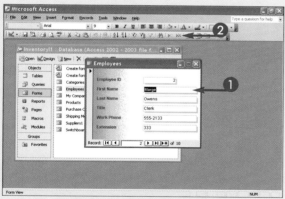

❶ In the form window, navigate to the record you want to delete.

You can use the navigation bar to display different records in your table.

❷ Click the **Delete Record** button (⧉) on the Standard toolbar.

You can also click the **Edit** menu and then **Delete Record**.

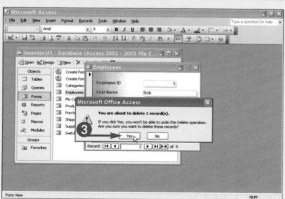

Access displays a warning box about the deletion.

❸ Click **Yes**.

Access permanently removes the record.

Change Form Views

You can customize your form using Design view. In Design view, each object appears as a separate, editable element in the form. For example, you can edit both the field box that contains the data as well as the field label identifying the data.

Change Form Views

① Click the **View** ▾.

② Click **Design View**.

● Access displays the form's design.

③ Click the **View** ▾.

④ Click **Form View**.

Access returns the form to its default view.

If you make any changes to the form design, Access prompts you to save the changes before closing the form.

Move a Field

You can move a field to another location on the form if you prefer. When you select a field for editing, the field label is selected as well, making it easy to move both the field and the label at the same time.

Move a Field

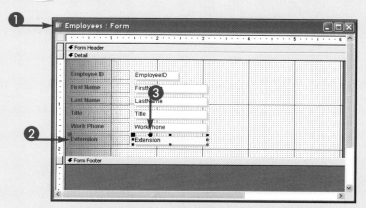

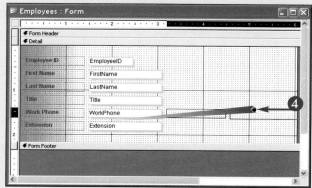

① Open the form you want to edit in Design view.

Note: See the previous section, "Change Form Views," to learn how to switch to Design view.

② Click the field you want to edit.

Access surrounds the field with selection handles and includes the field label.

③ Move the mouse pointer over the top of the field.

The ▷ changes to ✋.

④ Drag the field to a new location on the form.

Access repositions the field.

Delete
a Field

You can delete a field you no longer need in a form. When you remove a field, you remove both the data box and the field label. Removing a form field does not remove the field from the table upon which the form is based.

Delete a Field

1 Open the form you want to edit in Design view.

   Note: *See the section "Change Form Views," earlier in this chapter, to learn how to switch to Design view.*

2 Click the field you want to delete.

   Access surrounds the field with selection handles and includes the field label.

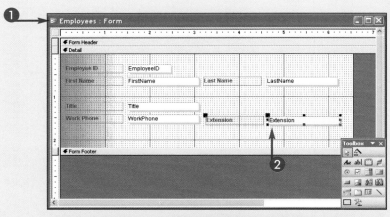

3 Press **Delete**.

● Access removes the field and label from the form.

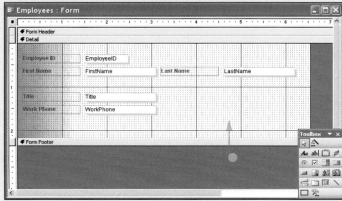

Add a Field

You can add new fields to your form, selecting from a list of available table fields. After you add a field, you can move it where you want it to go.

See the section "Move a Field," earlier in this chapter, to learn how to reposition fields in Design view.

Add a Field

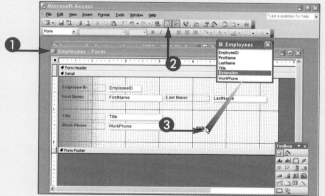

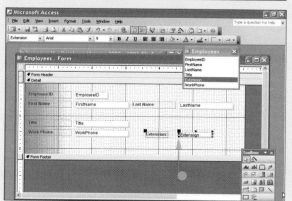

① Open the form you want to edit in Design view.

Note: *See the section "Change Form Views," earlier in this chapter, to learn how to switch to Design view.*

② Click the **Field List** button (▦).

The Field List box appears.

③ Drag the field you want to add from the Field List box and drop it onto the form.

● Access adds the field to the form.

You can reposition the field, if needed.

Note: *See the section "Move a Field," earlier in this chapter, to learn how to move a field in Design view.*

Sort Records

One of the easiest ways to manipulate your database data is to perform a sort. Sorting allows you to put your database records in a logical order to match any criteria you specify. For example, with a contacts database, you might want to sort the records alphabetically or based on zip code. You can sort in ascending order or descending order.

You can sort records in a table, or you can use a form to sort records. See Chapter 18 to learn more about Access tables. See Chapter 19 to learn about forms.

Sort Records

SORT A TABLE

1 Open the table you want to sort.

2 Click the column header for the field you want to sort.

3 Click a sort button.

Click **Sort Ascending** ([↓]) to sort the records in ascending order.

Click **Sort Descending** ([↓]) to sort the records in descending order.

● Access sorts the table records based on the field you choose.

In this example, the records are sorted alphabetically by country.

● In the prompt box that appears when you close the table, click **Yes** to make the sort permanent or **No** to leave the original order intact.

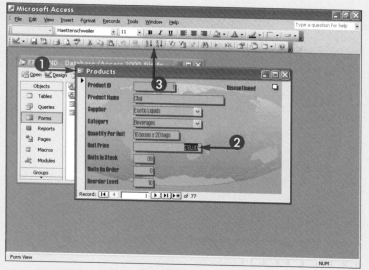

SORT USING A FORM

1. Open the form you want to use.

2. Click in the field you want to sort.

3. Click a sort button.

   Click **Sort Ascending** (⚟) to sort the records in ascending order.

   Click **Sort Descending** (⚟) to sort the records in descending order.

Access sorts the records.

- You can use the navigation buttons to view the sorted records.

  Note: See Chapter 19 to learn how to navigate records in Form view.

What happens if I have empty records and perform a sort?

If you perform a sort on a field without any data for some of your records, those records are included in the sort. Any empty fields are sorted first when you perform an ascending sort or last with a descending sort.

How do I remove a sort order?

With the sorted table open, click the **Records** menu and then click **Remove Filter/Sort**. This removes the sort order and returns the table to its original order. You can also use this technique to remove a sort from a query or report.

Filter Records

You can use the filter feature to view only specific records that meet your criteria. For example, you may want to view all the clients buying a particular product or anyone in a contacts database that has a birthday in June. You can use an Access filter to temporarily filter out all the records except those you want to view.

Filter Records

APPLY A SIMPLE FILTER

1. Open the form to which you want to apply a filter.

2. Click the field that contains the criteria you want to filter.

3. Click the **Filter By Selection** button (▣).

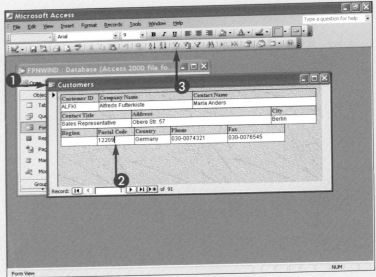

Access filters the records.

In this example, Access found only one record matching the filter criteria.

● You can use the navigation buttons to view the filtered records.

Note: See Chapter 19 to learn how to navigate records in Form view.

To undo a filter, click the **Records** menu and then **Remove Filter/Sort**.

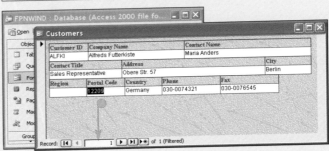

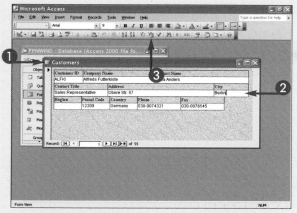

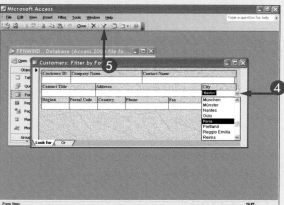

FILTER BY FORM

1 Open the form to which you want to apply a filter.

2 Click the field that contains the criteria you want to filter.

3 Click the **Filter By Form** button (⊞).

A blank form appears.

4 Click the ⊡ for the field you want to filter and click a criteria.

You can set additional filter criteria for other fields as needed.

5 Click the **Apply Filter** button (⊠).

Access filters the records.

To return the database to its original order, you can click the **Remove Filter** button (⊠).

Can I filter by exclusion?

Yes. You can filter out records that do not contain the search criteria you specify. To do so, first click in the field you want to filter in the form, click the **Records** menu, click **Filter**, and then click **Filter Excluding Selection**. Access filters the records for any that do not contain the data found in the field you selected.

What can I do with an advanced filter?

To filter by multiple fields, open the Advanced filter where you can designate multiple criteria for a filter. Click the **Records** menu, click **Filter**, and then click **Advanced Filter/Sort** to open the feature. Start by choosing a primary field for the filter and specify the criteria, and then enter secondary fields as needed. When you are ready to filter the records, click ⊠.

Perform a Simple Query

You can use a query to extract information you want to view in a database. Queries are especially useful when you want to glean data from two or more tables. Queries are similar to filters, but offer you greater control over the records you want to view. You can use the Query Wizard to help you select which fields you want to include in the analysis.

Perform a Simple Query

CREATE A QUERY WITH THE WIZARD

1 Click the **Queries** object in the database window.

2 Double-click the **Create query by using wizard** option.

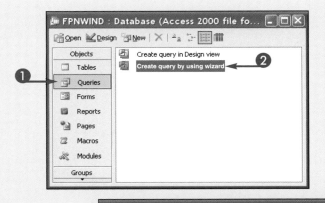

The Simple Query Wizard opens.

3 Click the **Tables/Queries** ⊡.

4 Click a table containing the fields on which you want to base the query.

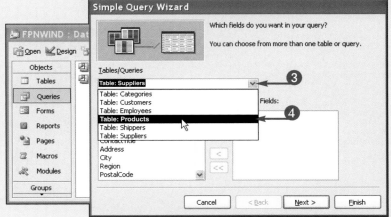

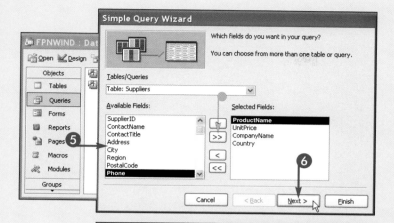

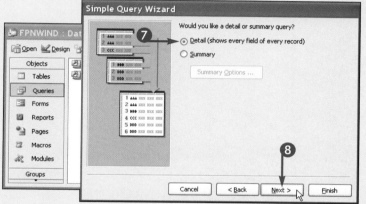

⑤ Double-click each field you want to include in the query.

● To add all the sample fields, click the **Add All** button (>>).

Access adds the fields to the list.

You can repeat Steps **3** and **4** to choose another table from which to add fields.

Note: *When using fields from two or more tables, the tables must have a prior relationship.*

⑥ Click **Next**.

⑦ Select an option for the amount of detail you want for the query report (○ changes to ◉).

⑧ Click **Next**.

What types of relationships exist between tables?

You can use relationships between tables to bring related information together for analysis. If you create your database using a template, Access has already defined some table relationships for you. For example, one table might include customer names and addresses, while another table might contain orders placed by your customers. By defining a relationship between the two tables, you can create queries to find all customers ordering the same product. You can click **Tools** and then **Relationships** to define relationships between your tables.

Are there other types of queries I can create?

Yes. When you click the **Queries** object in the database window and then click 🔳, the New Query dialog box appears and you can choose from several other query types to create a query. For example, the Crosstab Query Wizard helps you to group related information for a summary.

Perform a Simple Query *(continued)*

During the process of creating a new query, the wizard asks you to give the query a unique name. All queries you create are saved in the Queries objects in the database window. You can open a query in Design view to make changes to the fields used in the query.

Perform a Simple Query *(continued)*

9 Type a name for the query.

● Select this option to open the query after finishing the wizard (○ changes to ⊙).

● If you select this option, an additional wizard step asks you to select the values for the summary.

10 Click **Finish**.

A query datasheet appears listing the fields.

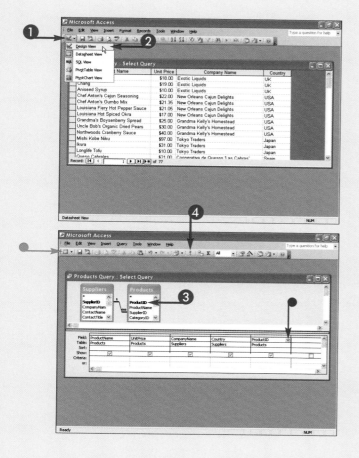

EDIT A QUERY

1 With the query open, click the **View** ▾.

2 Click **Design View**.

Access displays the query in Design view.

Each list box displays fields from a table.

3 Double-click a field to add it to the query.

● You can specify criteria here.

4 To run the query after making any edits, click the **Run Query** button (❗).

● To return to the datasheet again, click the **View** ▾ and then click **Datasheet view**.

How do I add another table to my query?

Switch to Design view, click the **Query** menu, and then click **Show Table**. This opens the Show Table dialog box where you can add another table to the query and choose from among the available fields to customize the query.

Can I sort or filter my query?

Yes. You can use the sorting and filtering features to further define your query results. To learn how to sort data, see the section "Sort Records," earlier in this chapter. To learn how to apply a filter, see the section "Filter Records," also earlier in this chapter.

Create a
Report

You can use the Report tool to turn any table, form, or query into a professional and polished report document. The Report Wizard walks you through all the steps necessary to turn your database data into an easy-to-read printout.

Create a Report

① Click the **Reports** object in the database window.

② Double-click the **Create report by using wizard** option.

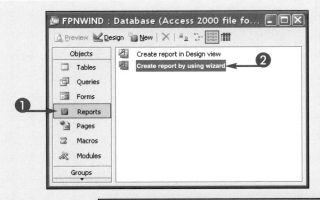

The Report Wizard appears.

③ Click the **Tables/Queries** ☑.

④ Click a table containing the fields on which you want to base the report.

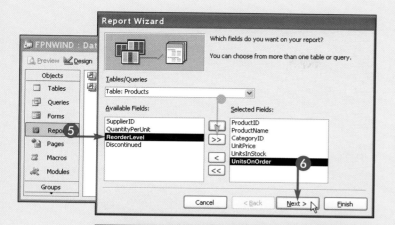

5. Double-click each field you want to include in the report.

● To add all the sample fields, click the **Add All** button (>>).

6. Click **Next**.

The next wizard screen asks how you want to group related data in the report.

7. Double-click the field you want to use to group the data.

● A sample of the grouping appears here.

8. Click **Next**.

SIMPLIFY IT

Can I choose different fields from different tables to create a report?
Yes. First choose fields from one table, and then follow Steps **3** and **4** in this section to select another table containing fields you want to use in the report. You can choose fields from more than one table or query for your Access report.

How do I remove a field I do not want in the report?
With the first Report Wizard screen open, you can click a field you previously placed in the Selected Fields list box and click the **Subtract** button (<) to remove the field. To remove all the fields and start over again with the list, click the **Subtract All** button (<<).

continued

Create a
Report *(continued)*

As the Report Wizard walks you through the steps for building a report, you are asked to decide upon a sort order and a layout for the report's appearance. After you create the report, you can print it.

Create a Report (continued)

The next wizard screen asks you how you want to set the sort order.

9 Click the first ☑ and click a sort field.

You can add more sort fields as needed.

10 Click **Next**.

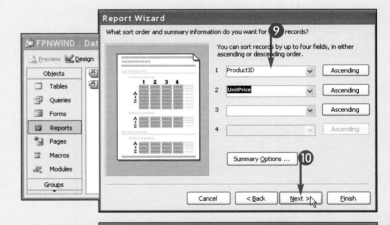

The next wizard screen asks you to select a layout for the report.

11 Select a layout option (○ changes to ◉).

● You can set the page orientation for a report using these options.

12 Click **Next**.

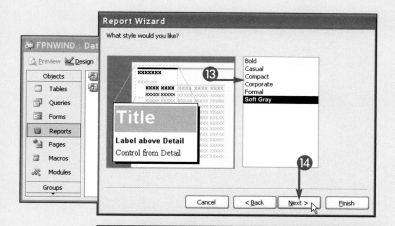

⑬ Click a style for the report.

⑭ Click **Next**.

⑮ Type a name for the report.

⑯ Click **Finish**.

Access creates the report and displays the report in Print Preview mode.

How do I print a report?

To print a report from Print Preview, click the **Print** button (🗐) on the toolbar. You can also click the **File** menu and then click **Print** to open the Print dialog box and assign any printing options before printing the report.

How can I customize a report in Access?

You can further customize a report using Design view. You can change the formatting of fields, move fields around, and more. To learn more about switching to Design view, see Chapter 19.

Part VI

Outlook

Outlook is a personal information manager for the computer desktop. You can use Outlook to manage your calendar, keep track of a contacts list, organize lists of things to do, create notes, and communicate with the online community. You can perform a wide variety of everyday tasks from the Outlook window, including sending and receiving e-mail messages, scheduling appointments, tracking a project's status, and organizing an address book of contacts.

In this part, you learn how to put Outlook to work for you using each of the major components to manage everyday tasks.

View Outlook Components

Microsoft Outlook features five main components: Mail, Calendar, Contacts, Tasks, and Notes. You can switch between components depending on the task you want to perform.

You can use Outlook to manage everyday tasks and e-mail correspondence. Outlook works much like a personal organizer, containing components for certain tasks, such as a Mail folder for e-mail tasks and a Calendar folder for scheduling appointments.

View Outlook Components

USE THE NAVIGATION PANE

1 Click the button in the Navigation pane for the component you want to open.

Note: *If the Navigation pane is not displayed, you can press* **Alt** + **F1** *to quickly view the pane again.*

● Outlook displays the component.

In this example, the Tasks component is displayed.

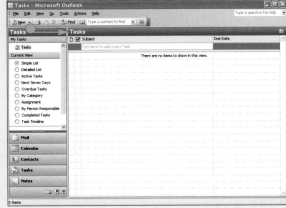

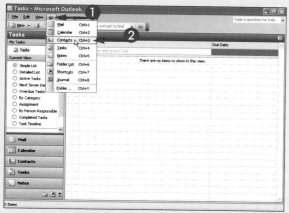

USE THE GO MENU

① Click **Go**.

② Click an Outlook component.

● Outlook displays the component.

In this example, the Contacts component is displayed.

Depending on the component, Outlook offers different ways to view the information using the View menu or View buttons on the toolbar.

Can I customize which component opens by default when I start Outlook?

By default, Outlook opens the Inbox for your Mail tasks as soon as you start the program. To start with another component instead, follow these steps:

① Click **Tools**.

② Click **Options**.

③ In the Options dialog box, click the **Other** tab and then **Advanced Options**.

④ In the Advanced Options dialog box, click **Browse**.

⑤ In the Select Folder dialog box, click the component you want to set as the default component.

⑥ Click **OK**.

⑦ Click **OK** to exit the remaining open dialog boxes and apply the new setting.

Schedule an Appointment

You can use Outlook's Calendar component to keep track of your schedule. You can add notations on the calendar to remind yourself of appointments and other important events. When adding new appointments to the Calendar, you fill out appointment details, such as the name of the person you are meeting with, and the start and end times of the appointment.

Schedule an Appointment

① Open the Calendar component.

Note: See the previous section, "View Outlook Components," to learn how to open a component.

② Click the date for which you want to set an appointment.

③ Double-click the time slot for the appointment you want to set.

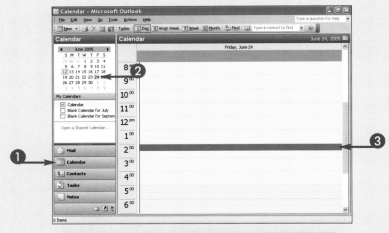

Outlook opens the Appointment window.

④ Type a subject for the appointment.

Outlook adds the subject to the window's title.

⑤ Type a location for the appointment.

⑥ Click the **End time** ☑ and set an end time for the appointment.

● If you did not select the correct time slot in Step **3**, you can click the **Start time** ☑ and click a start time.

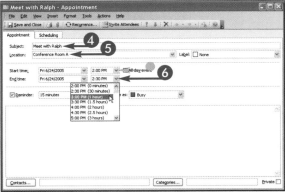

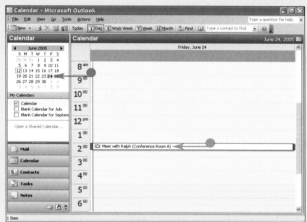

- To add a reminder about the appointment, leave the **Reminder** option selected (☑), and then click ☑ to set a reminder option.

- You can type any notes about the appointment here.

⑦ Click the **Save and Close** button (🖫).

- Outlook displays the appointment in the Calendar.

  To view the appointment details again or make changes, double-click the appointment to reopen the Appointment window.

- Any days on which you have an appointment scheduled appear bold in the Date Navigator.

How do I receive a reminder before an appointment?
If you add the Reminder option to an appointment, Outlook displays a prompt box at the designated time to remind you about the appointment. The Outlook program window must be running for the reminder audio beep to sound and the reminder prompt box to appear. You can leave Outlook open, but keep the program window minimized on your taskbar to work on other programs.

What does the Label option do?
You can click the **Label** ☑ and assign color labels to the appointment. You can use labels to help organize appointments in your calendar. For example, you might label all work-related appointments as Business and all nonwork appointments as Personal.

Schedule a Recurring Appointment

If your schedule includes many of the same appointments over and over again, such as weekly sales or department meetings, you can set the appointment as a recurring appointment. Outlook adds the appointment to each week or month as you require.

You can use this same technique to set recurring meetings and events on your Outlook Calendar.

Schedule a Recurring Appointment

① Open the Calendar component and the Appointment window for the appointment you want to schedule in a recurring pattern.

Note: See the previous section, "Schedule an Appointment," to learn how to open an Appointment window.

② Click the **Recurrence** button (⟳).

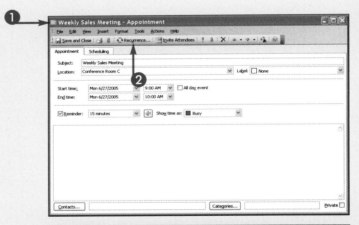

Outlook displays the Appointment Recurrence dialog box.

③ Select the Recurrence pattern you want to set.

● You can also set a range of the recurrence if the appointments continue only for a set number of weeks or months.

④ Click **OK**.

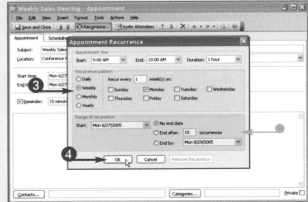

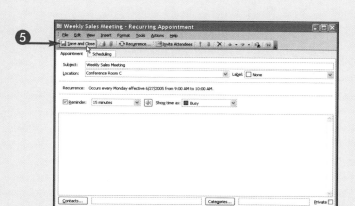

⑤ Click the **Save and Close** button (🖫).

Outlook displays the appointment in the Calendar.

● Recurring appointments show a recurrence icon next to the appointment on the Calendar.

How do I delete an appointment from the Calendar?
To remove an appointment, right-click the appointment on the Calendar and click **Delete**. You can also press the Delete key. Outlook immediately deletes the appointment from your schedule.

Is there an easy way to set an appointment with one of my contacts?
Yes. You can quickly create an appointment with anyone in your Contacts list. In the Contacts component, right-click over the contact you want to schedule an appointment with and click **New Appointment with Contact**. This opens the Appointment window and you can set up details concerning the appointment, such as the date and time.

Schedule an Event

> If you need to track an activity that lasts the entire day or spans several days, such as an anniversary or a conference, you can schedule the date as an event. Events appear as banners at the top of the scheduled date.

Schedule an Event

① Click **Actions**.

② Click **New All Day Event**.

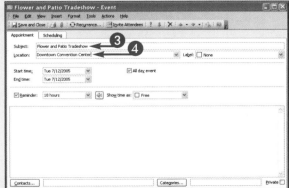

Outlook displays the Event window, which looks the same as the Appointment window.

③ Type a subject for the event.

Outlook adds the subject to the window's title.

④ Type a location for the event, if applicable.

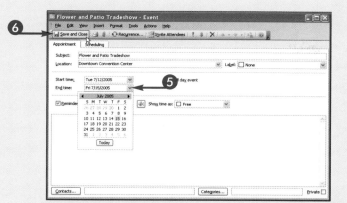

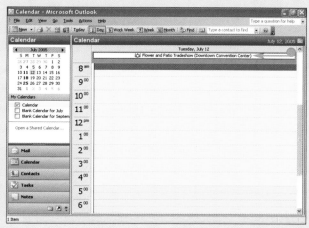

⑤ Set a start time and end time for the event.

You can click ⊡ to display a pop-up calendar of dates.

You can also add notes about the event, add a reminder, or assign a label to the event.

⑥ Click ⊡.

● Outlook displays the event as a banner in the Calendar for the date of the event.

To edit an event, double-click the event banner.

How do I edit a reminder?
To change the details about a reminder you add to any appointment or event, reopen the Appointment window for the appointment or event, click the **Reminder** ⊡ and change the setting. To remove the reminder entirely, deselect the **Reminder** option (☑ changes to ☐). To change the sound associated with the reminder, click the **Reminder Sound** button (⧉) and use the **Browse** button to assign another sound file.

How do I add a holiday to my calendar?
Holidays do not appear by default in Outlook. You can add a holiday by clicking **Tools**, **Options**, and then clicking the **Calendar Options** button in the **Preferences** tab. This opens the Calendar Options dialog box. Click the **Add Holidays** button and click the country whose holidays you want to add to the calendar.

Plan a Meeting

If you use Outlook on a Microsoft Exchange Server network, you can use the Plan a Meeting feature to schedule meetings with other users. You can send e-mail messages inviting attendees, track responses, and designate resources, such as conference rooms or equipment.

Plan a Meeting

① Click **Actions**.

② Click **Plan a Meeting**.

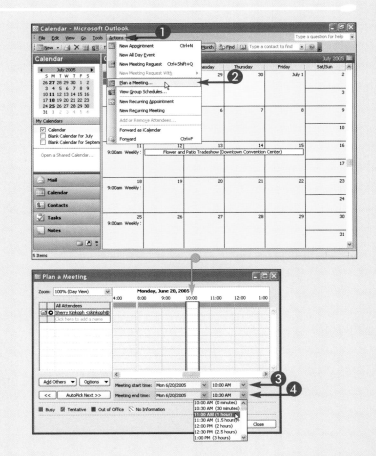

Outlook displays the Plan a Meeting window.

③ Click ⬇ and set a meeting start date and time.

● You can also click the time in the Meeting pane.

④ Click ⬇ and set a meeting end time.

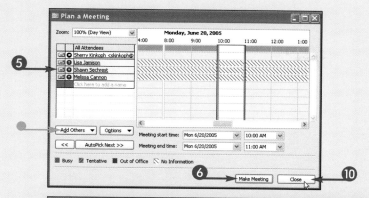

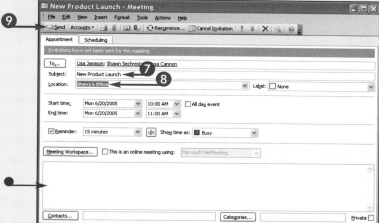

5 Type the names of the attendees.

When you press Tab after typing the first attendee name, Outlook automatically checks for the person's name in your Contacts list.

● You can also click **Add Others** and select attendee names.

6 Click **Make Meeting**.

7 Type a subject for the event.

Outlook adds the subject to the window's title.

8 Type a location for the event, if applicable.

● You can type a message to the attendees here.

9 Click the **Send** button (🖃).

Outlook e-mails an invitation to each attendee.

Note: *See Chapter 22 to learn more about e-mailing with Outlook.*

10 Click **Close** to close the Plan a Meeting window.

How do I know if people respond to my meeting invitation?
To see who is attending the meeting you must open the Plan a Meeting window and click the **Scheduling** tab. To open the window, double-click the meeting appointment in your calendar. To respond to an invitation yourself, simply click the appropriate button at the top of the e-mail message in Outlook's Mail component.

How do I publish my calendar so others can see it on the network?
To publish your calendar, click **Tools**, **Options**, and then **Calendar Options** on the **Preferences** tab. Click **Free/Busy Options** to open the Free/Busy Options dialog box and turn on any publishing features you want to set.

Create a New Contact

You can use the Contacts component to keep a list of people you contact the most, such as family, coworkers, or clients. You can keep track of information such as addresses, e-mail addresses, phone numbers, and more.

Create a New Contact

① Open the Contacts component.

Note: See the section "View Outlook Components," earlier in this chapter, to learn how to open a component.

② Click the **New** button (📇).

Outlook displays the Contact window.

③ Fill in the contact's information on the General tab.

You can press **Tab** to move from field to field.

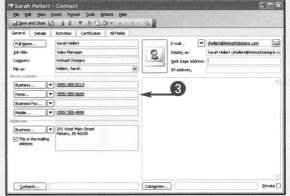

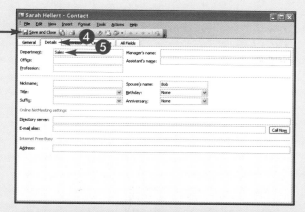

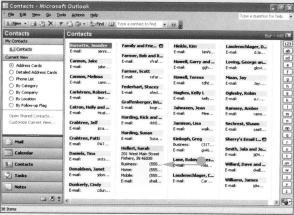

4 Click the **Details** tab.

5 Fill in additional information about the contact, as needed.

6 Click 🖫 .

● Outlook saves the information and displays the contact in the Contacts list.

To edit contact details, double-click the contact to reopen the Contact window.

Can I import a list of contacts from another program?
Yes. Click the **File** menu and then **Import and Export** to open the Import and Export Wizard. The wizard walks you through the steps for importing a list of contacts from other sources, including Outlook Express.

How do I send an e-mail to a contact?
You can right-click over the contact name and click **New Message to Contact**. This opens the Message window where you can type a message to the contact. To learn more about e-mailing with Outlook, see Chapter 22.

Create a New Task

You can use Outlook's Task component to keep track of things you need to do, such as a daily list of activities or project steps you need to complete. You might find the Task component useful in an office environment for tracking items you must fulfill for a work assignment, or for items other people must complete to help you finish an important project.

Create a New Task

① Open the Tasks component.

Note: See the section "View Outlook Components," earlier in this chapter, to learn how to open a component.

② Click the **New** button (🗒).

Outlook displays the Task window.

③ Type a subject for the appointment.

Outlook adds the subject to the window's title.

④ Type a due date for the task.

⑤ Click the **Status** ▾ and click a progress option.

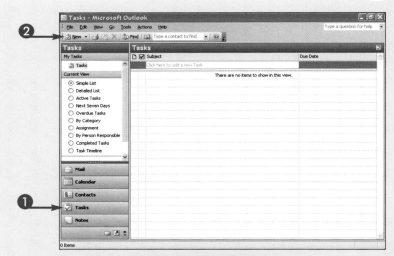

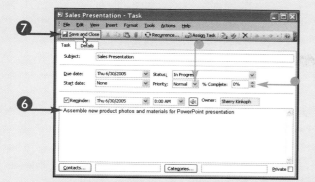

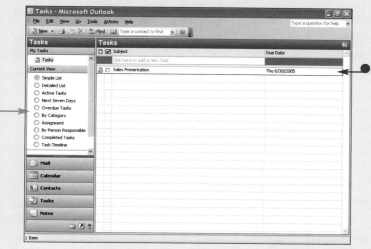

6 Type a note or details about the task here.

● You can set a priority level for the task using this option.

● To set a completion amount, click here.

7 Click 🖫.

● Outlook displays the task in the Tasks list.

To view the task details again or make changes, double-click the task to reopen the Task window.

● To change your view of tasks in the Tasks list, select a view option (○ changes to ◉).

How do I mark a task as completed?

You can click the check box next to the task name to mark the task as complete. Completed tasks appear with a strikethrough on the Tasks list. To remove a task completely from the list, right-click the task and click **Delete**.

Can I turn a task into an e-mail?

Yes. You can assign a task to another user by turning the task into an e-mail message. Right-click the task and click **Assign Task** to open the Task window. You can add an e-mail address and a message concerning the task, and then send the message. To learn more about e-mailing in Outlook, see Chapter 22.

Add a Note

You can use the Notes component to create notes for yourself. Much like an electronic version of yellow sticky notes, Outlook's Notes allow you to jot down ideas and thoughts, or any note text you want to remind yourself of later. You can attach Outlook Notes to other items in Outlook as well as drag them onto the Windows desktop for easy viewing.

Add a Note

1 Open the Notes component.

Note: *See the section "View Outlook Components," earlier in this chapter, to learn how to open a component.*

2 Click the **New** button ().

Outlook displays a yellow note.

3 Type your note text.

4 When you finish, click the **Close** button (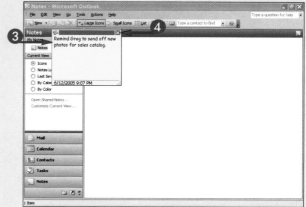).

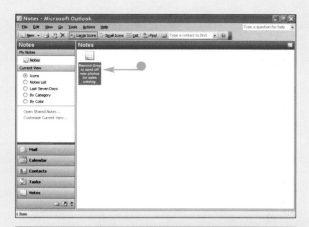

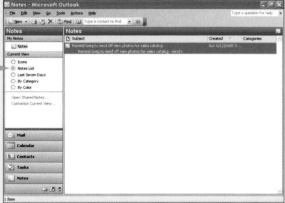

● Outlook adds the note to the Notes list.

To view the note again or make changes, double-click the note to reopen the note window.

● To change your view of notes in the Notes list, select a view option (○ changes to ◉).

In this example, the Notes List view appears.

Can I forward the note to another user?
Yes. You can turn any note into an instant e-mail attachment. Simply right-click the note in the Notes list, and then click **Forward** to open an e-mail Message window. You can address the note and add any additional message text. To learn more about e-mailing with Outlook, see Chapter 22.

How do I delete notes I no longer want?
Right-click over the note in the Notes list and click **Delete** or press Delete . Outlook immediately deletes the note. To delete multiple notes at the same time, press and hold the Ctrl key while clicking the notes and then press Delete .

Organize Outlook Items

You can store your Outlook items, whether they are messages, tasks, or notes, in folders. By default, Outlook creates a set of folders for you to use when you install the program, including e-mail folders for managing incoming, outgoing, and deleted messages. You can use the Folders list to move items from one folder to another and create new folders in which to store Outlook items.

Organize Outlook Items

VIEW THE FOLDER LIST

1. Click **Go**.
2. Click **Folder List**.

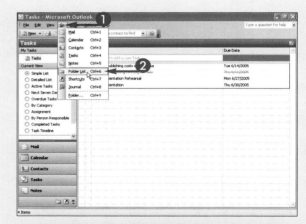

Outlook displays the Folder List pane.

3. Click the folder whose contents you want to view.

- Outlook displays the folder's contents.

To move an item to another folder, click and drag the item and drop it on the folder name.

CREATE A NEW FOLDER

① Click **File**.

② Click **New**.

③ Click **Folder**.

The Create New Folder dialog box appears.

④ Type a name for the new folder.

⑤ Click the **Folder contains** ▾ and choose an item type.

⑥ Click the parent folder in which to store the new folder.

⑦ Click **OK**.

Outlook creates the new folder.

How do I delete an item from a folder?
Select the item you want to delete, and then click the **Delete** button (⊠) or press Delete . The deleted items are immediately placed in the Deleted Items folder. To empty the folder, click **Tools** and then click **Empty "Deleted Items" Folder**. To delete an entire folder and all of its items, click the folder name in the Folder list and press Delete .

Can I create subfolders for my work items and home items?
Yes. You can create as many folders as you need for each type of Outlook item or a variety of items. For example, you might create a subfolder in your Inbox folder to place all the corporate correspondence you send and receive, or create a folder in the Tasks folder for a special project.

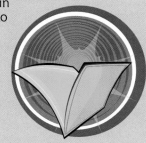

Compose and Send a Message

You can use Outlook to create and send e-mail messages. When you compose a message, you can designate the e-mail address of the person or persons you are sending it to, and type your message text. You can also give the message a subject title to help the recipients know what the message is about.

You need to log on to your Internet connection in order to send a message. If you compose a message while offline, the message is stored in Outlook's Outbox folder until it is sent.

Compose and Send a Message

① Click the **Mail** button (⬚) in the Navigation pane.

② Click the **New** button (⬚).

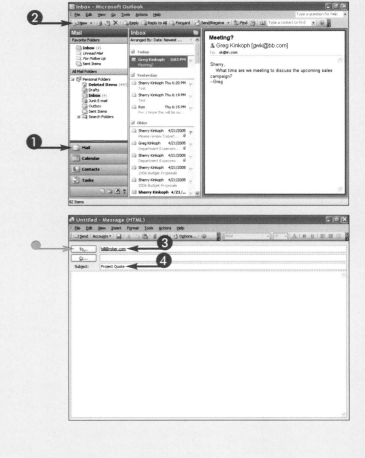

Outlook opens an untitled message window.

③ Type the recipient's e-mail address.

● If the e-mail address is already in your Address Book, click **To** and select the recipient's name.

If you enter more than one e-mail address, separate each with a semicolon (;) and a space.

④ Type a subject title for the message.

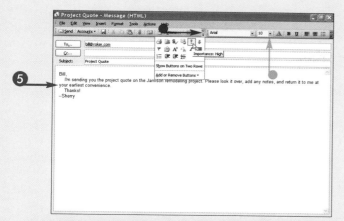

⑤ Type the message text.

● You can use Outlook's formatting buttons to control the appearance of your message text.

● To set a priority level for the message, click here and click **Importance: High** (🛈) or **Importance: Low** (⬇).

Note: By default, the message priority level is considered Normal.

⑥ Click the **Send** button (📧).

Outlook sends the e-mail message.

Note: You must be logged on to your Internet account in order to send the message.

Where can I find messages I previously sent?
You can click the **Sent Items** folder to view a list of e-mail messages you previously sent. The Sent Items folder is one of the main Mail folders found in Outlook. To view a message from the Sent Items list, simply double-click the message to open it in a new window.

How do I carbon copy someone in my message?
You can use the Cc field to copy the message to another recipient besides the main recipient. You can click **Cc** to open the Address Book and select the person's name. To send a copy of the message without revealing the Cc recipient's name, use the blind carbon copy feature. Click **Cc**, click the person's name, and then click **Bcc**.

Read an Incoming Message

You need to log on to your Internet connection in order to receive e-mail messages.

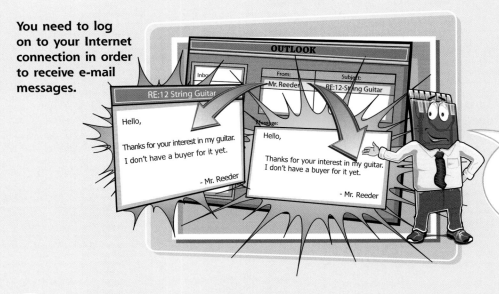

When you open Outlook's Mail feature, you can retrieve and view incoming e-mail messages. You can view a message in a separate message window or in the Reading pane.

Read an Incoming Message

① Click the **Mail** button (▣) in the Navigation pane.

② Click the **Send/Receive** button (▣).

Outlook accesses your e-mail account and downloads any waiting messages.

Note: *You must be connected to your Internet account to download messages.*

● If the Inbox is not in view, click the **Inbox** folder.

③ Click the message you want to view.

● The message appears in the Reading pane.

You can also double-click the message to open it.

You can now read and respond to the message.

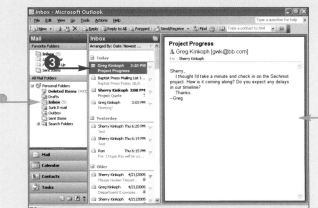

Turn Off the Reading Pane

In today's world of spam e-mails, you may prefer not to leave the Outlook Reading pane on when working with incoming and outgoing messages. You can turn off Outlook's Reading pane to prevent viewing of unsolicited e-mails and free up on-screen workspace to view more of your message lists.

Turn Off the Reading Pane

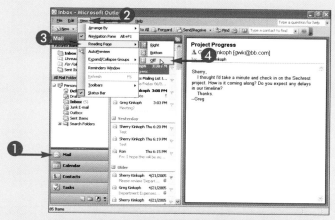

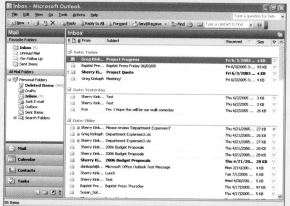

① Click the **Mail** button (📧) in the Navigation pane.

② Click **View**.

③ Click **Reading Pane**.

④ Click **Off**.

Outlook closes the Reading pane.

To turn the pane on again, simply repeat these steps and select the **Right** or **Bottom** options instead.

Reply to or Forward a Message

You can reply to an e-mail message by sending a return message to the original sender. You can also forward the message to another recipient.

You need to log on to your Internet connection in order to send e-mail messages.

Reply to or Forward a Message

REPLY TO A MESSAGE

① Open the message you want to answer.

Note: See the section "Read an Incoming Message," earlier in this chapter, to learn how to view an e-mail message.

② Click the **Reply** button (📧) to reply to the original sender.

To reply to everyone who received the original message, click the **Reply to All** button (📧).

③ Type any return message you want to add to the e-mail.

④ Click 📧.

Outlook sends the e-mail message.

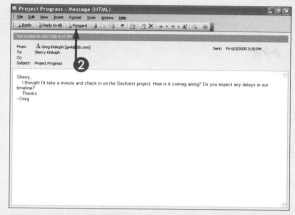

FORWARD A MESSAGE

① Open the message you want to forward.

Note: See the section "Read an Incoming Message," earlier in this chapter to learn how to view an e-mail message.

② Click the **Forward** button (🖼️).

③ Type any message you want to add to the e-mail.

④ Click 🖼️.

Outlook forwards the e-mail message.

How do I get rid of the original message in my reply?

By default, Outlook retains the original message when you click the **Reply** or **Reply to All** commands. To turn off the feature, follow these steps:

① Click **Tools**.

② Click **Options**.

The Options dialog box appears.

③ In the **Preferences** tab, click **E-mail Options**.

④ Click the **When replying to a message** 🔽 and click **Do not include original message**.

⑤ Click **OK** to exit each dialog box and apply the new setting.

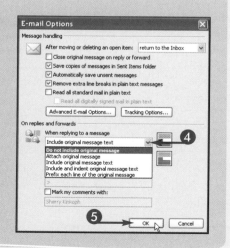

Add a Sender to Your Address Book

You can add the e-mail address of any message you receive to your Outlook Address Book. This makes it easy to send e-mails to the person at a later time.

Add a Sender to Your Address Book

1 Open the e-mail message of the sender you want to save.

Note: See the section "Read an Incoming Message," earlier in this chapter, to learn how to open the message window.

2 Click the icon () next to the sender's name.

3 Click **Add to Outlook Contacts**.

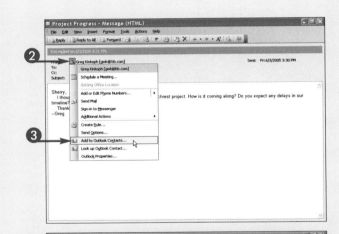

● The Contact window opens with the sender's name and e-mail address already filled in.

4 Click the **Save and Close** button ().

The e-mail address is saved.

Note: The next time you want to send a message to the person, click **To** in the message window and choose the name from the Address Book.

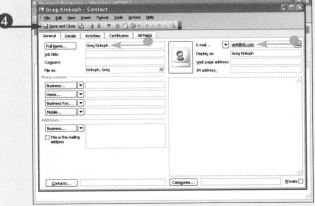

Delete a Message

To keep your computer's storage capacity at its peak, remember to purge the Deleted Items folder regularly.

You can remove messages from your Inbox to eliminate clutter and keep your folder manageable. When you delete a message, Outlook moves it to the Deleted Items folder. You can remove all the deleted Outlook items at your leisure.

Delete a Message

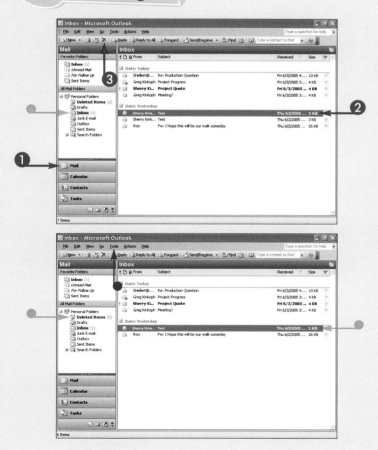

① Click the **Mail** button (⬛) in the Navigation pane.

● If the Inbox is not in view, click the **Inbox** folder.

② Click the message you want to remove from the Inbox.

③ Press **Delete** or click the **Delete** button (✕) on the toolbar.

Outlook deletes the message from the Inbox and adds it to the Deleted Items folder.

● You can click the **Deleted Items** folder to view the message you deleted.

● To empty the Deleted Items folder, click the **Tools** menu and click **Empty "Deleted Items" Folder**.

Attach a File to a Message

You can send files stored on your computer to other e-mail recipients. For example, you might send an Excel file to a work colleague, or send a digital photo of your child's birthday to a relative.

Attach a File to a Message

1 Open and address the message you want to send.

   Note: See the section "Compose and Send a Message," earlier in this chapter, to learn how to create an e-mail message.

2 Click the **Insert File** button (📎).

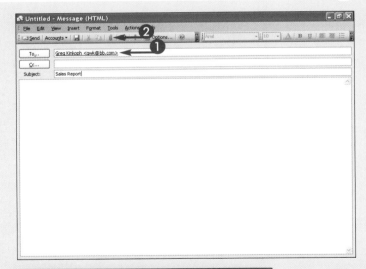

The Insert File dialog box appears.

3 Navigate to the folder or drive containing the file you want to send.

4 Click the filename.

5 Click **Insert**.

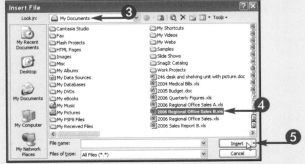

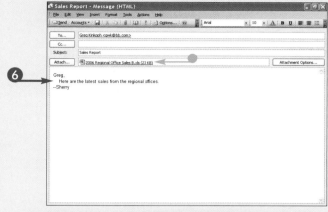

Outlook adds the file attachment to the message and displays the **Attach** button and field.

● The Attach field includes the filename and the file size.

⑥ Type any message text you want to send.

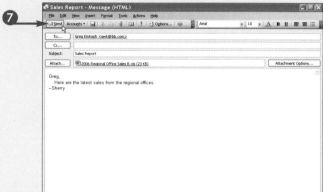

⑦ Click .

Outlook sends the e-mail message and attachment.

Note: Some Internet providers and e-mail systems are not set up to handle large file attachments. Check with the recipient to see if his system can receive the attachment size you want to send.

How do I open an attachment someone sends me?
You can double-click the attachment filename to open the item. When you do, a prompt box appears warning you about opening attachments and presenting options to open or save the file. If you click **Open**, the associated program opens and displays the file. Never open a file unless you trust the source who sent it. If you click **Save**, you can save the attachment to a folder or drive on your computer.

Why does Outlook block some file attachments?
Some attachments, such as those ending with the extensions .bat, .exe, .vbs, and .js, are associated with viruses, and Outlook automatically blocks the files. Always use a good virus protection program to help keep your computer safe from unwanted viruses.

Screen Junk
E-mail

Junk e-mail, also called spam, is overabundant on the Internet and often finds its way onto your computer. You can safeguard against wasting time viewing unsolicited messages by setting up Outlook's Junk E-mail feature. You can target e-mail from specific Web domains and make sure it gets deposited into the Outlook Junk E-mail folder.

Screen Junk E-mail

VIEW JUNK E-MAIL OPTIONS

① Click **Actions**.

② Click **Junk E-mail**.

③ Click **Junk E-mail Options**.

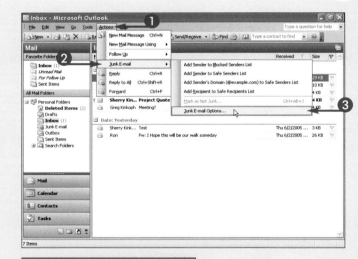

The Junk E-mail Options dialog box appears.

You can use the various tabs to view junk e-mail settings, blocked domains, and safe senders.

● You can select one of these options to control the level of junk e-mail filtering Outlook applies (○ changes to ◉).

● You can select this option to permanently remove any junk e-mail you receive (☐ changes to ☑).

④ Click **OK**.

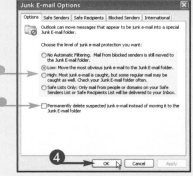

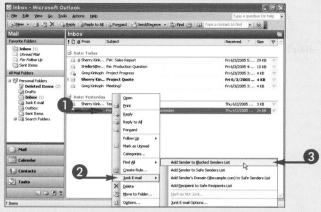

DESIGNATE A MESSAGE AS JUNK

1 Right-click over the message.

2 Click **Junk E-mail**.

3 Click **Add Sender to Blocked Senders List**.

A prompt box appears.

4 Click **OK**.

Outlook adds the sender's e-mail address to the list of filtered domain names and moves the message to the Junk E-mail folder.

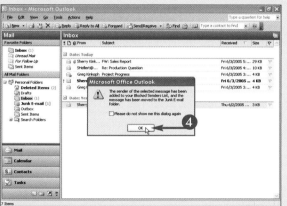

How can I restore a junk e-mail to my safe list?

If you accidentally send a message to the Junk E-mail folder, you can correct the action and remove it from the filter. First, click the Junk E-mail folder. Right-click the message you want to restore. From the menu that appears, click **Junk E-mail** and then **Mark as Not Junk**. Outlook restores the message and removes it from the filter list.

How do I keep my mailbox manageable?

You can use the Mailbox Cleanup feature to tidy up your Outlook mailbox, delete old e-mail messages, archive messages, and more. To use the feature, click the **Tools** menu and then click **Mailbox Cleanup**. The Mailbox Cleanup dialog box appears, offering options for moving, deleting, or archiving messages.

Create a Message Rule

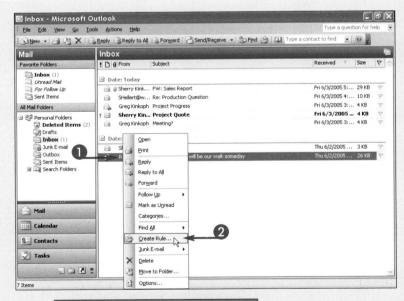

You can use rules to help control messages that meet a specific set of conditions, such as placing messages from a certain sender or domain directly into a folder of your choosing as soon as the message arrives in the Inbox. Rules are also useful in filtering out unwanted spam messages.

Create a Message Rule

① Right-click on the message on which you want to base a rule.

② Click **Create Rule**.

The Create Rule dialog box appears.

③ Select the conditions you want to apply (☐ changes to ☑).

④ Select the **Move e-mail to folder** option (☐ changes to ☑).

The Rules and Alerts dialog box appears.

5 Click the folder where you want the messages stored.

6 Click **OK**.

7 Click **OK**.

The next time you receive a message matching the criteria you specified, Outlook places the message directly into the folder you selected.

How can I add more criteria to a message rule?
You can click **Advanced Options** in the Create Rule dialog box to display the Rules Wizard and view additional options you can set concerning the message. The Rules Wizard includes several sets of criteria you can set, such as exceptions to the rule, actions, and even a dialog box for naming the rule. Click the **Next** and **Back** buttons to view all the available criteria you can set.

How do I remove a rule I no longer want?
To delete a rule from Outlook's list, click the **Tools** menu and click **Rules and Alerts** to open the Rules and Alerts dialog box. Click the rule you want to delete and click **Delete**. If you have more than one e-mail account, you must first select the correct Inbox for the account containing the rule.

Part VII

Publisher

Publisher is a desktop publishing program you can use to design and produce a variety of publications. You can create anything from a simple business card to a complex brochure. Publisher installs with a large selection of pre-designed publications that you can use as templates to build your own desktop publishing projects. For example, you can use Publisher to create a professional newsletter for your company or a simple flyer advertising your garage sale.

In this part, you learn how build and fine-tune all kinds of publications and tap into Publisher's formatting features to make each document suit your own design and needs.

Create a
Publication

You can use Publisher to create all kinds of publications, such as brochures, flyers, newsletters, letterhead, and more. Publisher installs with a wide variety of publication types, including preset designs that control the layout and formatting of the publication. To start a new publication, simply select a design from the New Publication task pane.

Create a Publication

① Click a publication category from the New Publication pane.

● If the New Publication pane is not displayed, click **View** and then **Task Pane**.

Note: *See Chapter 1 to learn more about working with the Office task panes.*

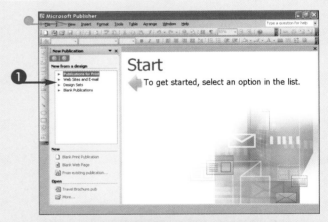

● You can use the scroll bar to scroll through the available publications.

② Click a publication type.

Depending on the publication you pick, additional subcategories may appear.

● Publisher displays samples of the publications here.

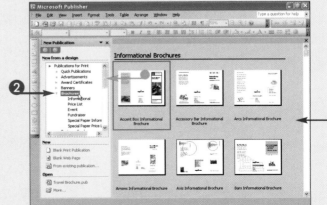

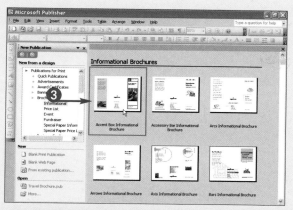

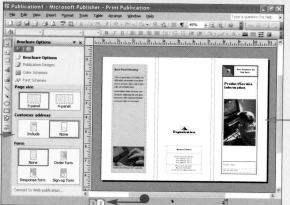

③ Click the publication design you want to create.

● Publisher creates the publication.

● Depending on the publication you choose, any additional options you can set for the document appear in the Options pane.

● If the publication has more than one page, you can click a page number to view a page.

Note: *After creating a publication, you can save it to reuse later. See Chapter 2 to learn how to open and save Office files.*

How do I change the design of my publication?
You can click the **Publication Designs** link in the task pane to view other graphical designs you can apply to the publication. To change the color scheme, click the **Color Schemes** link and select from a range of preset color schemes for the publication. If the task pane is not displayed, click the **View** menu and then click **Task Pane**. To learn more about working with the Office task panes, see Chapter 1.

What types of publications can I make in Publisher?
Publisher groups publications into three main categories: Print Publications, Web Publications, and E-mail Publications. Among the many print publications you can find advertisements, banners, business cards, greeting cards, programs, and resumes, just to list a few. The Web publications category helps you to create Web pages for posting on the Internet. The E-mail Publications category helps you create publications for electronic distribution, such as e-mail newsletters, event announcements, and more. Be sure to browse among all the categories and subcategories to find just the right publication for your needs.

Create a Blank Publication

You can create a blank publication and populate it with your own text boxes and design a layout to suit your project. You might create a blank presentation to maintain total control over all the elements you want to place in a publication design.

Create a Blank Publication

1 Click the **Blank Publications** category from the New Publication task pane.

● If the New Publication task pane is not displayed, click **View** and then **Task Pane**.

Note: *See Chapter 1 to learn more about working with the Office task panes.*

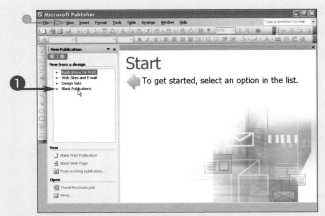

● You can use the scroll bar to scroll through the available publication types.

● Publisher displays samples of the blank publications here.

2 Click a design.

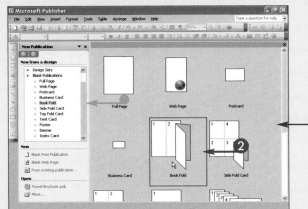

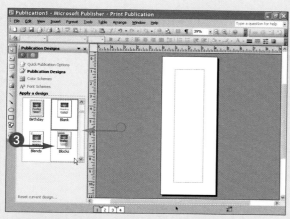

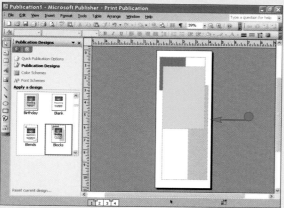

- You can use the scroll bar to scroll through the available designs.

③ Click the design you want to apply.

- Publisher applies the design to the blank publication.

  You can now add your own text boxes and pictures to the document.

  Note: *See the section "Add a New Text Box," later in this chapter, to learn more about adding text to a blank publication.*

What does the Blank Print Publication link do?

If you click the **Blank Print Publication** link at the bottom of the New Publication pane, Publisher immediately creates a full-page blank publication for you. You can then assign a design and add your own text boxes and pictures as needed. If you click the **Blank Web Page** link, you can create a blank Web page instead.

How do I select another publication to create?

You can click ⊙ to move back a task pane and select another blank publication to create. The ⊙ and ⊙ buttons move back and forth between task pane steps, so you can use these buttons to change the publication before you commit to building the document.

Zoom In and Out

You can use the Zoom feature to control the magnification of your publication. By default, Publisher displays your document in a zoomed-out view so you can see all the elements. When you begin working with the publication and add text and formatting, you can zoom in to better see what you are doing.

Zoom In and Out

SPECIFY A MAGNIFICATION

① Click the area of the publication where you want to change the zoom magnification.

When you click an object on the page, Publisher surrounds it with selection handles.

② Click the **Zoom** ⬝.

③ Click a percentage.

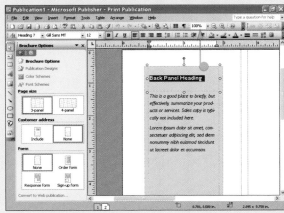

● Publisher changes the magnification setting for your publication.

In this example, the publication is zoomed 100 percent.

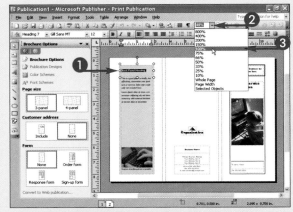

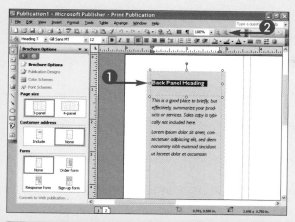

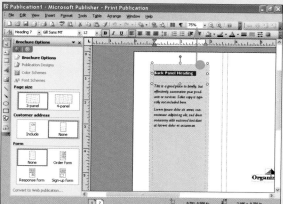

USE ZOOM BUTTONS

1 Click the area of the publication where you want to change the zoom.

2 Click the **Zoom Out** (🔍) or **Zoom In** (🔍) button.

You can click the Zoom buttons multiple times to change the level of magnification.

● Publisher changes the magnification setting for your publication.

In this example, the publication is zoomed out.

How can I free up more workspace on-screen?

You can close the task pane to quickly free up on-screen workspace. Click the pane's ⓧ button, or click **View** and then **Task Pane**. A check mark next to the command indicates the pane is displayed. No check mark indicates the pane is hidden. To view the pane again, click **View** and then **Task Pane**. See Chapter 1 to learn more about working with the Office task panes.

Is there a quicker way to zoom my publication?

You can press F9 on the keyboard to quickly zoom in and out of a publication. To quickly view the entire page in the work area, press Ctrl + Shift + L.

Add
Text

When you create a new publication based on a style and design, Publisher inserts a layout for the text and displays placeholder text in the text boxes, also called *objects* or *frames*. The placeholder text gives you an idea of the text formatting applied by the design and what sort of text you might place in the text box.

Add Text

① Click the text object you want to edit.

You may need to zoom in first to see the text object.

Note: *See the previous section, "Zoom In and Out," to learn how to magnify your view.*

Publisher surrounds the selected object with handles and highlights the placeholder text within.

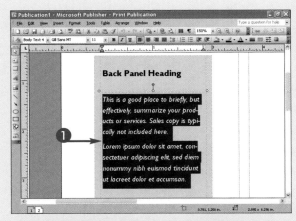

② Type your own text.

Publisher replaces any placeholder text with the new text you type.

Click anywhere outside of the text object to deselect the text box.

Note: *See Chapter 24 to learn how to apply formatting to objects.*

You can continue entering text to build your publication.

To edit the text at any time, click the text box and make your changes.

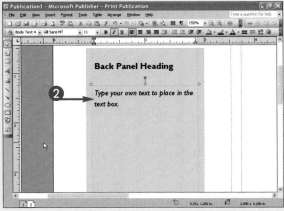

Add a New Text Box

You can add new text boxes to a publication and type your own text. For example, you may need to add a new text box to an empty area in your layout to include additional information, or you may need to add new text boxes to a blank publication.

Add a New Text Box

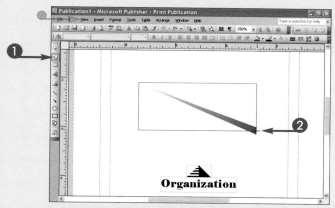

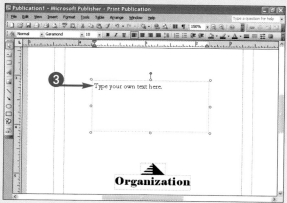

❶ Click the **Text Box** button (⬜) on the Objects toolbar.

● If the Objects toolbar is not displayed, click **View**, **Toolbars**, and then **Objects**.

The ⃝ changes to +.

❷ Click and drag the text box to the size you want to insert.

❸ Type the text you want to insert into the text box.

Click anywhere outside of the text object to deselect the text box.

Note: *See Chapter 24 to apply formatting to objects and to move and resize text box objects.*

Add a Picture to a Publication

You can add digital photographs or other picture files to your Publisher creations. For example, you might add a photo of your company's latest product to a new brochure, or include a snapshot of the new baby on a family e-mail newsletter.

Add a Picture to a Publication

① Click the **Picture Frame** button (🖼) on the Objects toolbar.

● If the Objects toolbar is not displayed, click **View**, **Toolbars**, and then **Objects**.

② Click **Picture from File**.

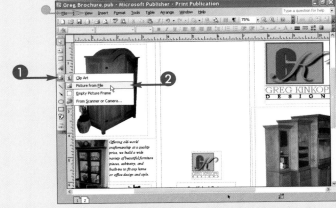

The ⌖ changes to +.

③ Click and drag the frame to the size you want to insert.

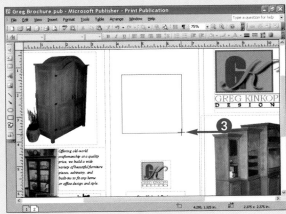

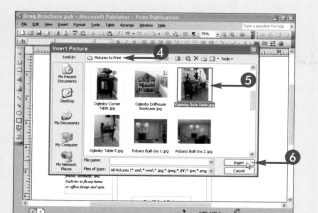

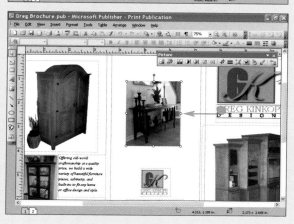

The Insert Picture dialog box appears.

④ Navigate to the folder containing the picture file you want to use.

⑤ Click the filename.

⑥ Click **Insert**.

● Publisher inserts the picture file and displays the Picture toolbar.

You can move and resize the picture, if needed.

Note: See Chapter 24 to learn how to resize objects in Publisher.

How do I fill in an existing picture object?

If the publication design you select already has a picture object in the layout, you can replace the placeholder image with another picture file on your computer. Right-click the placeholder picture and click **Change Picture** and then **From File**. This opens the Insert Picture dialog box and you can select a file from your own computer to use in the publication.

How do I delete a picture object I no longer need?

To remove any object in a publication, whether it is a picture, a text box, or any other object, click the object to select it. Next, press the `Delete` key. Publisher immediately removes the object from the page. You can select more than one object to delete by pressing and holding the `Ctrl` key while clicking each object.

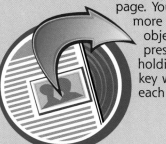

Add Clip Art
to a Publication

You can illustrate a publication with artwork found in Publisher's Clip Art collection. Clip art is simply predrawn artwork. You can search for a specific type of clip art to suit your project needs. The Clip Art collection includes a wide variety of clip art images.

You can also draw your own artwork, such as simple shapes or arrows, using the tools found on the Drawing toolbar. See Chapter 26 to learn more about the Office graphics features.

Add Clip Art to a Publication

① Click the **Picture Frame** button (🖻) on the Objects toolbar.

● If the Objects toolbar is not displayed, click **View**, **Toolbars**, and then **Objects**.

② Click **Clip Art**.

Note: You can also draw your own shapes to use as art. See Chapter 26 to learn how to use the Office drawing tools.

The Clip Art task pane opens.

③ Type a keyword describing the type of clip art you want to insert.

④ Click **Go**.

Note: To learn more about inserting clip art into Office projects, see Chapter 26.

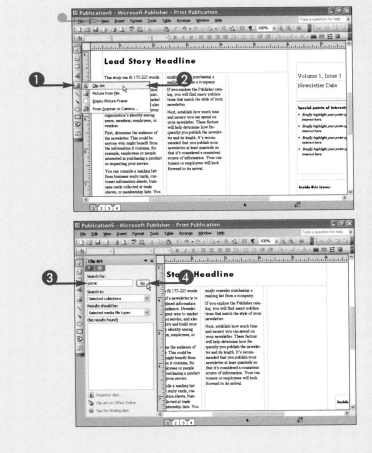

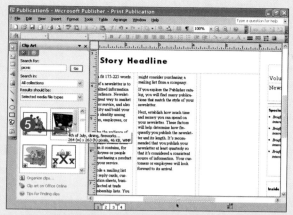

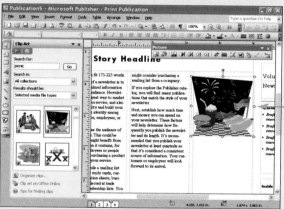

The Clip Art task pane displays any possible matches.

You can use the scroll bar to view the clip art choices.

Note: *If the search did not produce any results, try another keyword.*

5 Click the clip art you want to insert.

● Publisher inserts the clip art and displays the Picture toolbar.

You can move and resize the clip art, if needed.

Note: *See Chapter 24 to learn how to resize objects in Publisher.*

I cannot find a clip art image to use. Is there another place I can look for clip art?

You can look for more clip art images on the Web. For example, you can click the **Clip art on Office Online** link at the bottom of the Clip Art pane to search the Microsoft Web site for clip art to suit your project. You can also find free clip art images on the Internet. Simply conduct a Web search for free clip art to find out what is available for downloading.

How can I add a border to my clip art?

To add a border to your clip art, select the clip art object, click the **Line/Border Style** button (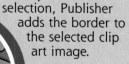) on the Picture toolbar, and then click a style. As soon as you make a selection, Publisher adds the border to the selected clip art image.

Change the Text Font and Size

When you change the text font, you are changing the design of the characters. When you change the font size, you are changing the height of the characters.

You can control the font and size of your publication text. By default, when you assign a publication design, Publisher uses a predefined set of formatting for the text, including a specific font and size.

Change the Text Font and Size

① Click the text object or select the text you want to format.

② Click the **Font** ⊡ on the Formatting toolbar.

③ Click a font.

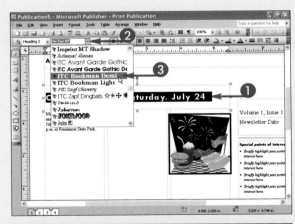

● Publisher applies the new font.

④ Click the **Font Size** ⊡.

⑤ Click a size.

Publisher applies the new size.

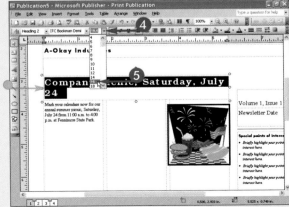

Change the Text Style

You can change the style of your publication text by applying the Bold, Italics, or Underline formatting. For example, you might need to make a paragraph bold to stand out in a newsletter article, or change a flyer heading to italics for emphasis.

Bold, italics, and underlining are considered basic formatting options and applying one or more to your text is one of the quickest ways to change the appearance of your publication.

Change the Text Style

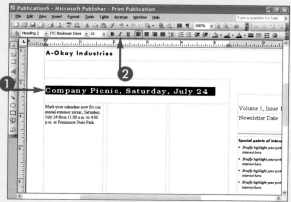

1. Click the text object or select the text you want to format.

2. Click a formatting button on the Formatting toolbar.

   Click **Bold** (**B**) to make text bold.

   Click **Italic** (*I*) to italicize text.

   Click **Underline** (U) to add an underline to the text.

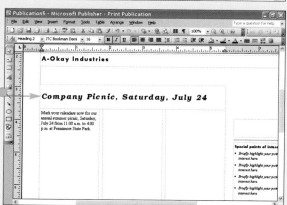

● Publisher applies the new style.

   In this example, both bold and italics are applied to the article title.

Change Text Alignment

You can use Publisher's alignment commands to change the way in which text is positioned horizontally in a text object box. Depending on the publication design you select, alignment is preset to best suit the publication type. You can change the alignment to suit your own needs.

Change Text Alignment

① Click the text object or select the text you want to format.

② Click an alignment button on the Formatting toolbar.

Click the **Align Left** button (▤) to left-align text.

Click the **Center** button (▤) to center text.

Click the **Align Right** button (▤) to right-align text.

Click the **Justify** button (▤) to justify text between the left and right margins of the text object.

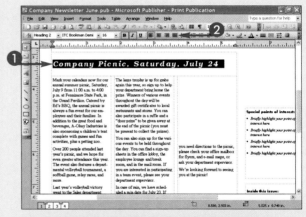

● Publisher applies the new alignment.

In this example, the article title is now centered in the text object.

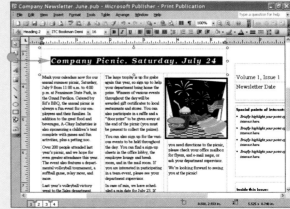

Change
Text Color

> You can add color to your text to enhance the appearance of a publication or add emphasis to your text. When selecting text colors, be careful not to choose a color that makes your text difficult to read.

Change Text Color

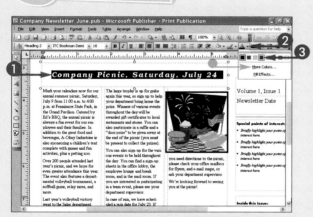

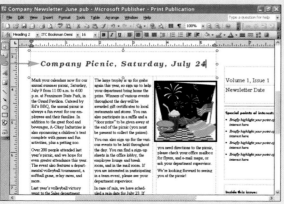

1. Click the text object or select the text you want to format.

2. Click the **Font Color** button (⬛) on the Formatting toolbar.

3. Click a color.

   By default, Publisher displays colors associated with the design.

- To choose another color, click the **More Colors** option.

- Publisher immediately applies the color to the text.

   In this example, red is applied to the text.

Control
Text Wrap

You can control the way in which a text object wraps text around a picture object or any other object in a publication. For example, you may want a column of text to wrap tightly around a clip art object. The text wrapping controls offer you several ways to control how text flows around another object on the page. You can set anything from a tight-fitting text wrap to no text wrapping at all.

Control Text Wrap

① Click the picture object or other object you want to edit.

② Click the **Text Wrapping** button (⊞) on the Picture toolbar.

● If the Picture toolbar is not displayed, click **View**, **Toolbars**, and then **Picture** to open the toolbar.

③ Click a text wrapping option.

● You can also click **Arrange** and then **Text Wrapping** for text wrapping options.

● Publisher immediately applies the text wrapping.

In this example, tight text wrapping is applied.

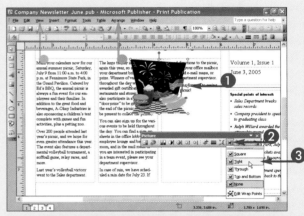

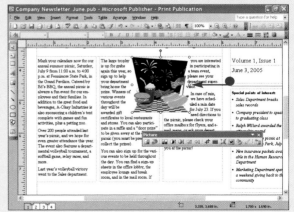

Add a Border

You can add a border to any object in a publication, including text boxes, clip art, and pictures. For example, adding a border around a text box can help set off the text from other elements on the publication page. Borders can also help add emphasis to artwork or give your layout better definition. When assigning borders, you can control the line thickness of the border, called *line style* in Publisher.

Add a Border

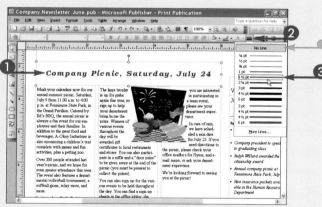

① Click the object you want to edit.

② Click the **Line/Border Style** button (▤) on the Formatting toolbar.

③ Click a line style.

● To remove a border instead, click **No Line**.

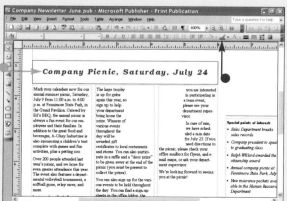

● Publisher immediately applies the border to the object.

In this example, a border is added to a text object.

● You can also change the color of any border or line using the **Line Color** button (▨).

Move a Publication Object

> You can move a publication object to better suit your layout. For example, when building a publication from a blank document, you may need to move text objects or picture objects around to create a better layout.

Move a Publication Object

① Click the object you want to move.

Publisher surrounds the selected object with handles.

② Move ⌖ over the edge of the object until ⌖ changes to ✛.

③ Drag the object to a new location.

● Publisher moves the object.

In this example, a text box is moved.

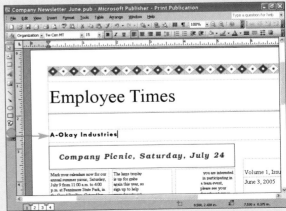

Resize a Publication Object

You can resize a publication object to improve the appearance of the object or the layout. For example, you may need to resize a clip art object to make it bigger, or resize a text object to fit more text into the box.

Resize a Publication Object

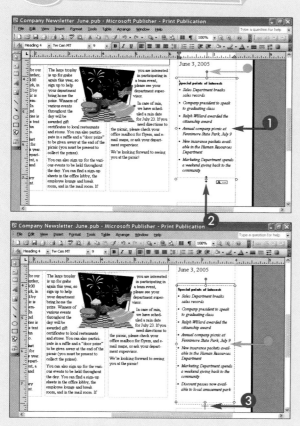

① Click the object you want to resize.

● Publisher surrounds the selected object with handles.

② Move ▷ over the edge of the object until ▷ changes to ↕.

You can also rotate an object by clicking and dragging the green rotation handle at the top of the selected object.

③ Click and drag the handle to resize the object.

● When you release the mouse button, Publisher resizes the object.

In this example, a text box is resized.

Connect
Text Boxes

You can link text boxes to create a relationship between the text in each box. For example, you may want to connect two text boxes so the text flows from one to another, such as two columns in a newsletter. You can also break a text box connection to turn a grouped text box into two separate boxes. You can use the Connect Text Boxes toolbar to navigate and connect text boxes in a publication.

Connect Text Boxes

LINK TEXT BOXES

① Click the first text box you want to connect.

② Click the **Create Text Box Link** button (🖼) on the Connect Text Boxes toolbar.

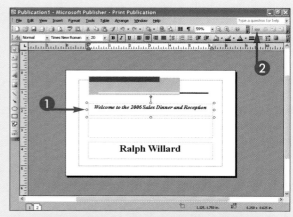

The ⬚ changes to 🖂.

③ Click the text box to which you want to link.

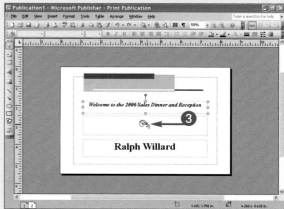

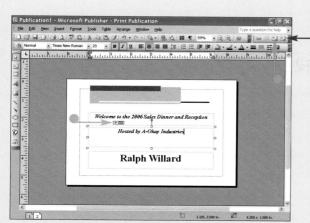

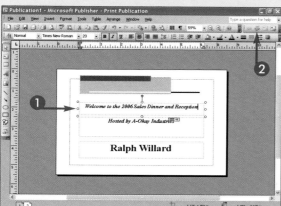

- Publisher links the two boxes and displays a link icon (⬅ ▭).

- You can click the **Previous Text Box** button (▣) to return to the previous text box.

- You can click the **Next Text Box** button (▣) to move to the next text box.

BREAK A LINK

1️⃣ Click the first text box you want to disconnect.

2️⃣ Click the **Break Link** button (▤) on the Connect Text Boxes toolbar.

What happens if my text exceeds the size of my text box?

When you add too much text to a text object, it is called *overflow*. You can correct overflow text by connecting it to an adjacent text box to flow into it using the Connect Text Boxes toolbar. Another option is to click the **Format** menu and click **AutoFit Text** to choose from three text-fitting options to help resolve the situation. You can also enlarge the size of the current text box or reduce the font size of the text to make it fit.

Why does Publisher reduce my font size to fit my text in a box?

With some publication designs, AutoFitting is turned on by default and Publisher tries to fit your text to the space provided. To turn the feature off, right-click the text box and click **Format Text Box** to open the Format Text Box dialog box. Click the **Text Box** tab and select the **Do not fit** option (◯ changes to ◉) to turn the feature off.

Edit the Background Page

When assigning backgrounds, always be mindful of the legibility of your publication text. If you choose a busy background, the publication may be difficult to read.

You can change the background of your publication page by assigning a new background color, gradient effect, or texture. You can apply a background to the current page, or to all the pages in your publication.

Edit the Background Page

① Click **Format**.

② Click **Background**.

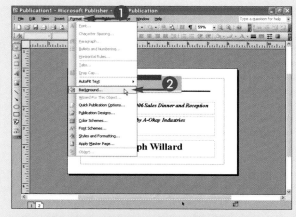

The Background pane opens.

③ Click a background tint.

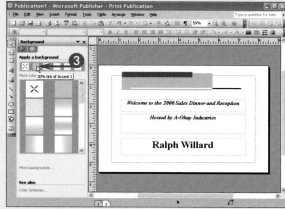

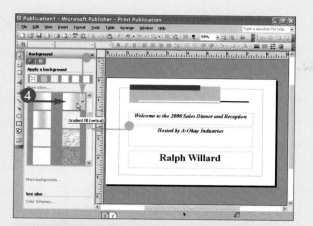

Publisher displays a list of backgrounds in the list box.

● You can use the scroll box to scroll through the list of background selections.

④ Click the background you want to apply.

● To apply the background to all the pages, click the ⊡ and click **Apply to All Pages**.

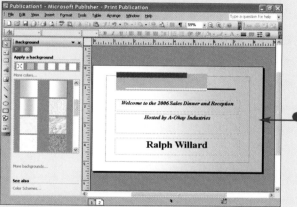

● Publisher assigns the background to the publication.

In this example, a gradient background is added to the page.

How do I remove a background I no longer want?

To remove a background, reopen the Background pane and click the **No Color** option, the selection with a large ✕ in the middle. Publisher immediately removes the background and returns the publication to the original background setting.

Can I assign backgrounds other than what is shown in the Background pane?

Yes. You can assign color backgrounds, turn a picture into a background, and more. To add a color background, click the **More colors** link in the Background pane and choose a color. Click the **More backgrounds** link to open the Fill Effects dialog box where you can assign a different gradient effect, background texture, or turn a picture into a background.

Part VIII

Internet and Graphics

Many of the Office programs share a set of tools for adding graphic elements to a project, such as clip art, pictures, and shapes. The Office applications also share Internet functionality, and offer features for turning Office files into Web pages.

In this part, you learn how to utilize the Office Internet tools to turn files into HTML content, access the Internet, and more. You also learn how to bring visual impact to your Office files by drawing your own shapes, inserting clip art, creating text effects, and adding photographs. Learn how to use the graphic editing tools to crop an image, enhance a picture, and download additional visual resources from the Web.

Create an HTML File

You can turn your Microsoft Office files into HTML documents that you can post on the Web. When you activate the Save As Web page command, you can create a file containing all the necessary HTML coding required to create a Web page that can be read by other Web browsers.

Create an HTML File

① Click **File**.

② Click **Save as Web Page**.

Note: The Save As dialog box only displays the Web page options when you activate the Save as Web Page command.

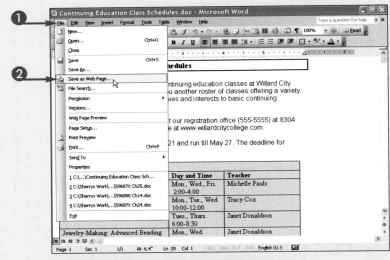

The Save As dialog box appears.

③ Navigate to the folder where you want to save the file.

④ Click **Change Title**.

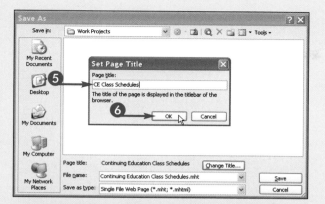

The Set Page Title dialog box appears.

⑤ Type a title.

⑥ Click **OK**.

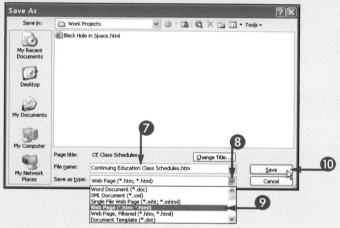

⑦ Type a name for the file.

⑧ Click the **Save as type** ▾.

⑨ Click **Web Page (*.htm; *.html)**.

⑩ Click **Save**.

The file is saved as a Web page.

What does the Publish button do?

If turning an Excel worksheet or PowerPoint slide into a Web page, and you are ready to publish the Web page to a server, you can click **Publish** in the Save As dialog box to open the Publish as Web Page dialog box. You can then use the Publish as Web Page dialog box to add spreadsheet functionality to the page and designate a server path and filename. When you activate the **Publish** command, Microsoft Office publishes the page and opens it in your default browser to display the information.

Can I add interactivity to my Web page?

If you turn a worksheet into a Web page in Excel, you can allow others to manipulate your data on a Web page. Simply select the **Add Interactivity** option in the Save As dialog box (☐ changes to ☑). When this feature is activated, Excel saves the data and adds interactivity to the page. Other users who have Office Web components can view the page, and make changes to the data they are viewing.

Preview a File as a Web Page

Before you turn a file into Web content, you can preview how the data will look as a Web page. For example, you might want to check out how an Excel chart looks next to a range of cells, or view how your data's formatting appears in a browser window.

Preview a File as a Web Page

① Click **File**.

② Click **Web Page Preview**.

Your default Web browser opens and displays the data as a Web page.

③ Click ⊠ to close the browser window.

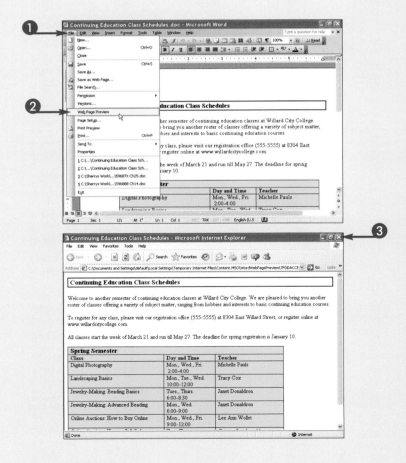

Set Alternative Text for an Object

When preparing a file for display on the Web, you can set alternative text for any picture or shape objects that appear on the sheet. Many users choose to turn off pictures and other graphic objects to save on downloading time when viewing Web pages. By including alternative text, you can accurately describe what the object is so users can decide whether to view the image.

You can set alternative text for any kind of picture, shape, or other drawn object you place in a file.

Set Alternative Text for an Object

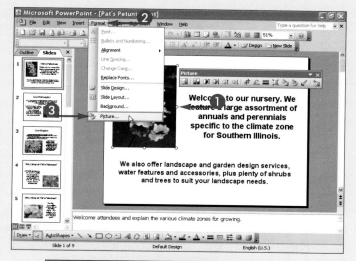

1 Select the object to which you want to add alternative text.

2 Click **Format**.

3 Click the name of the object.

In this example, the Picture command is selected.

The Format dialog box for the object appears.

4 Click the **Web** tab.

5 Type the alternative text for the object.

6 Click **OK**.

The alternative text is assigned.

Note: See the section "Create an HTML File," earlier in this chapter, to learn how to turn a Microsoft Office file into a Web page.

Add a Hyperlink

You can insert hyperlinks into your files that, when clicked, open a Web page. When linking to a Web page, you must designate the URL, which stands for Uniform Resource Locator, the unique address that identifies the Web page.

You can also use hyperlinks to link to other files on your computer. You must designate the address or path of the page you want to link to when adding links to a file.

Add a Hyperlink

① Select the text or image you want to use as a hyperlink.

② Click **Insert**.

③ Click **Hyperlink**.

● You can also click the **Insert Hyperlink** button (🔗) on the Standard toolbar.

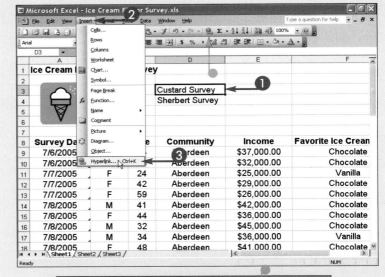

The Insert Hyperlink dialog box appears.

④ Click the type of document to which you want to link.

⑤ Select the page or type the address or URL of the page to which you want to link.

● To browse the Internet to look for the page, you can click this button (🔍) and open your default browser window.

⑥ Click **OK**.

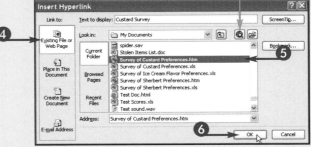

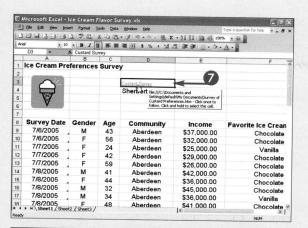

The hyperlink is created.

⑦ To test the link, click the link.

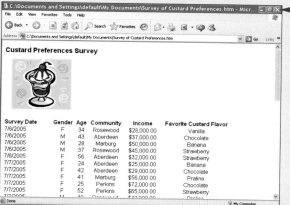

The default Web browser opens and displays the designated page.

● You can click ☒ to close the browser window.

How do I edit a link?

To change a link, such as edit the Web page URL, you can reopen the Edit Hyperlink dialog box and make any necessary changes. Right-click the link and click **Edit Hyperlink** from the shortcut menu. The Edit Hyperlink dialog box appears. You can use the dialog box to change the hyperlink text, address, or the type of page you want to use in the link.

How do I remove a hyperlink?

You can right-click a link and click **Remove Hyperlink** from the shortcut menu. The associated link is removed and the original text or image remains. To remove a hyperlink from the Edit Hyperlink dialog box, you can click **Remove Link**.

Use the Web Toolbar

Using your Internet connection, you can access the Web directly from Word, Excel, PowerPoint, or Access using the Web toolbar features. For example, you can use the Web toolbar to open a URL you type, open your default home page, or display a page from your Favorites folder. When you activate any of the toolbar features, your default Web browser opens to display the actual Web page.

You must be connected to the Internet in order to use the Web toolbar features.

Use the Web Toolbar

① Click **View**.

② Click **Toolbars**.

③ Click **Web**.

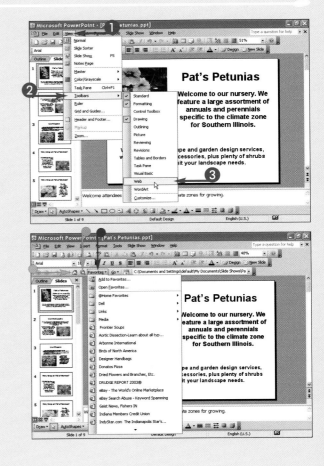

The Web toolbar appears.

● To view your default home page, click the **Start Page** button (🏠).

● To perform a Web search, click the **Search the Web** button (🔍).

● To view your list of bookmarked pages, click **Favorites** and then click the page you want to view.

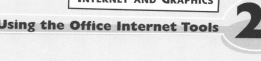

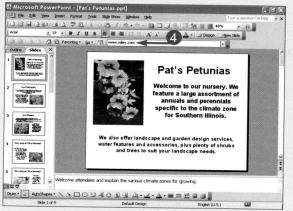

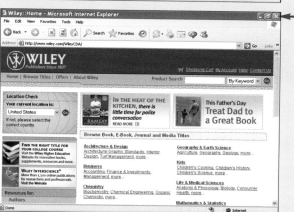

④ To view a specific Web page, type the URL here.

⑤ Press **Enter**.

Your default browser opens and displays the page.

⑥ Click ☒ to close the browser window and return to Excel.

What does the Show Only Web Toolbar button do?
You can click the **Show Only Web Toolbar** button (▣) on the Web toolbar to hide all the other toolbars but keep the Web toolbar in view. To display all the other toolbars again, simply click ▣. The button toggles between hiding and displaying the other toolbars.

Can I customize the Web toolbar?
Yes. You can customize any of the Office toolbars to show just the buttons you use the most. For example, you might want to add buttons to the Web toolbar for previewing and publishing Web pages. To learn more about creating custom toolbars, see Chapter 1.

Draw AutoShapes

You can use the Microsoft Office drawing tools to draw your own shapes and graphics for your documents, worksheets, slides, and publications. One of the fastest ways to add a drawing is to create an AutoShape. You can choose from a library of predrawn shapes in the AutoShapes palette.

AutoShapes are just one of several features you can find on the Drawing toolbar in Word, Excel, and PowerPoint. The toolbar also includes tools for controlling the color and thickness of the lines and shapes you draw. You can also find the AutoShapes tool on the Objects toolbar in Publisher. Graphics tools are not available in Outlook or Access.

Draw AutoShapes

① Click **View**.

② Click **Toolbars**.

③ Click **Drawing**.

Note: See Chapter 1 to learn more about Microsoft Office toolbars.

Note: In Publisher, you can click the AutoShapes tool on the Objects toolbar to draw shapes.

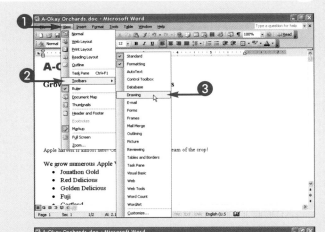

The Drawing toolbar appears at the bottom of the program window.

④ Click **AutoShapes**.

⑤ Click an AutoShape category.

⑥ Click an AutoShape.

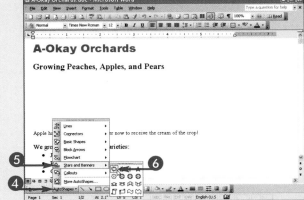

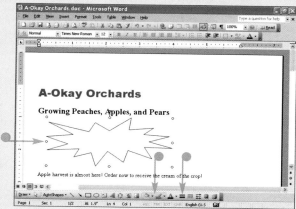

The ⌖ changes to ✛.

7️⃣ Click and drag on the work area to draw the desired shape.

● When you release the mouse, the program completes the shape.

Note: *You can move and resize the object or edit it with the Drawing toolbar buttons. See the section "Move and Resize an Object" to learn more.*

● You can use these buttons to define the fill color, line thickness, and color of the shape after drawing the shape.

SIMPLIFY IT

How do I draw a basic shape with the drawing tools?

The Drawing toolbar includes Oval and Rectangle tools for drawing basic circular or rectangular shapes. You can fill the shapes with any fill color or leave them empty. You can also apply shadows to the shapes to give them more depth. To draw a basic shape, display the Drawing toolbar and follow these steps:

1️⃣ Click 🔘 to draw ovals or 🔲 to draw rectangles.

The ⌖ changes to ✛.

2️⃣ Click and drag in the work area to draw the shape.

● You can make any selections from the line thickness, line color, or fill color settings before or after you draw the shape.

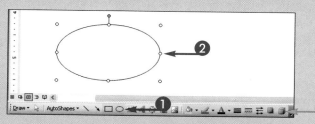

Insert Clip Art

You can add interest to your Office files by inserting clip art images. Clip art is simply predrawn artwork. You might use clip art to illustrate a document or to add visual impact to a worksheet. Word, Excel, PowerPoint, and Publisher install with the Office clip art collection. In addition, you can look for more clip art on the Web using the Clip Art task pane.

Insert Clip Art

1 Click where you want to add clip art.

You can also move the clip art to a particular location after you insert the art.

2 Click **Insert**.

3 Click **Picture**.

4 Click **Clip Art**.

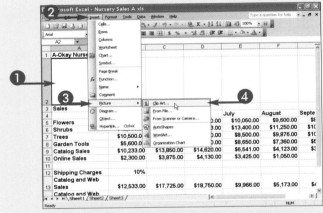

The Clip Art task pane opens.

Note: *See Chapter 1 to learn more about Office task panes.*

5 To search for a particular category of clip art, type a keyword or phrase here.

● To search in a particular collection, click the **Search in** ⌄ and click a collection.

● You can also search for clip art on the Office Web site by clicking this link.

6 Click **Go**.

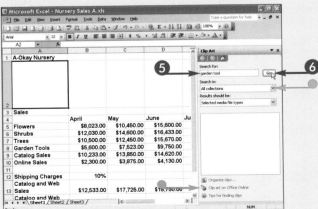

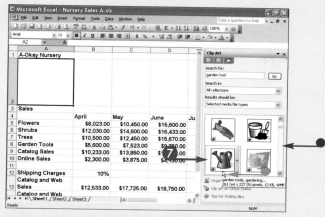

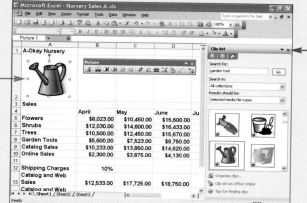

The Clip Art task pane displays any matches for the keyword or phrase you typed.

● You can use the scroll arrows to move through the list of matches.

● To view information about a clip art image, move ↳ over the image.

7 To add a clip art image, click the image.

● The clip art is inserted and the Picture toolbar appears on-screen.

You can resize or move the clip art, if needed.

Note: See the section "Move and Resize an Object," later in this chapter, to learn more.

To deselect the clip art, click another area on the work area.

● You can click ✕ to close the pane.

How do I search for a particular type of clip art, such as a photo or sound file?
To search for a particular type of media, click the **Results should be** ☑. The drop-down menu displays a list of different media types. You can select or deselect which types to include in your search. If you leave the **All media types** check box selected (☑), you can search for a match among all the available media formats.

How do I find details about the clip art?
To find out more about the clip art's properties in the Clip Art task pane, move ↳ over the image, click the ☑, and then click **Preview/Properties**. This opens the Preview/Properties dialog box and you can learn more about the file size, filename, file type, its creation date, and more.

View Clip Art with the Clip Organizer

You can use the Microsoft Clip Organizer to view clip art collections on your computer. You can also insert clip art from the Organizer window and place it in your Office file.

View Clip Art with the Clip Organizer

1. Display the Clip Art task pane.

   Note: See the previous section to learn how to open the pane.

2. Click **Organize clips**.

The Microsoft Clip Organizer window opens.

3. Click the **Collection List** button (🗐), if the list is not already viewable.

4. Click a collection ⊞ to expand the collection list.

5. Click a category.

   If some categories include subcategories, click a category ⊞ to expand the list.

   ● The Clip Organizer displays thumbnails of available clip art.

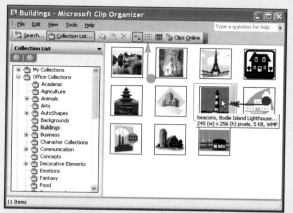

- You can use these buttons to change how clip art is listed in the window.

- To view information about a clip art image, move ▷ over the image.

  To add a clip art image to the file, drag the clip art to your work area.

- You can click the **Search** button (🔍) to display settings for conducting a search for clip art on your computer.

⑥ When finished viewing clip art, click ☒.

The Microsoft Clip Organizer window closes.

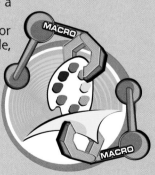

Is there a way to add the same clip art image every time I use the program?
Yes. You can create a macro that inserts the clip art image or any other image file, such as a logo, when you activate the macro keystrokes. To learn more about creating macros, see the Office Help files.

Can I copy clip art from one collection to another?
Yes. You can copy clip art from one collection and paste it into another collection using the Microsoft Clip Organizer. Simply click the clip art you want to copy, and then use the **Copy** (📋) and **Paste** (📋) buttons on the Microsoft Clip Organizer's toolbar to copy and paste the clip art.

Download Clip Art from the Web

You must log on to your Internet connection to view the Office Web pages and download clip art.

You can look for additional clip art to use in your Office files by perusing the Microsoft Office Web site. You can download clip art and import it into a clip collection in the Microsoft Clip Organizer.

Download Clip Art from the Web

① Display the Clip Art task pane.

Note: See the section "Insert Clip Art," earlier in this chapter, to learn how to open the pane.

② Click **Clip art on Office Online**.

Note: You must first log on to your Internet connection before clicking the Web site link.

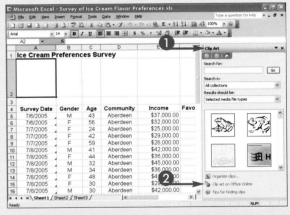

Your default Web browser opens to the Office Web site.

③ Click a clip art category link.

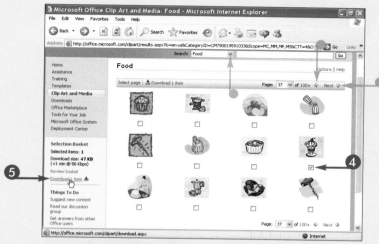

Clip art for that category appears.

● To look for a particular media format, click the **Search** ⌄ and choose a format.

● You can use the navigation links (◁ and ▷) to move through the clip art pages.

④ Select an image to download (☐ changes to ☑).

The clip art is added to your download basket.

⑤ When you are ready to download the images, click the **Download** link and follow the download instructions as prompted.

● When the download is complete, the clip art is added to the Clip Organizer window where you can view it in the Downloaded Clips category.

Note: *See the previous section to learn how to add clip art from the Clip Organizer to your Office files.*

Where else can I find clip art collections to use with my Office programs?

You can purchase clip art collections from computer and office supply stores, as well as find clip art collections to buy on the Internet. For example, if you need to use a lot of work-related clip art, you can look for a business collection of clip art, and you can also find collections geared toward certain industries, such as architecture and banking. You can also find clip art for free on the Web, but most sites require registration or a subscription for their services.

Can I use any artwork I find on the Internet in my workbooks?

No. Be very careful about using copyrighted images. Most images on the Internet are protected by copyrights, and you cannot reuse them without permission. If you do use a copyright-protected image, be sure to cite its source and the terms under which you are permitted to use it.

Insert an Image File

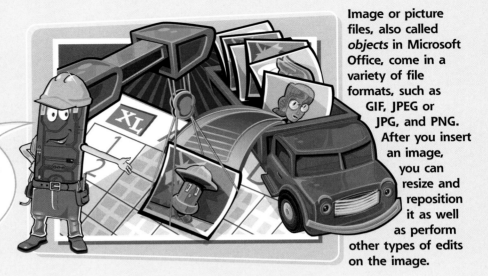

Image or picture files, also called *objects* in Microsoft Office, come in a variety of file formats, such as GIF, JPEG or JPG, and PNG. After you insert an image, you can resize and reposition it as well as perform other types of edits on the image.

You can illustrate your Office files with images stored on your computer. For example, if you have a photo or graphic file from another program that relates to your Excel data, you can insert it onto the worksheet. If you have a company logo, you can insert it onto a Word document.

Insert an Image File

① Click the area where you want to add an image.

You can also move the image to a particular location after inserting it onto the page.

② Click **Insert**.

③ Click **Picture**.

④ Click **From File**.

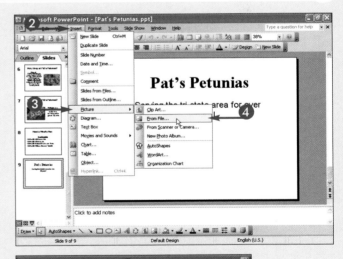

The Insert Picture dialog box appears.

⑤ Navigate to the folder or drive containing the image file you want to use.

● To browse for a particular file type, click ⊡ and choose a file format.

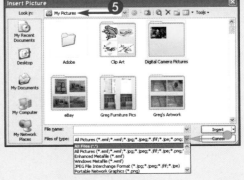

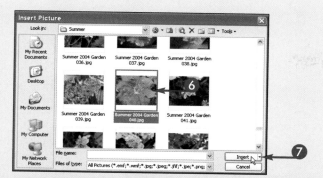

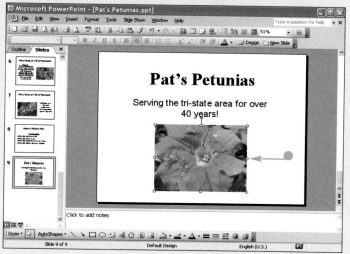

⑥ Click the filename.

⑦ Click **Insert**.

● The image is added to the file.

Depending on the program you are using, the Picture toolbar might also appear.

You may need to resize or reposition the image to fit the space.

Note: *See the section "Move and Resize an Object," later in this chapter, to learn more.*

To remove an image you no longer want, click the image and press Delete.

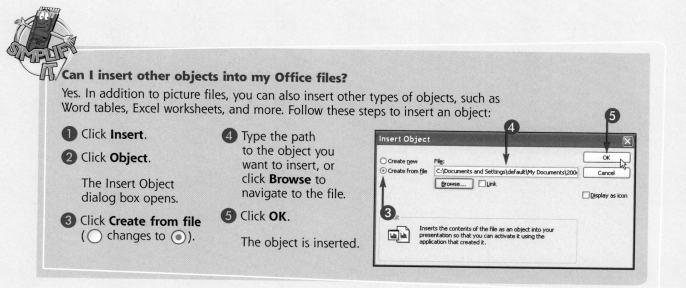

Can I insert other objects into my Office files?

Yes. In addition to picture files, you can also insert other types of objects, such as Word tables, Excel worksheets, and more. Follow these steps to insert an object:

① Click **Insert**.

② Click **Object**.

The Insert Object dialog box opens.

③ Click **Create from file** (○ changes to ⊙).

④ Type the path to the object you want to insert, or click **Browse** to navigate to the file.

⑤ Click **OK**.

The object is inserted.

Insert a WordArt Object

You can use the WordArt feature to turn text into interesting graphic objects to use in your Office files. For example, you can create arched text to appear over a range of data in Excel or vertical text to appear next to a paragraph in Word. You can create text graphics that bend and twist, or display a subtle shading of color.

Insert a WordArt Object

① Click **Insert**.

② Click **Picture**.

③ Click **WordArt**.

● You can also click the **WordArt** button (□) on the Drawing toolbar.

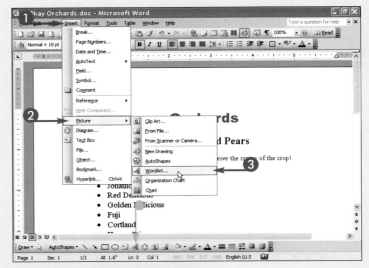

The WordArt Gallery dialog box appears.

④ Click a WordArt style.

⑤ Click **OK**.

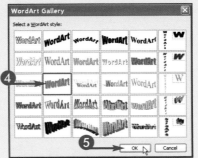

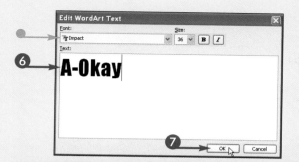

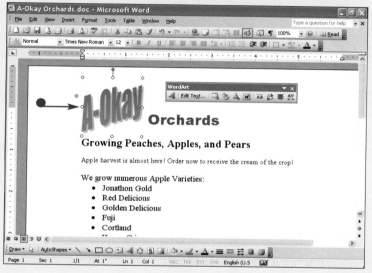

The Edit WordArt Text dialog box appears.

⑥ Type your WordArt text.

● You can change the font, size, and apply bold or italics using these settings.

⑦ Click **OK**.

● The WordArt object is added to your work area and the WordArt toolbar is displayed.

You can resize or move the image, if needed.

Note: *See the next section, "Move and Resize an Object," to learn more.*

How do I edit my WordArt text?
To edit any portion of a WordArt object, whether it is the text, font, or font size, you must reopen the Edit WordArt Text dialog box. Simply double-click the WordArt object on your worksheet or click **Edit Text** on the WordArt toolbar. When you open the Edit WordArt Text dialog box, you can make changes to the existing text, or type in all new text for the effect.

How do I change the WordArt style?
You can click the **WordArt Gallery** button (⬚) on the WordArt toolbar to quickly access the Gallery dialog box and select another style to apply. You can also click the **WordArt Shape** button (⬚) and choose another shape for the text.

Move and Resize
an Object

You can move and resize any clip art, image, or shape — called *objects* in the Microsoft Office programs — you place in a file. When you select an object, it is surrounded by handles that you can use to resize the object.

Move and Resize an Object

MOVE AN OBJECT

① Click the object you want to move.

The ⬚ changes to ✛.

② Drag the object to a new location on the worksheet.

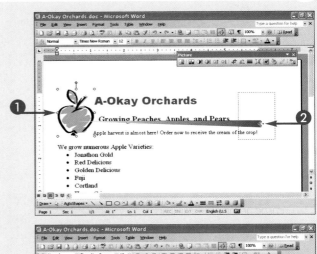

● The object is moved.

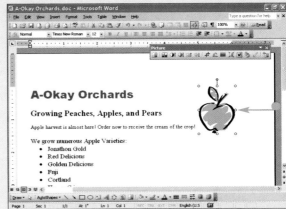

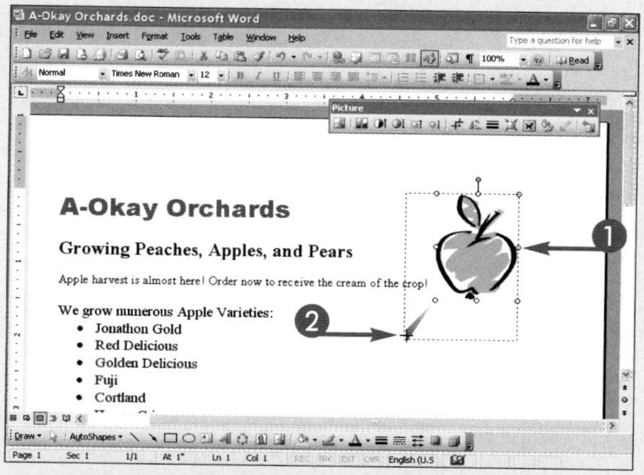

RESIZE AN OBJECT

1. Click the object you want to resize.
2. Drag a selection handle to resize the object.

   The changes to +.

- The object is resized.

Can I also use the Cut, Copy, and Paste commands to move or copy an object?
Yes. You can easily cut, copy, and paste objects around your files. Simply select an object and then apply the commands. You can click , , or on the Standard toolbar, or you can click the **Edit** menu to apply the commands.

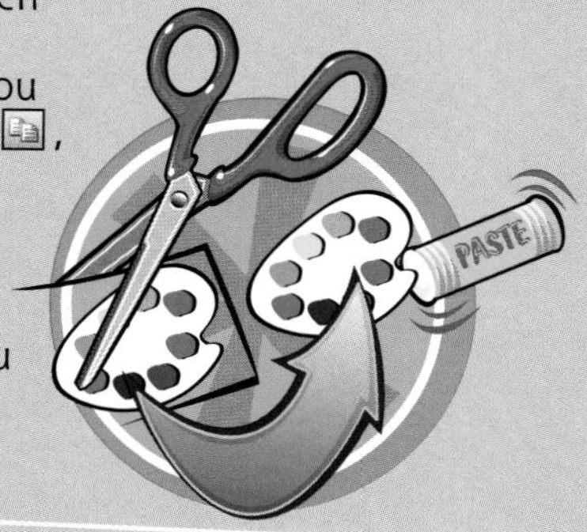

Can I resize an object and keep the scaling proportional?
To maintain an object's height-to-width ratio when resizing, press and hold Shift while dragging a resizing corner handle. To resize from the center of the object in two dimensions at the same time, press and hold Ctrl while dragging a corner handle.

Rotate and Flip Objects

You can rotate and flip objects you place on your documents, worksheets, slides, or publications to change the appearance of the objects. For example, you might flip a clip art image to face another direction, or rotate an arrow object to point elsewhere on the page.

Rotate and Flip Objects

ROTATE AN OBJECT

1. Click the object you want to rotate.

2. Click **Draw** on the Drawing toolbar.

   Note: See Chapter 1 to learn how to display toolbars.

3. Click **Rotate or Flip**.

4. Click **Free Rotate**.

   You can also rotate an object 90 degrees left or right.

   A rotation handle appears on the selected object.

5. Click and drag the handle to rotate the object.

   The ⓗ changes to ⟲.

   Note: To constrain the rotation to 15-degree angles, press and hold the **Shift** key while rotating the object.

   The object rotates.

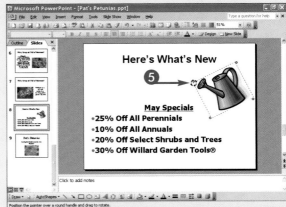

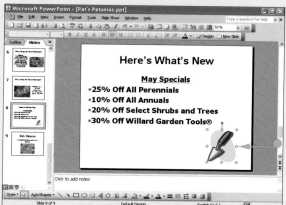

FLIP AN OBJECT

1. Click the object you want to flip.

2. Click **Draw** on the Drawing toolbar.

   Note: See Chapter 1 to learn how to display toolbars.

3. Click **Rotate or Flip**.

4. Click **Flip Horizontal** or **Flip Vertical**.

● The object is flipped.

How do I rotate text?

The easiest way to rotate text is to create a WordArt object to rotate. Learn how to create a WordArt object in the section "Insert a WordArt Object," earlier in this chapter. After you create the WordArt, you can rotate it using the steps shown in this section. You can also choose from several vertical text styles from the WordArt Gallery.

Is there a way to prevent anyone from moving or rotating an object on my worksheet?

As soon as you position an object the way you want it on the document, other users who have access to your file can make changes to the data, including changes to the objects in your files. The only way to prevent someone from making changes to your file is to assign a password or apply the read-only option. To learn more about protecting Office files with passwords, see Chapter 2.

Crop a Picture

> You can crop a picture you add to any Office file to create a better fit or to focus on an important area of the image. The Crop tool, located on the Picture toolbar, can help you crop out parts of the image you do not need. You can also crop clip art images.

Crop a Picture

1. Click the image you want to edit.

2. Click the **Crop** button ( ) on the Picture toolbar.

   - The image is surrounded with crop handles.

   - If the Picture toolbar is not displayed, click **View**, **Toolbars**, and then **Picture**.

   You can also right-click the image and click **Picture Toolbar** from the menu that appears.

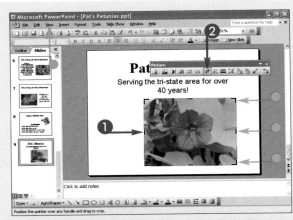

3. Click and drag a crop handle to crop out an area of the image.

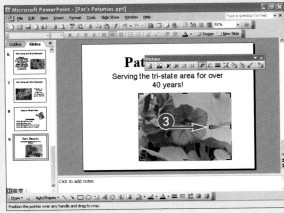

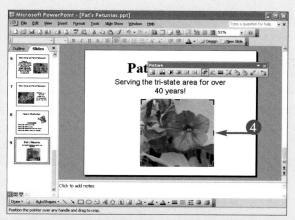

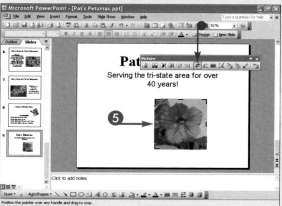

4 Release the mouse button.

The image is cropped.

5 Continue cropping other edges of the image as needed.

● You can click 🖽 again to turn off the Crop tool.

Note: *See the section "Move and Resize an Object," earlier in this chapter, to learn more.*

How can I reduce the overall file size of an image I use in an Office file?
Image files are notorious for consuming large amounts of file space, and when you insert a large image into a document or worksheet, it adds to the size of the file. You can use the **Compress Pictures** tool (🖾) on the Picture toolbar to reduce the resolution of an image or discard extra information from cropping the image. The Compress Pictures dialog box offers several options for helping to control the overall file size of an image.

How can I return the image to its original state before cropping?
You can click the **Reset Picture** button (🖾) on the Picture toolbar to reset the image to the size it appeared when first inserted onto your worksheet. Any cropping or other edits made to the image are discarded. You can also click the **Undo** button (🔄) on the Standard toolbar to undo each edit you made to the image.

Format
an Object

You can edit the objects you add to an Office file by accessing the Format dialog box. For example, for an AutoShape, you can make adjustments to the shape's color, alignment, and line thickness. Depending on the object, the Format dialog box may display different formatting options you can apply.

Format an Object

① Double-click the object you want to edit.

You can also right-click the object and click **Format** from the menu that appears.

● If you are editing clip art or an image, you can click the **Format Picture** button (⬚) on the Picture toolbar.

Note: *See Chapter 1 to learn how to display toolbars.*

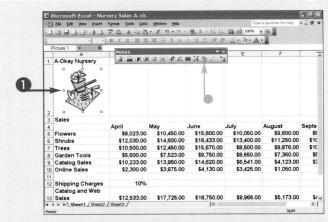

The Format dialog box appears.

If you edit clip art or an image, the dialog box is named Format Picture. If you edit a shape, the dialog box is named Format AutoShape.

② Click a tab and make any changes you need.

In this example, the **Colors and Lines** tab is used to make changes to the fill color or line or arrow colors of the object.

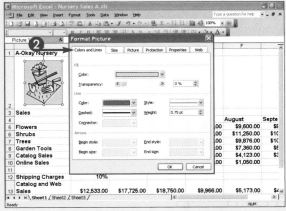

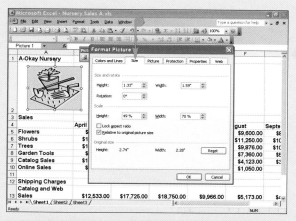

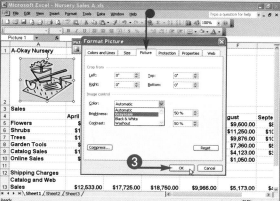

- In this example, the **Size** tab is used to make changes to the size and scale of the object.

- In this example, the **Picture** tab is used to make changes to the object's crop and appearance.

③ Click **OK**.

Any new settings you choose are immediately applied to the object.

What options do the other tabs in the Format Picture dialog box offer?

If your file has a password assigned, you can use the **Protection** tab in the Format Picture dialog box to lock the object. The **Properties** tab offers several options for controlling the positioning of the object. If you save the file as a Web page, you can use the **Web** tab to assign any alternative text for users who do not choose to view graphics in their Web browsers.

What kind of formatting changes can I make to clip art objects?

You can make subtle changes to predrawn art by adding a border around the clip art. You can use the **Colors and Lines** tab in the Format Picture dialog box to add a border, or you can use the **Line Style** (▤) and **Line Color** (▨) buttons on the Drawing toolbar to add a border. Depending on the clip art background, you can also make changes to the artwork's fill color or transparency setting.

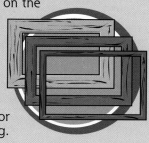

Index

Index

Index

M

mailbox management, Outlook, 327
margins
    cells, 169
    select text, 39
    set, 62–63
markup options, customize, 99
mathematical operators formulas, 141
media clips, slides, 201
meeting invitations, Outlook, 307
meetings, plan, 306–307
menu bar, 6
menus
    display, 10
    turn off, 11
merge table cells, 74
message rule, Outlook, 328–329
mixed cell references, 149
mouse click to select text, 39
move
    charts, 180
    fields, forms, 281
    fields, tables, 269
    objects, 378
    objects, publications, 350
    to range name, 145
    slide object, 222
    text, 40–41, 41
    worksheets, 125
move worksheets, 125
multiple columns and rows, insert, 113
Multiple Pages button, 24
multiple pieces of data, 27

N

navigate
    program windows, 6–7
    records, forms, 278
    tables, 257
Navigation pane, Outlook, 298
new contacts, Outlook, 308–309
New Record button, 277
new slides, add, 226
new tasks, Outlook, 310–311
new text object, add, 213
noncontiguous data, charts, 177
Normal view, 34, 199
notes, add, 312–313
number formats, 162–163
number functions, 153
number series, autofill, 111
numbered lists, 60–61

O

object linking and embedding (OLE), 28
objects
    flip, 381
    format, 384–385
    move, 378
    resize, 379
    rotate, 380
Office
    assign passwords to files, 30–31
    close files, 22
    cut, copy, paste data, 26–27
    exit, 5
    find files, 23
    help, 16–17
    link and embed data, 28–29
    menus, 10–11
    navigate program windows, 6–7
    open existing files, 21
    preview files, 24
    print files, 25
    save files, 20
    shortcuts, 5
    start, 4–5
    start new files, 18–19
    task panes, 8–9
    toolbars, 11–15
Office Assistant, 17
open
    attachments, Outlook, 325
    existing files, 21
Open dialog box, 21
operator precedence formulas, 141
organizational charts, 179
Outline view
    about, 34
    add slide text, 203
    PowerPoint, 198
Outlook
    add notes, 312–313
    add senders to address book, 322
    attach files to e-mail messages, 324–325
    calendar, 300–303
    components, 298–299
    compose e-mail messages, 316–317
    create message rule, 328–329
    create new contacts, 308–309
    create new tasks, 310–311
    delete messages, 323
    forward e-mail messages, 321
    Go menu, 299
    Navigation pane, 298
    organize items, 314–315
    plan meetings, 306–307
    read new messages, 318
    reply to messages, 320
    schedule appointments, 300–303
    screen junk e-mail, 326–327
    turn off Reading pane, 319
Outside Border button, 81
Overtype mode, 37

P

Page Border tab, 81
page breaks, insert, 91
page numbers
    insert, 90
    style, 91
Page Setup dialog box, 101
pane areas, PowerPoint, 199
paper size, change, 101
Paragraph dialog box, 65
paragraphs
    select text, 39
    spacing, 65
passwords
    assign, 30–31
    forgotten, 31
    remove, 31

Index

Index

Index

If this book helped you, check out these other Simplified® titles.

All designed for visual learners—just like you!

0-7645-8329-8

0-7645-9752-3

0-7645-9999-2

**For a complete listing of *Simplified*® titles
and other Visual books, go to wiley.com/go/visualtech**

Visual®
An Imprint of WILEY
Now you know.